CAPTA
LIVIN

Y: **ANDY DIGGLE**

DI GRANOV

ER: **ANDY DIGGLE**

EDDIE ROBSON (ISSUES #3 & 4)

TRATION: **ADI GRANOV**

GUSTIN ALESSIO

ERS: **VC's JOE CARAMAGNA**

PRODUCTION DESIGN: **MANNY MEDEROS**

ASSISTANT EDITORS: **JAKE THOMAS & JOHN DENNING**

EDITORS: **TOM BREVOORT** with **LAUREN SANKOVITCH**

EDITOR IN CHIEF: **AXEL ALONSO**

CHIEF CREATIVE OFFICER: **JOE QUESADA**

PUBLISHER: **DAN BUCKLEY**

EXECUTIVE PRODUCER: **ALAN FINE**

COVER ART: **ADI GRANOV**

CAPTAIN AMERICA CREATED BY **JOE SIMON & JACK KIRBY**

have any comments or queries about t   vels@panini.co.uk

RVEL
el.com
4 Marvel

MIX
Paper from
responsible sources
FSC® C016466

MARVEL GRAPHIC NOVEL **CAPTAIN AMERICA: LIVING LEGEND #**

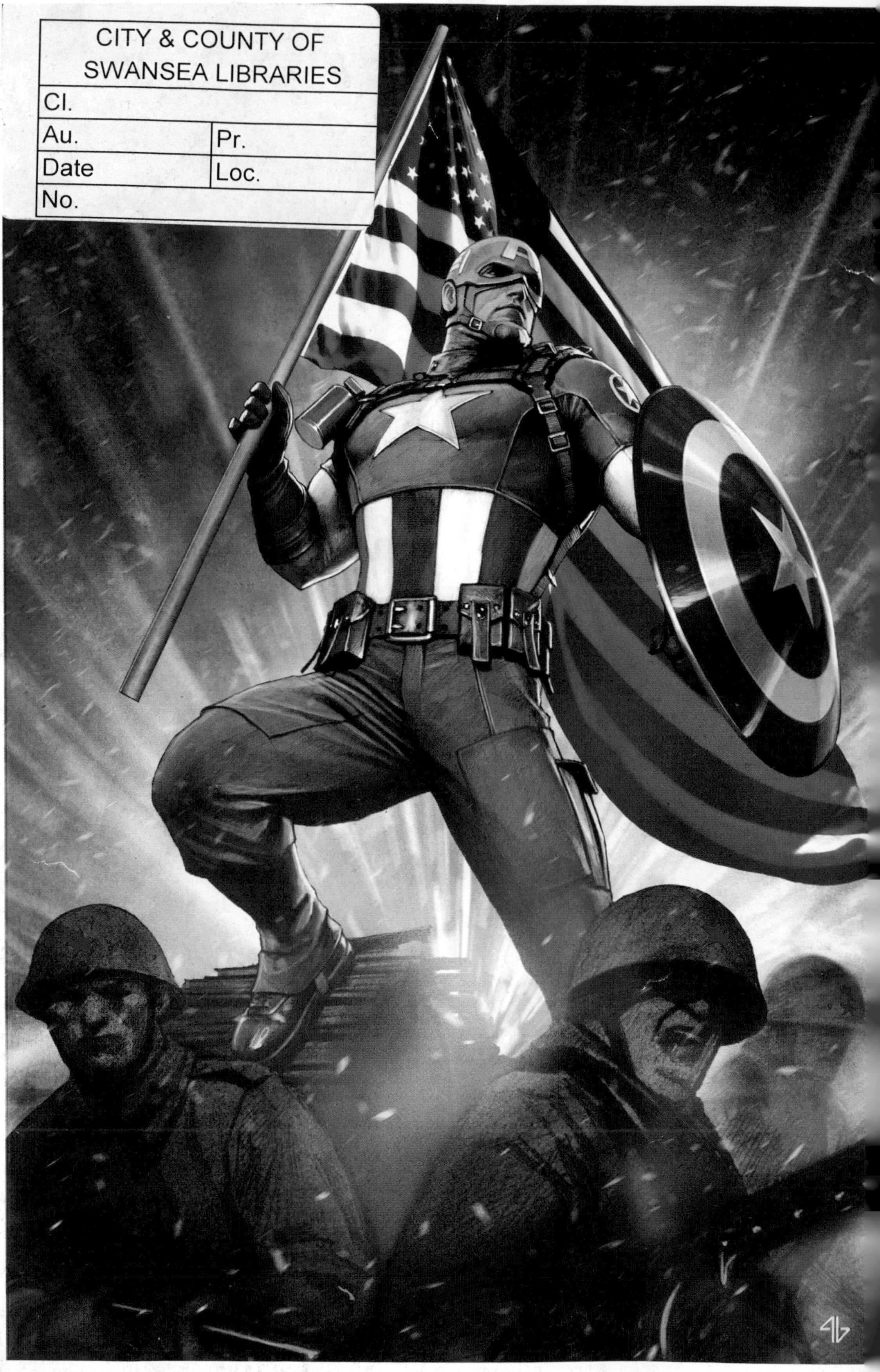

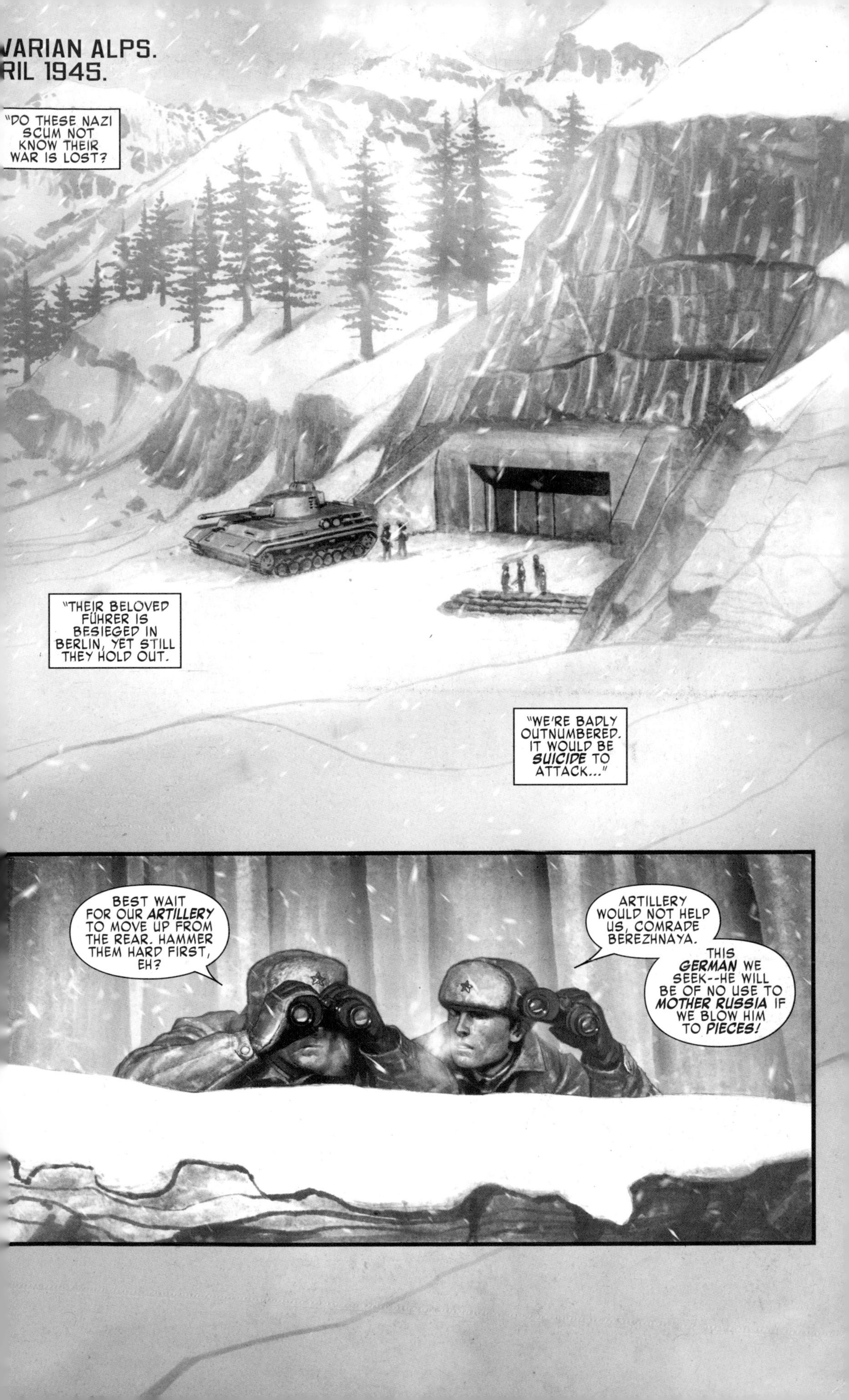

VARIAN ALPS.
RIL 1945.
"DO THESE NAZI SCUM NOT KNOW THEIR WAR IS LOST?
"THEIR BELOVED FÜHRER IS BESIEGED IN BERLIN, YET STILL THEY HOLD OUT.
"WE'RE BADLY OUTNUMBERED. IT WOULD BE SUICIDE TO ATTACK..."
BEST WAIT FOR OUR ARTILLERY TO MOVE UP FROM THE REAR. HAMMER THEM HARD FIRST, EH?
ARTILLERY WOULD NOT HELP US, COMRADE BEREZHNAYA.
THIS GERMAN WE SEEK--HE WILL BE OF NO USE TO MOTHER RUSSIA IF WE BLOW HIM TO PIECES!

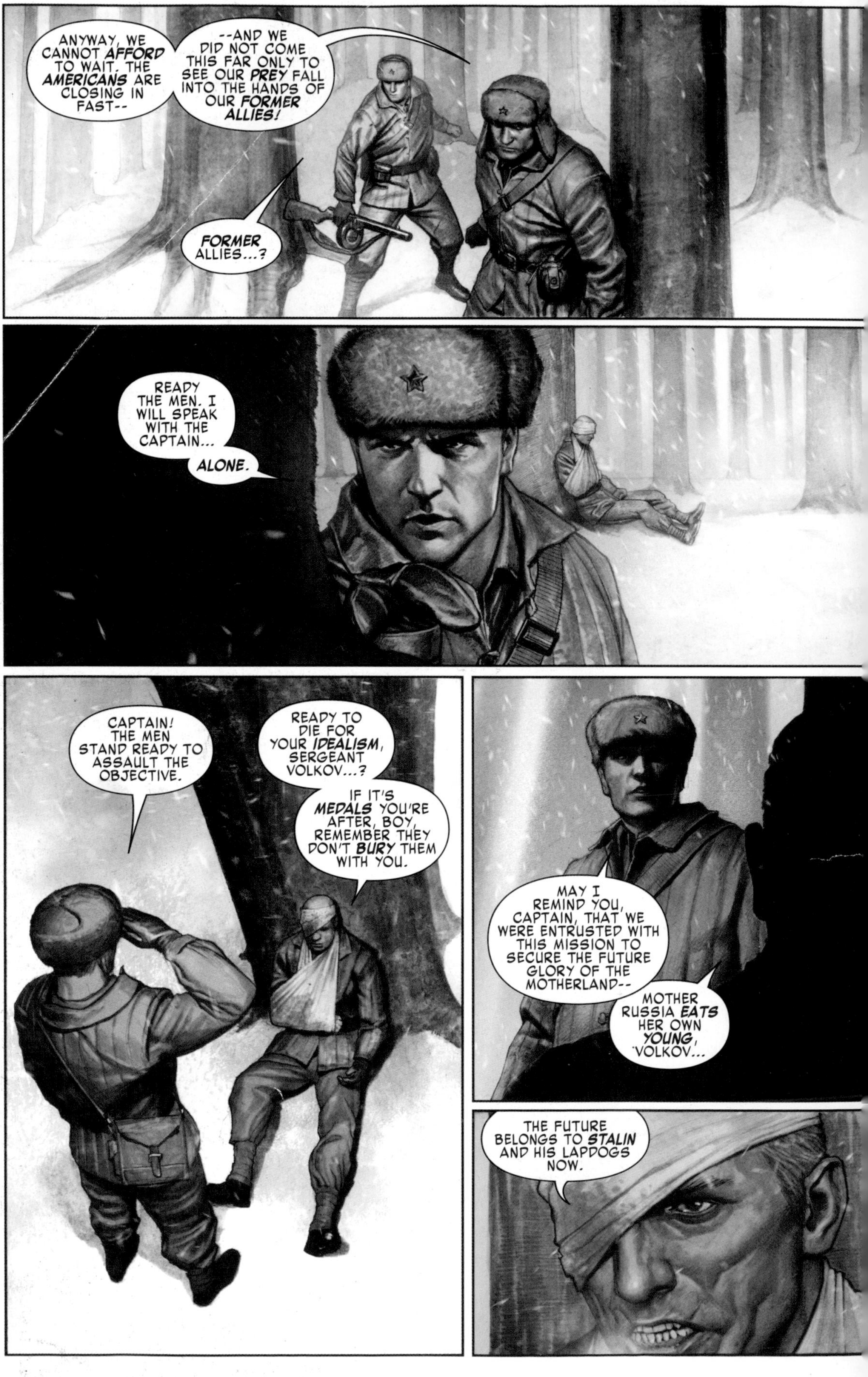
ANYWAY, WE CANNOT AFFORD TO WAIT. THE AMERICANS ARE CLOSING IN FAST--
--AND WE DID NOT COME THIS FAR ONLY TO SEE OUR PREY FALL INTO THE HANDS OF OUR FORMER ALLIES!
FORMER ALLIES...?
READY THE MEN. I WILL SPEAK WITH THE CAPTAIN... ALONE.
CAPTAIN! THE MEN STAND READY TO ASSAULT THE OBJECTIVE.
READY TO DIE FOR YOUR IDEALISM, SERGEANT VOLKOV...?
IF IT'S MEDALS YOU'RE AFTER, BOY, REMEMBER THEY DON'T BURY THEM WITH YOU.
MAY I REMIND YOU, CAPTAIN, THAT WE WERE ENTRUSTED WITH THIS MISSION TO SECURE THE FUTURE GLORY OF THE MOTHERLAND--
MOTHER RUSSIA EATS HER OWN YOUNG, VOLKOV...
THE FUTURE BELONGS TO STALIN AND HIS LAPDOGS NOW.

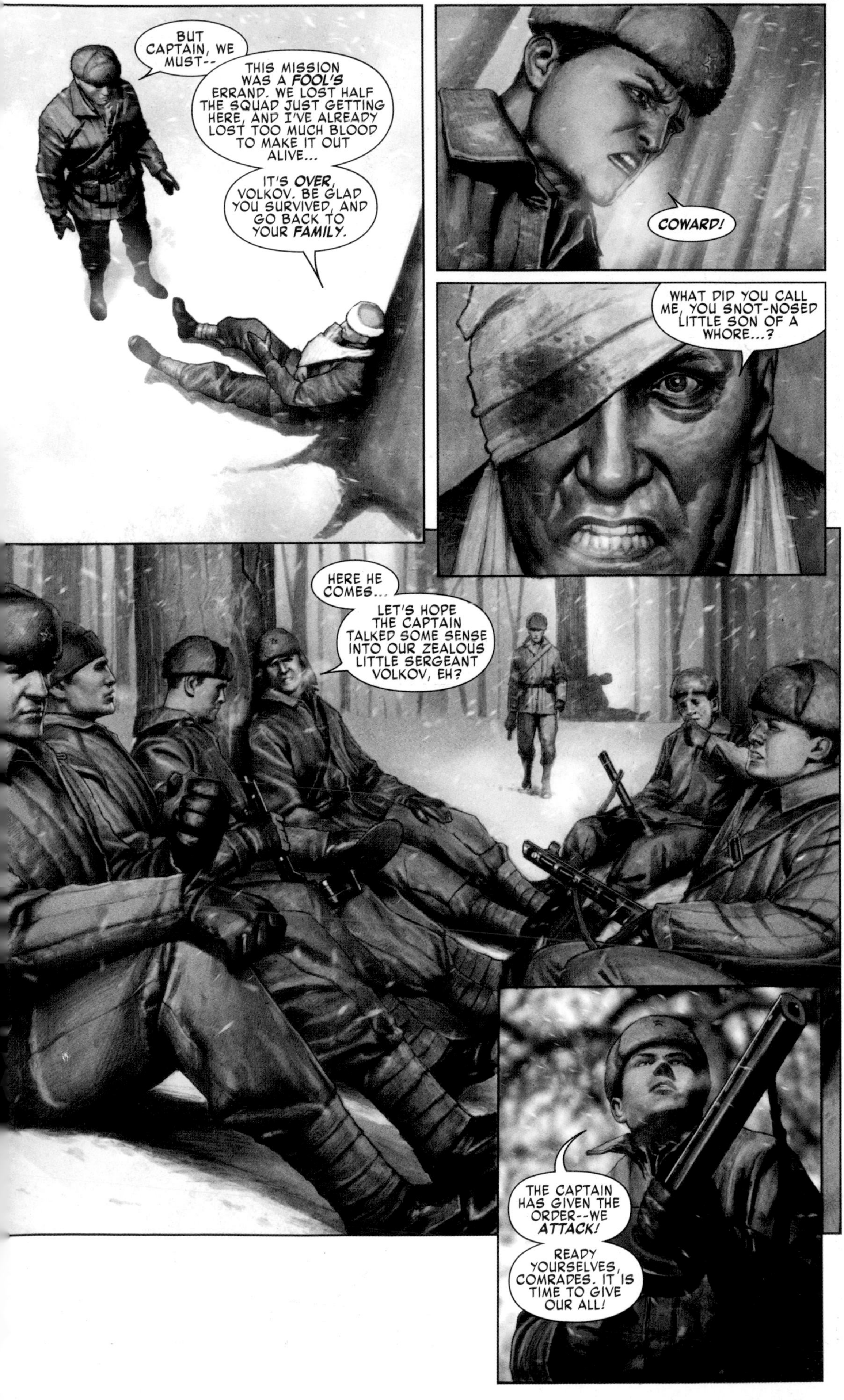
BUT CAPTAIN, WE MUST--
THIS MISSION WAS A FOOL'S ERRAND. WE LOST HALF THE SQUAD JUST GETTING HERE, AND I'VE ALREADY LOST TOO MUCH BLOOD TO MAKE IT OUT ALIVE...
IT'S OVER, VOLKOV. BE GLAD YOU SURVIVED, AND GO BACK TO YOUR FAMILY.
COWARD!
WHAT DID YOU CALL ME, YOU SNOT-NOSED LITTLE SON OF A WHORE...?
HERE HE COMES...
LET'S HOPE THE CAPTAIN TALKED SOME SENSE INTO OUR ZEALOUS LITTLE SERGEANT VOLKOV, EH?
THE CAPTAIN HAS GIVEN THE ORDER--WE ATTACK!
READY YOURSELVES, COMRADES. IT IS TIME TO GIVE OUR ALL!

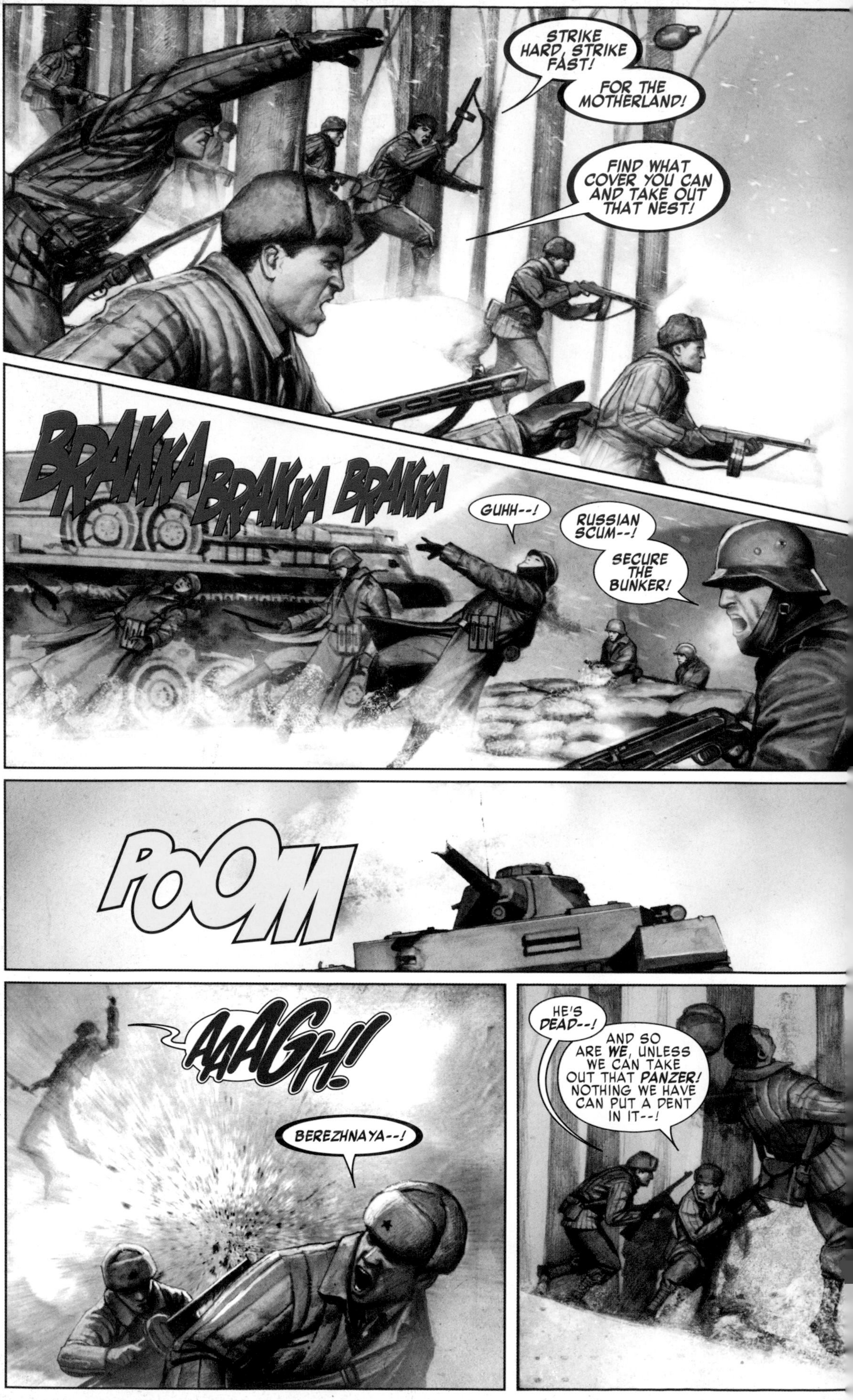

STRIKE HARD, STRIKE FAST!
FOR THE MOTHERLAND!
FIND WHAT COVER YOU CAN AND TAKE OUT THAT NEST!
BRAKKA BRAKKA BRAKKA
GUHH--!
RUSSIAN SCUM--!
SECURE THE BUNKER!
POOM
AAAGH!
BEREZHNAYA--!
HE'S DEAD--!
AND SO ARE WE, UNLESS WE CAN TAKE OUT THAT PANZER! NOTHING WE HAVE CAN PUT A DENT IN IT--!

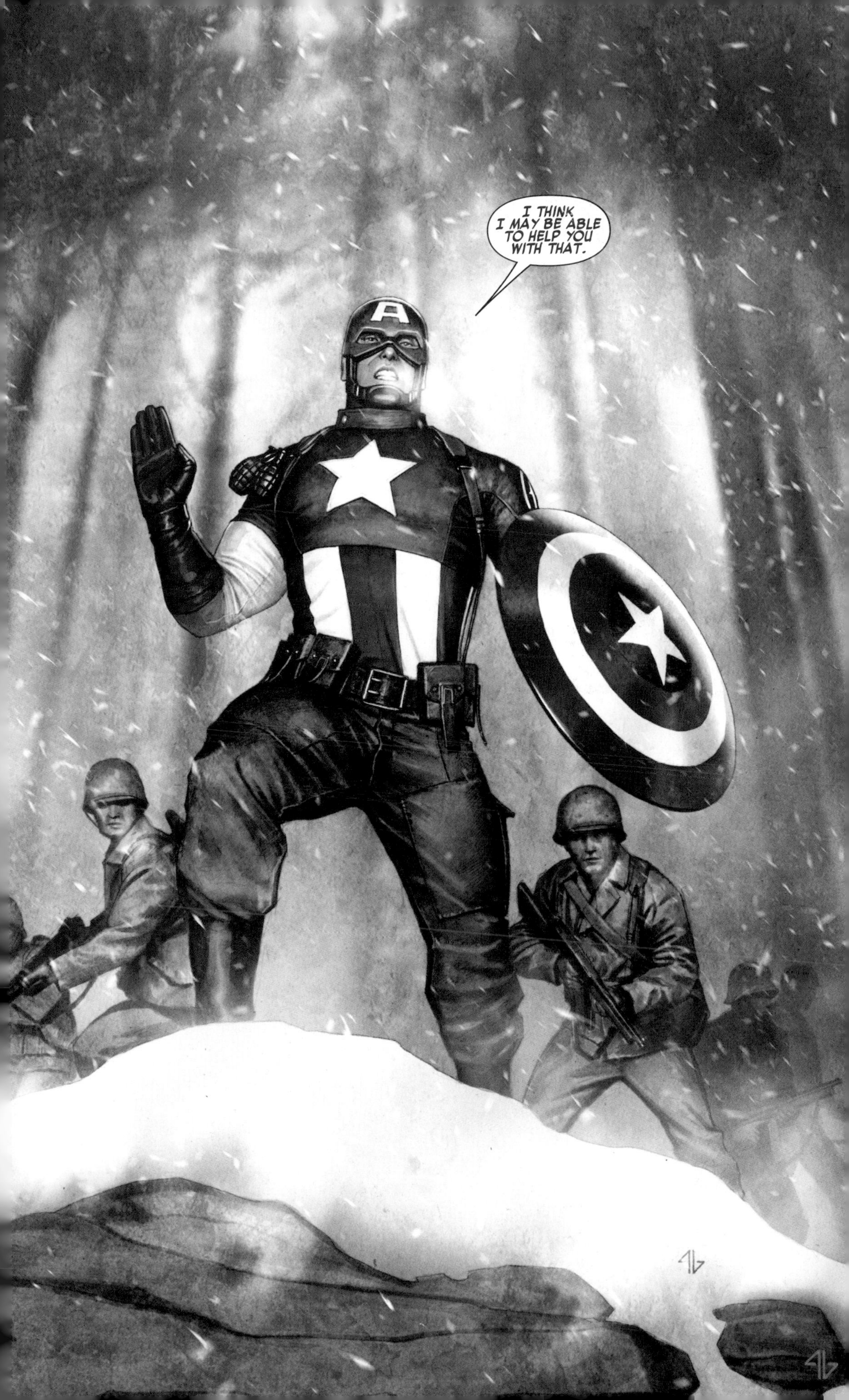
I THINK I MAY BE ABLE TO HELP YOU WITH THAT.

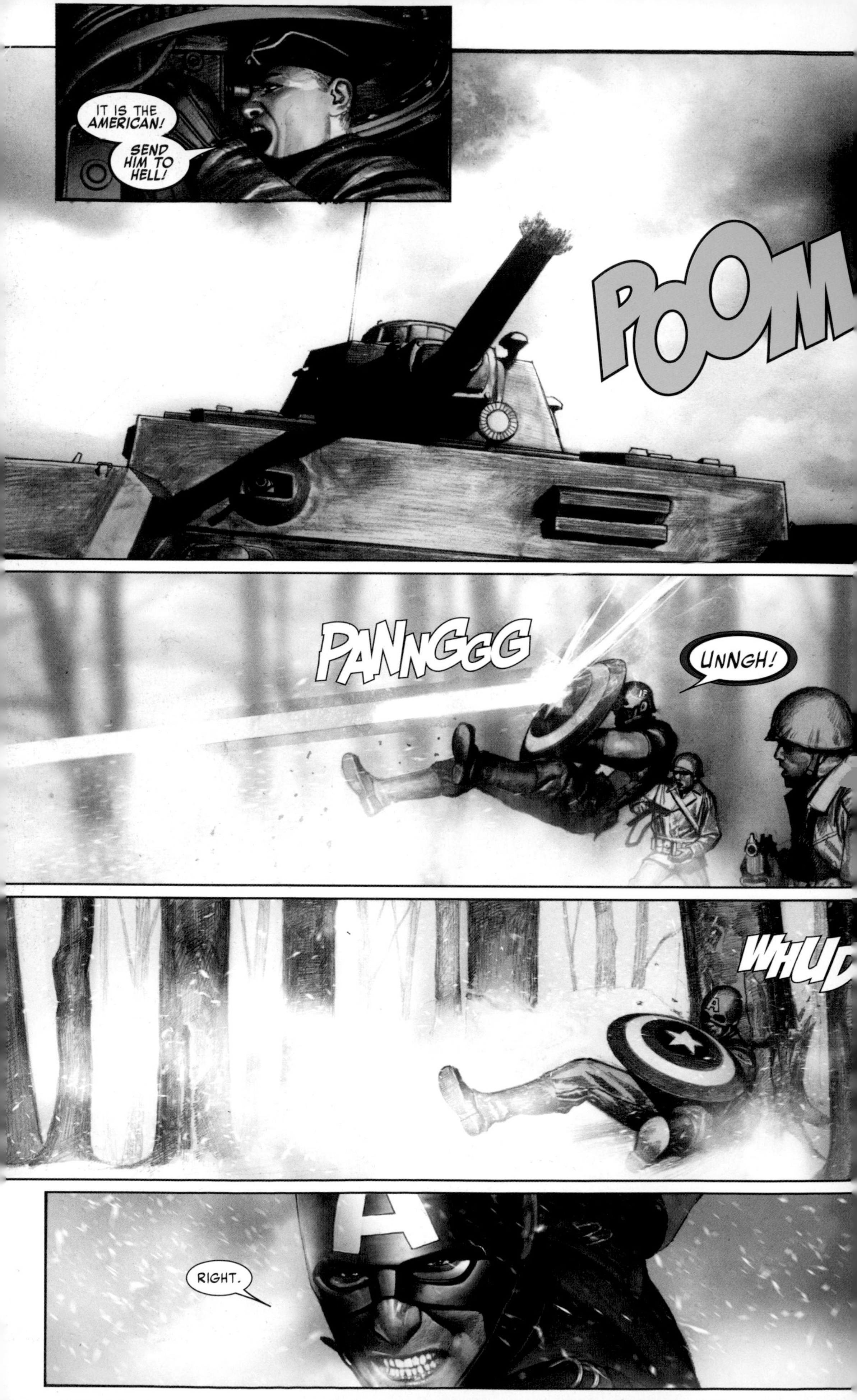
IT IS THE AMERICAN!
SEND HIM TO HELL!
POOM
PANNGGG
UNNGH!
WHUD
RIGHT.

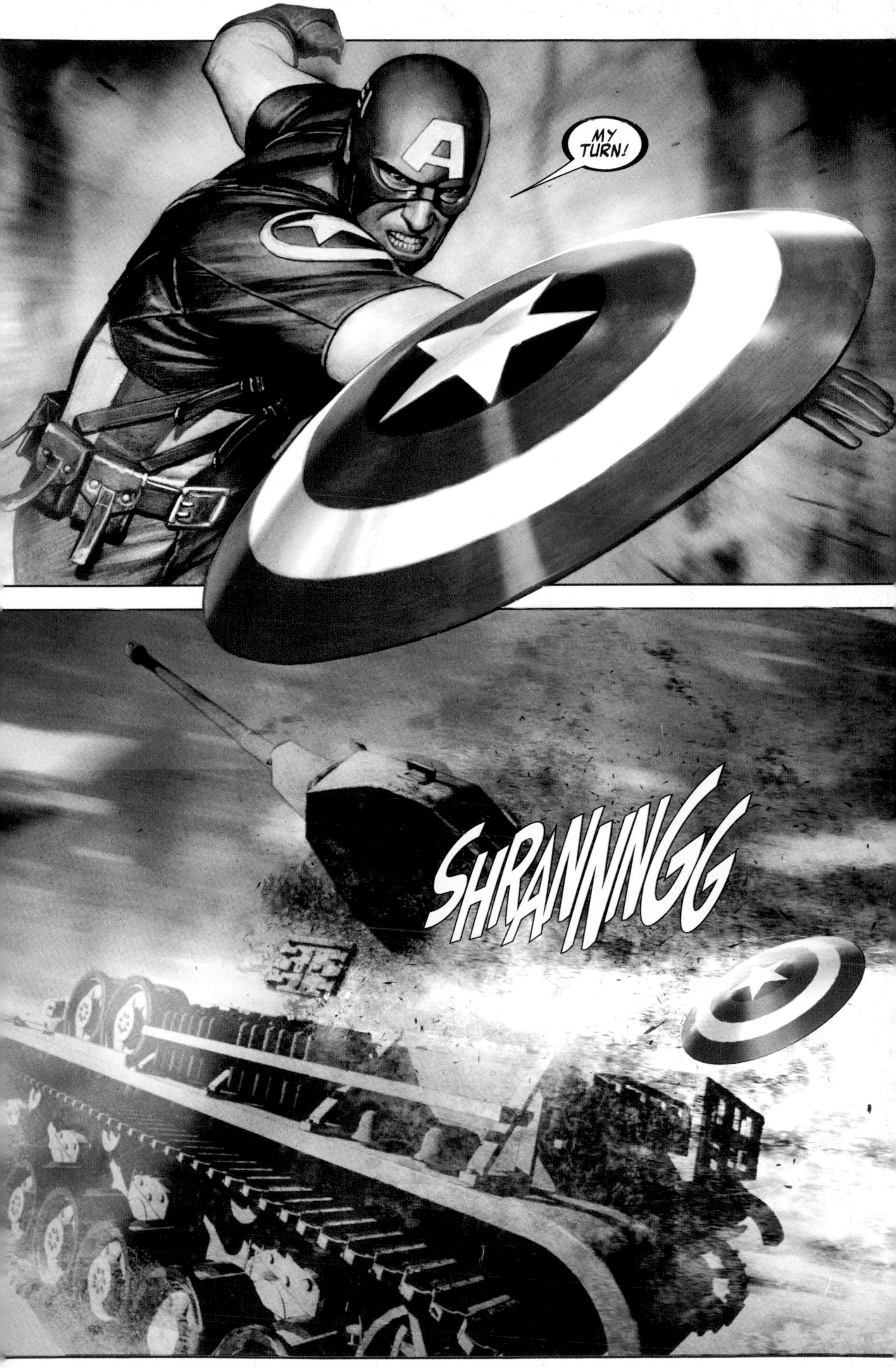
MY TURN!
SHRANNNGG

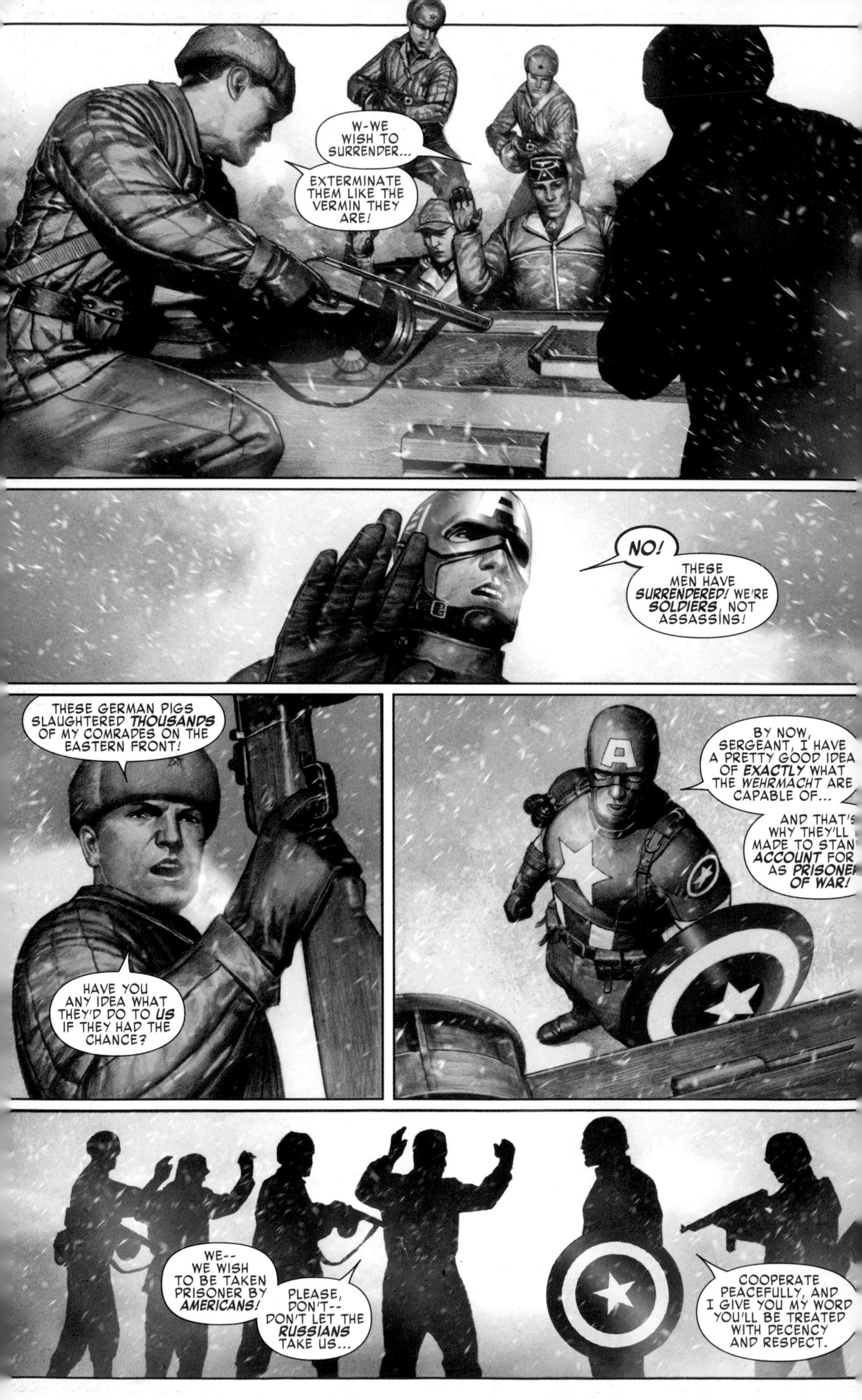
W-WE WISH TO SURRENDER...
EXTERMINATE THEM LIKE THE VERMIN THEY ARE!
NO! THESE MEN HAVE SURRENDERED! WE'RE SOLDIERS, NOT ASSASSINS!
THESE GERMAN PIGS SLAUGHTERED THOUSANDS OF MY COMRADES ON THE EASTERN FRONT!
HAVE YOU ANY IDEA WHAT THEY'D DO TO US IF THEY HAD THE CHANCE?
BY NOW, SERGEANT, I HAVE A PRETTY GOOD IDEA OF EXACTLY WHAT THE WEHRMACHT ARE CAPABLE OF...
AND THAT'S WHY THEY'LL MADE TO STAN ACCOUNT FOR AS PRISONE OF WAR!
WE-- WE WISH TO BE TAKEN PRISONER BY AMERICANS!
PLEASE, DON'T-- DON'T LET THE RUSSIANS TAKE US...
COOPERATE PEACEFULLY, AND I GIVE YOU MY WORD YOU'LL BE TREATED WITH DECENCY AND RESPECT.

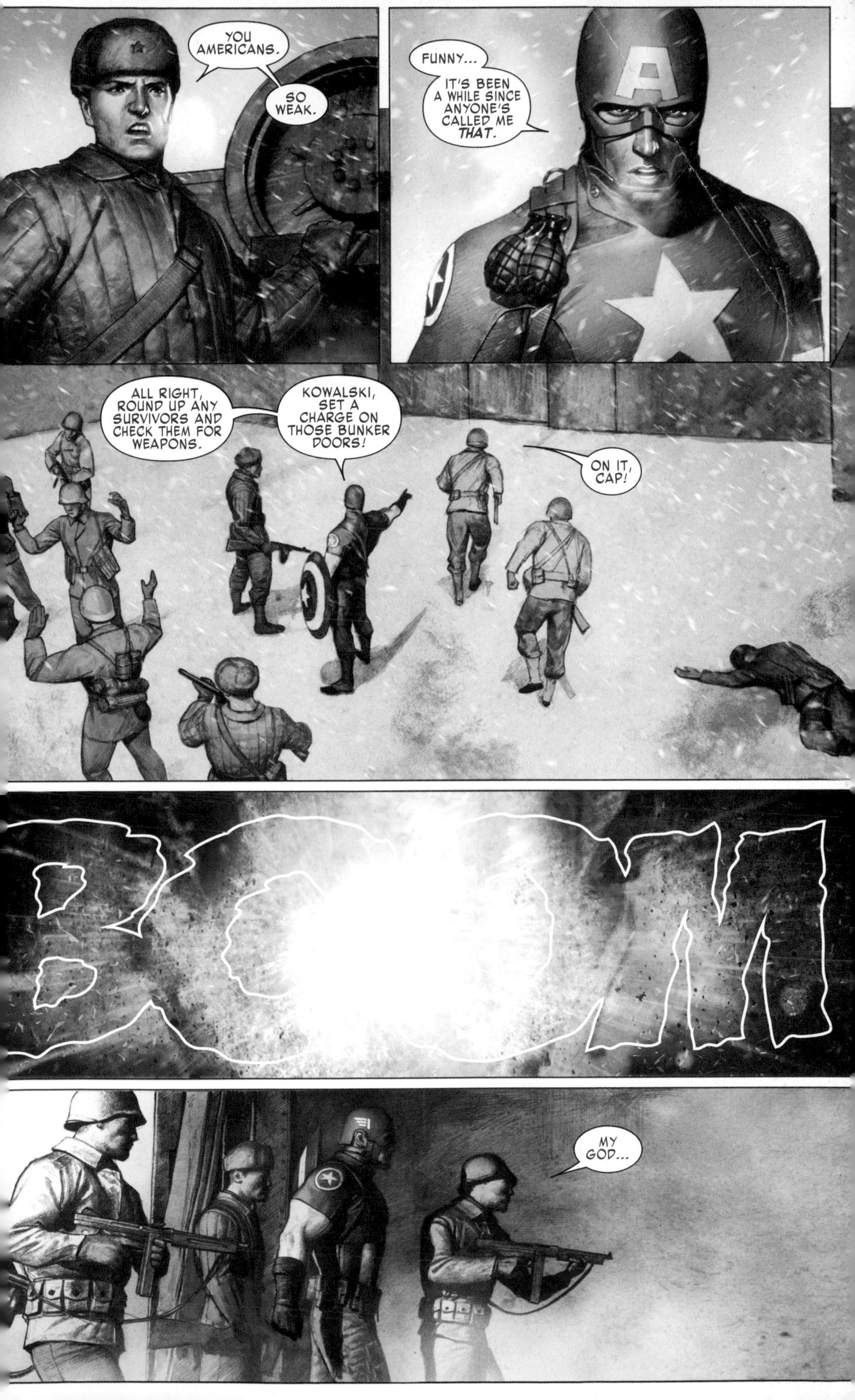
YOU AMERICANS.
SO WEAK.
FUNNY...
IT'S BEEN A WHILE SINCE ANYONE'S CALLED ME *THAT*.
ALL RIGHT, ROUND UP ANY SURVIVORS AND CHECK THEM FOR WEAPONS.
KOWALSKI, SET A CHARGE ON THOSE BUNKER DOORS!
ON IT, CAP!
BOOM
MY GOD...

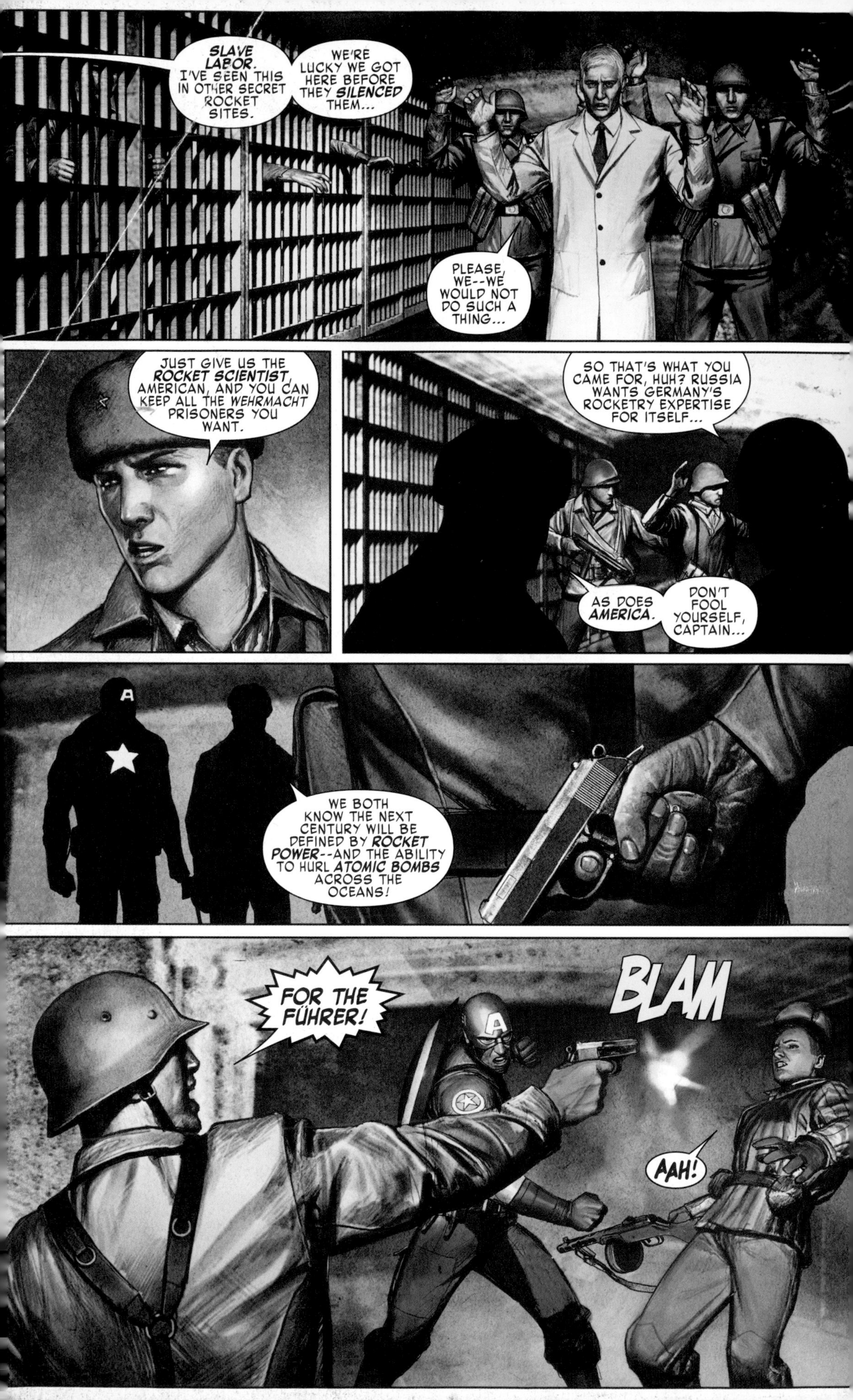
SLAVE LABOR. I'VE SEEN THIS IN OTHER SECRET ROCKET SITES.
WE'RE LUCKY WE GOT HERE BEFORE THEY SILENCED THEM...
PLEASE, WE--WE WOULD NOT DO SUCH A THING...
JUST GIVE US THE ROCKET SCIENTIST, AMERICAN, AND YOU CAN KEEP ALL THE WEHRMACHT PRISONERS YOU WANT.
SO THAT'S WHAT YOU CAME FOR, HUH? RUSSIA WANTS GERMANY'S ROCKETRY EXPERTISE FOR ITSELF...
AS DOES AMERICA.
DON'T FOOL YOURSELF, CAPTAIN...
WE BOTH KNOW THE NEXT CENTURY WILL BE DEFINED BY ROCKET POWER--AND THE ABILITY TO HURL ATOMIC BOMBS ACROSS THE OCEANS!
FOR THE FÜHRER!
BLAM
AAH!

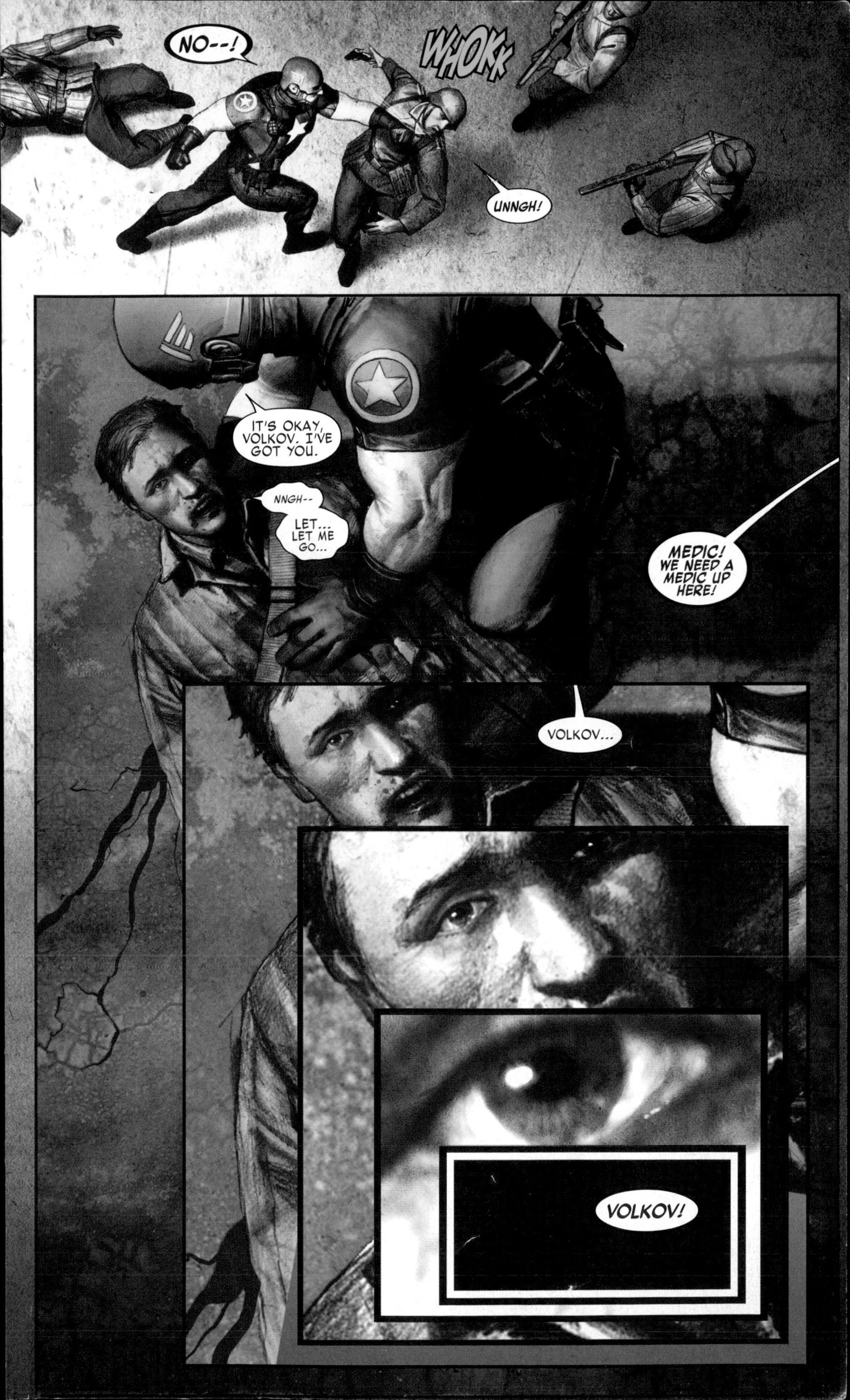
NO--!
WHOKK
UNNGH!
IT'S OKAY, VOLKOV. I'VE GOT YOU.
NNGH--
LET... LET ME GO...
MEDIC! WE NEED A MEDIC UP HERE!
VOLKOV...
VOLKOV!

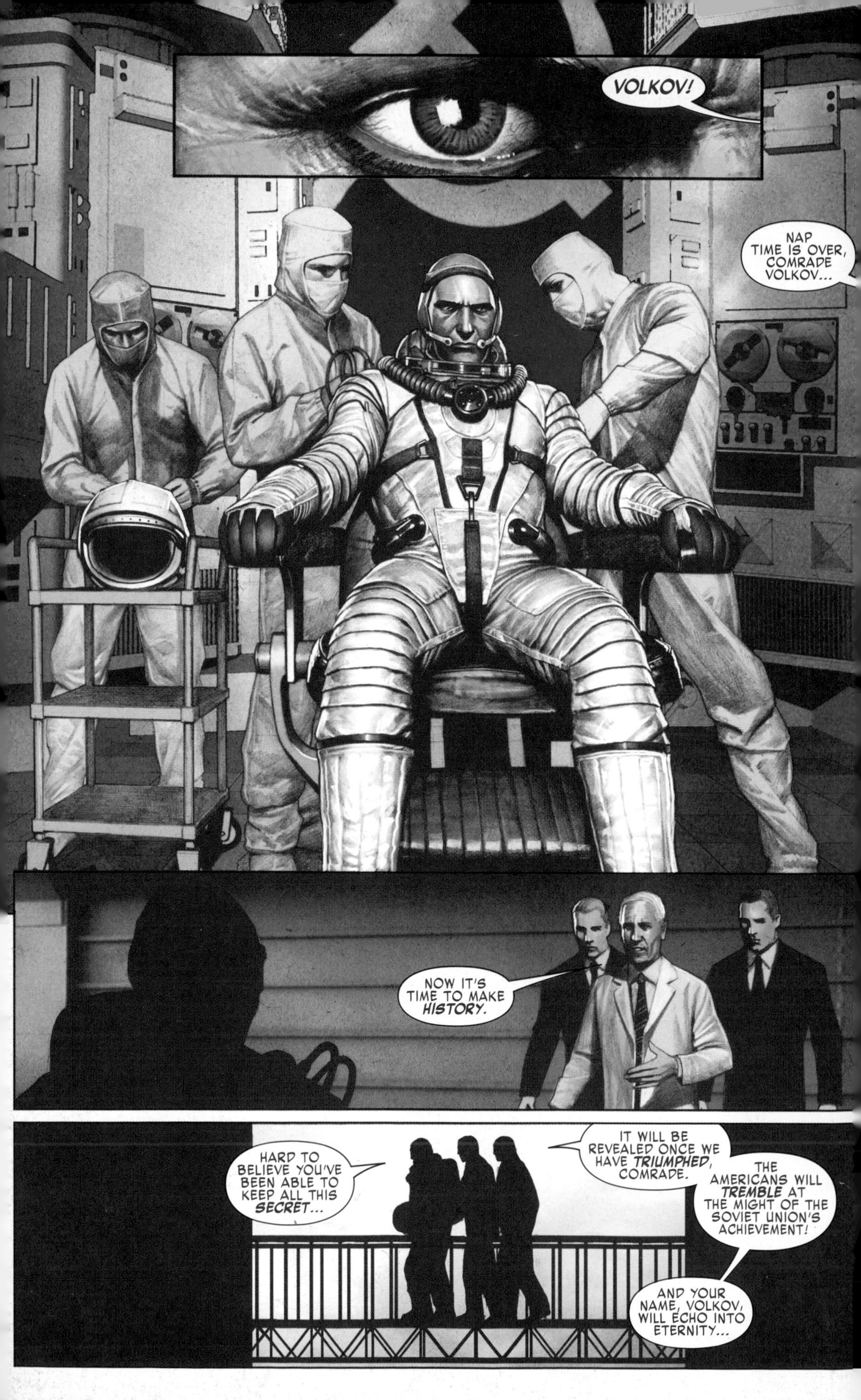
VOLKOV!
NAP TIME IS OVER, COMRADE VOLKOV...
NOW IT'S TIME TO MAKE HISTORY.
HARD TO BELIEVE YOU'VE BEEN ABLE TO KEEP ALL THIS SECRET...
IT WILL BE REVEALED ONCE WE HAVE TRIUMPHED, COMRADE.
THE AMERICANS WILL TREMBLE AT THE MIGHT OF THE SOVIET UNION'S ACHIEVEMENT!
AND YOUR NAME, VOLKOV, WILL ECHO INTO ETERNITY...

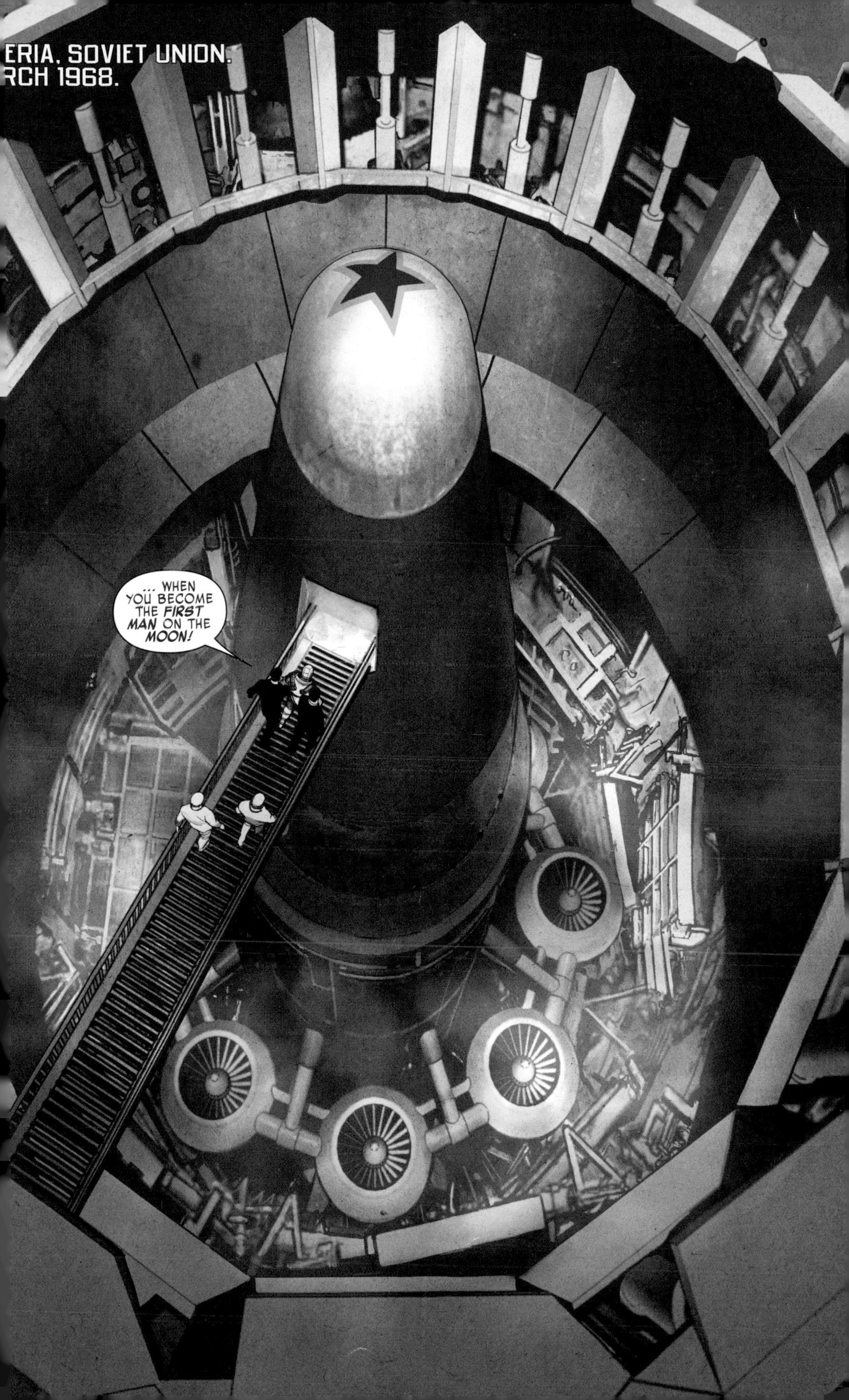
ERIA, SOVIET UNION.
RCH 1968.
... WHEN YOU BECOME THE FIRST MAN ON THE MOON!

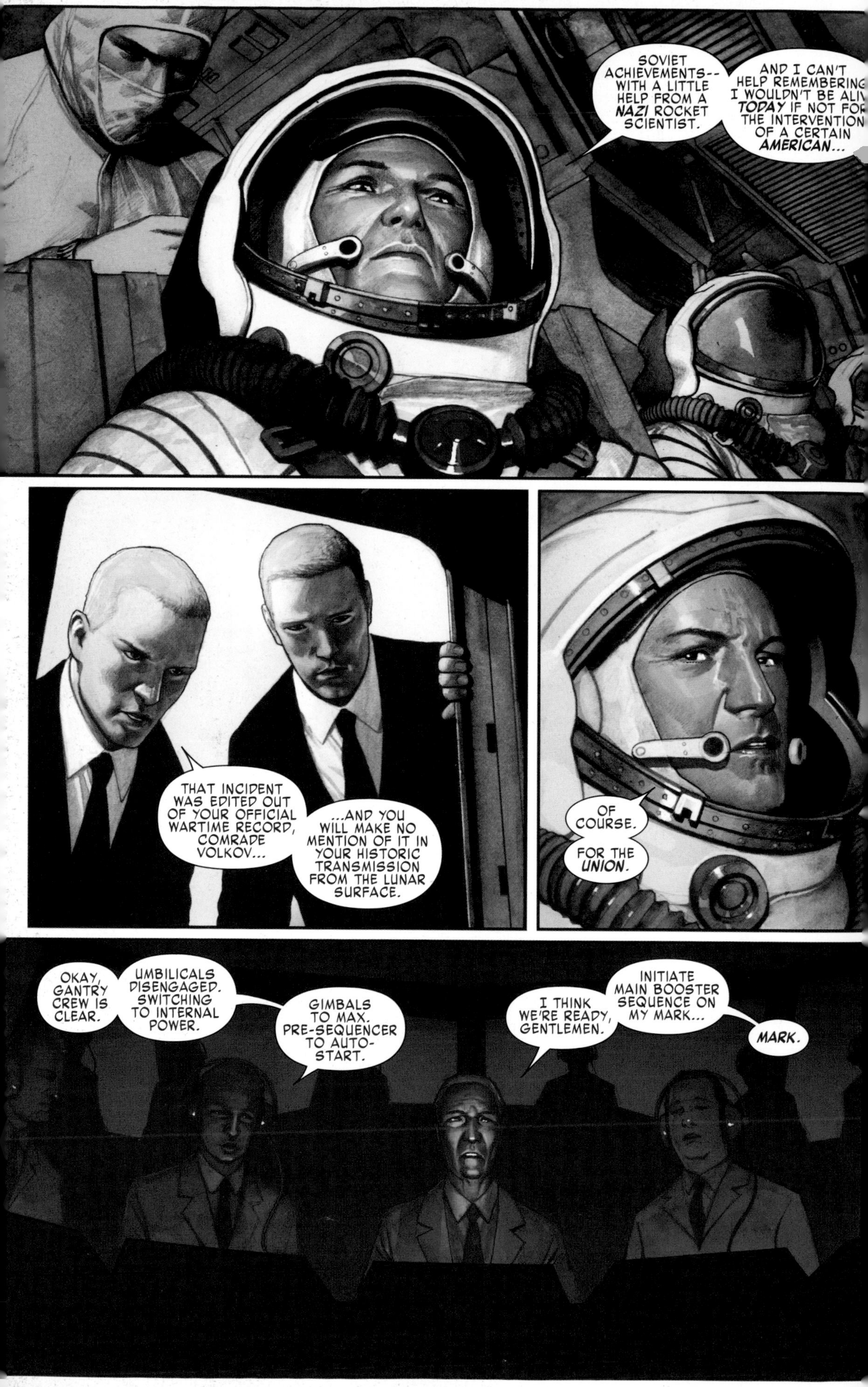
SOVIET ACHIEVEMENTS-- WITH A LITTLE HELP FROM A NAZI ROCKET SCIENTIST.
AND I CAN'T HELP REMEMBERING I WOULDN'T BE ALIV TODAY IF NOT FOR THE INTERVENTION OF A CERTAIN AMERICAN...
THAT INCIDENT WAS EDITED OUT OF YOUR OFFICIAL WARTIME RECORD, COMRADE VOLKOV...
...AND YOU WILL MAKE NO MENTION OF IT IN YOUR HISTORIC TRANSMISSION FROM THE LUNAR SURFACE.
OF COURSE.
FOR THE UNION.
OKAY, GANTRY CREW IS CLEAR.
UMBILICALS DISENGAGED. SWITCHING TO INTERNAL POWER.
GIMBALS TO MAX. PRE-SEQUENCER TO AUTO-START.
I THINK WE'RE READY, GENTLEMEN.
INITIATE MAIN BOOSTER SEQUENCE ON MY MARK...
MARK.

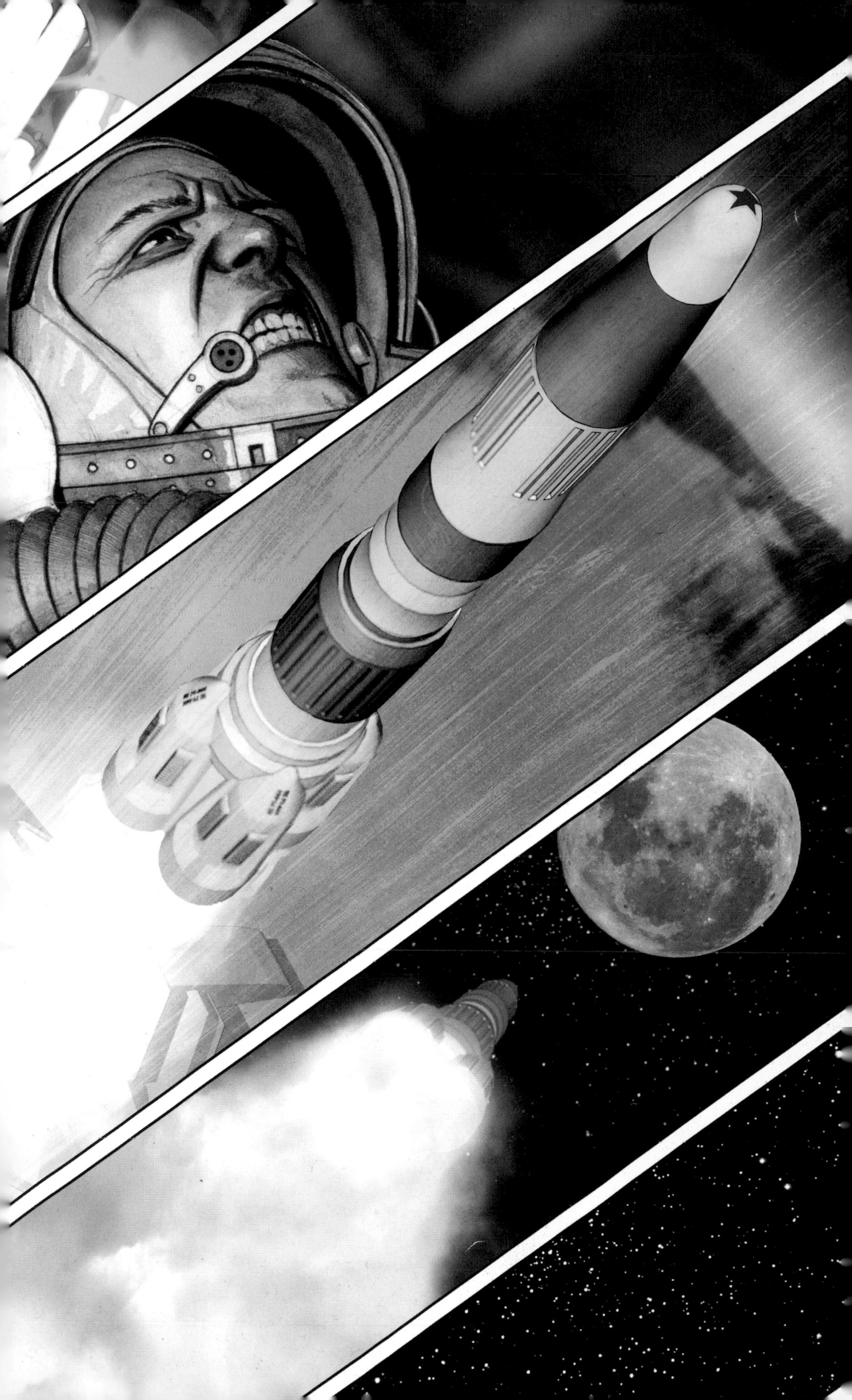

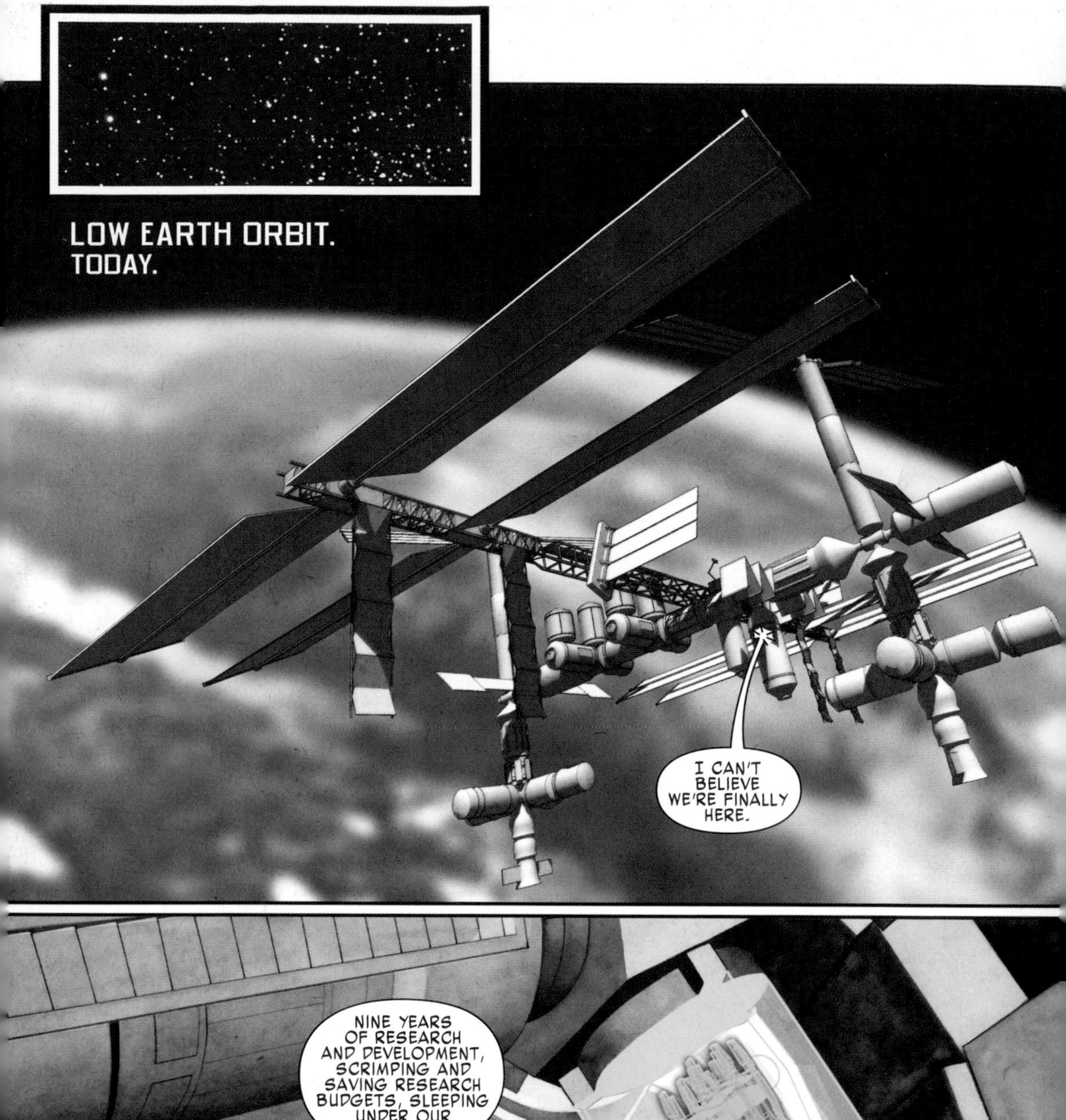
LOW EARTH ORBIT.
TODAY.
I CAN'T BELIEVE WE'RE FINALLY HERE.

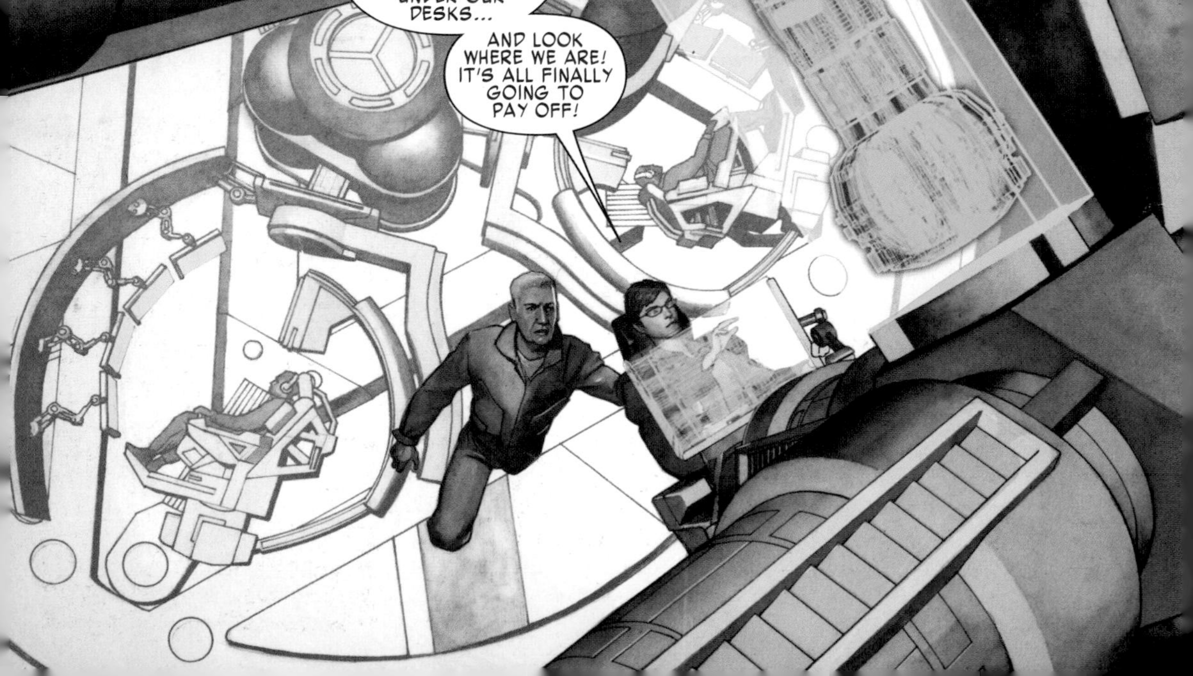
NINE YEARS OF RESEARCH AND DEVELOPMENT, SCRIMPING AND SAVING RESEARCH BUDGETS, SLEEPING UNDER OUR DESKS...
AND LOOK WHERE WE ARE! IT'S ALL FINALLY GOING TO PAY OFF!

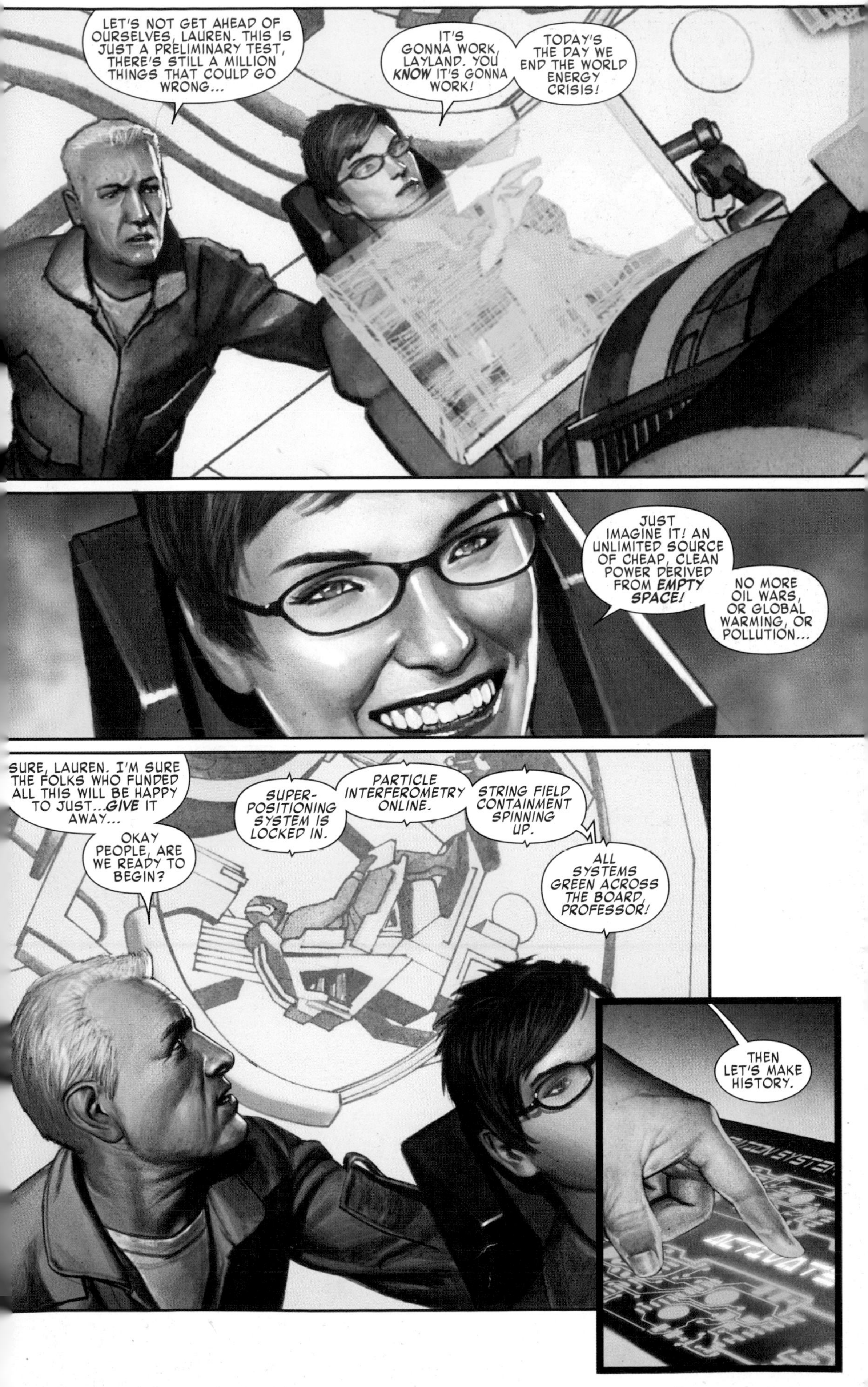
LET'S NOT GET AHEAD OF OURSELVES, LAUREN. THIS IS JUST A PRELIMINARY TEST, THERE'S STILL A MILLION THINGS THAT COULD GO WRONG...
IT'S GONNA WORK, LAYLAND. YOU **KNOW** IT'S GONNA WORK!
TODAY'S THE DAY WE END THE WORLD ENERGY CRISIS!
JUST IMAGINE IT! AN UNLIMITED SOURCE OF CHEAP, CLEAN POWER DERIVED FROM **EMPTY SPACE!**
NO MORE OIL WARS, OR GLOBAL WARMING, OR POLLUTION...
SURE, LAUREN. I'M SURE THE FOLKS WHO FUNDED ALL THIS WILL BE HAPPY TO JUST...**GIVE** IT AWAY...
OKAY PEOPLE, ARE WE READY TO BEGIN?
SUPER-POSITIONING SYSTEM IS LOCKED IN.
PARTICLE INTERFEROMETRY ONLINE.
STRING FIELD CONTAINMENT SPINNING UP.
ALL SYSTEMS GREEN ACROSS THE BOARD, PROFESSOR!
THEN LET'S MAKE HISTORY.
ACTIVATE

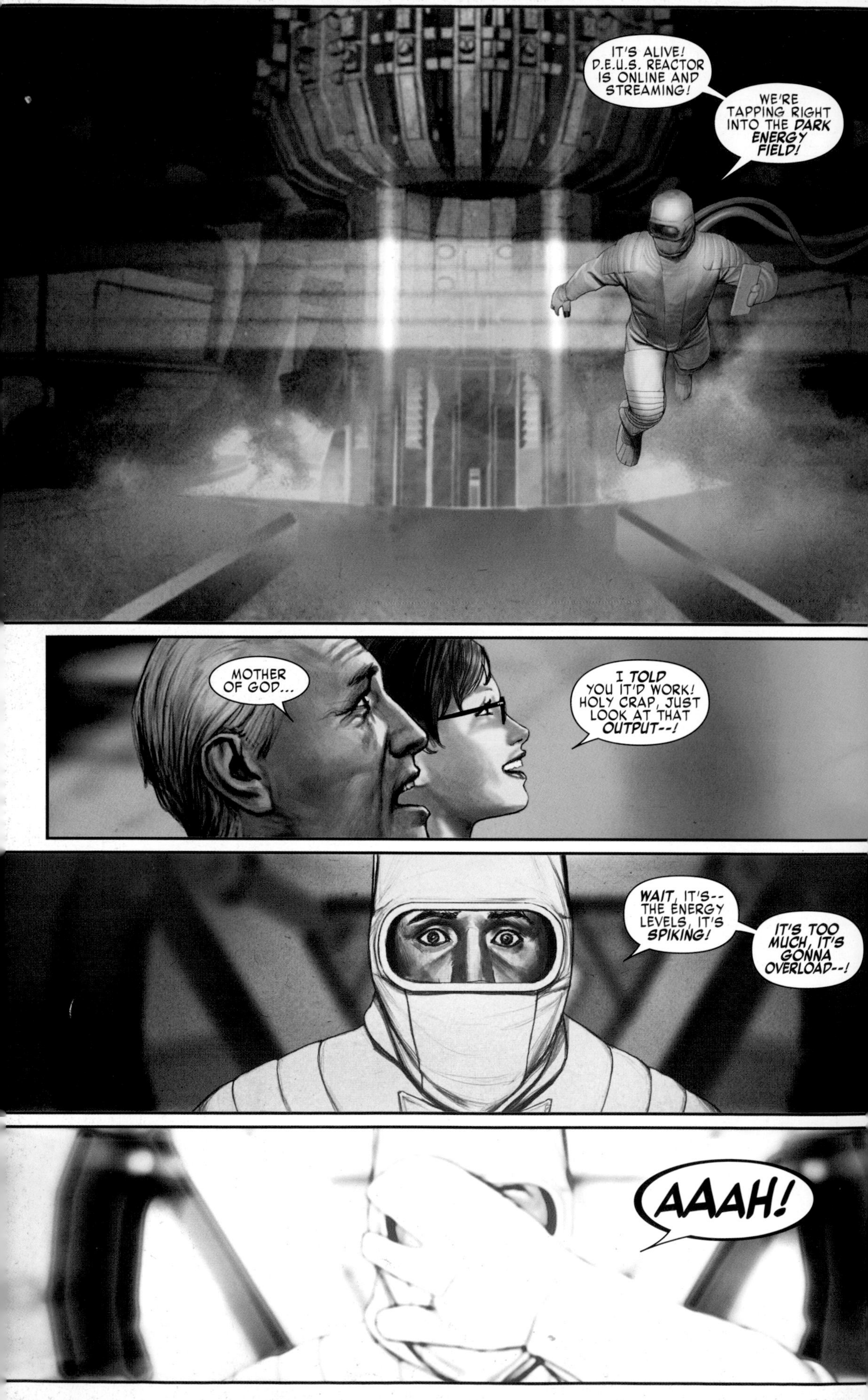
IT'S ALIVE! D.E.U.S. REACTOR IS ONLINE AND STREAMING!
WE'RE TAPPING RIGHT INTO THE DARK ENERGY FIELD!
MOTHER OF GOD...
I TOLD YOU IT'D WORK! HOLY CRAP, JUST LOOK AT THAT OUTPUT--!
WAIT, IT'S-- THE ENERGY LEVELS, IT'S SPIKING!
IT'S TOO MUCH, IT'S GONNA OVERLOAD--!
AAAH!

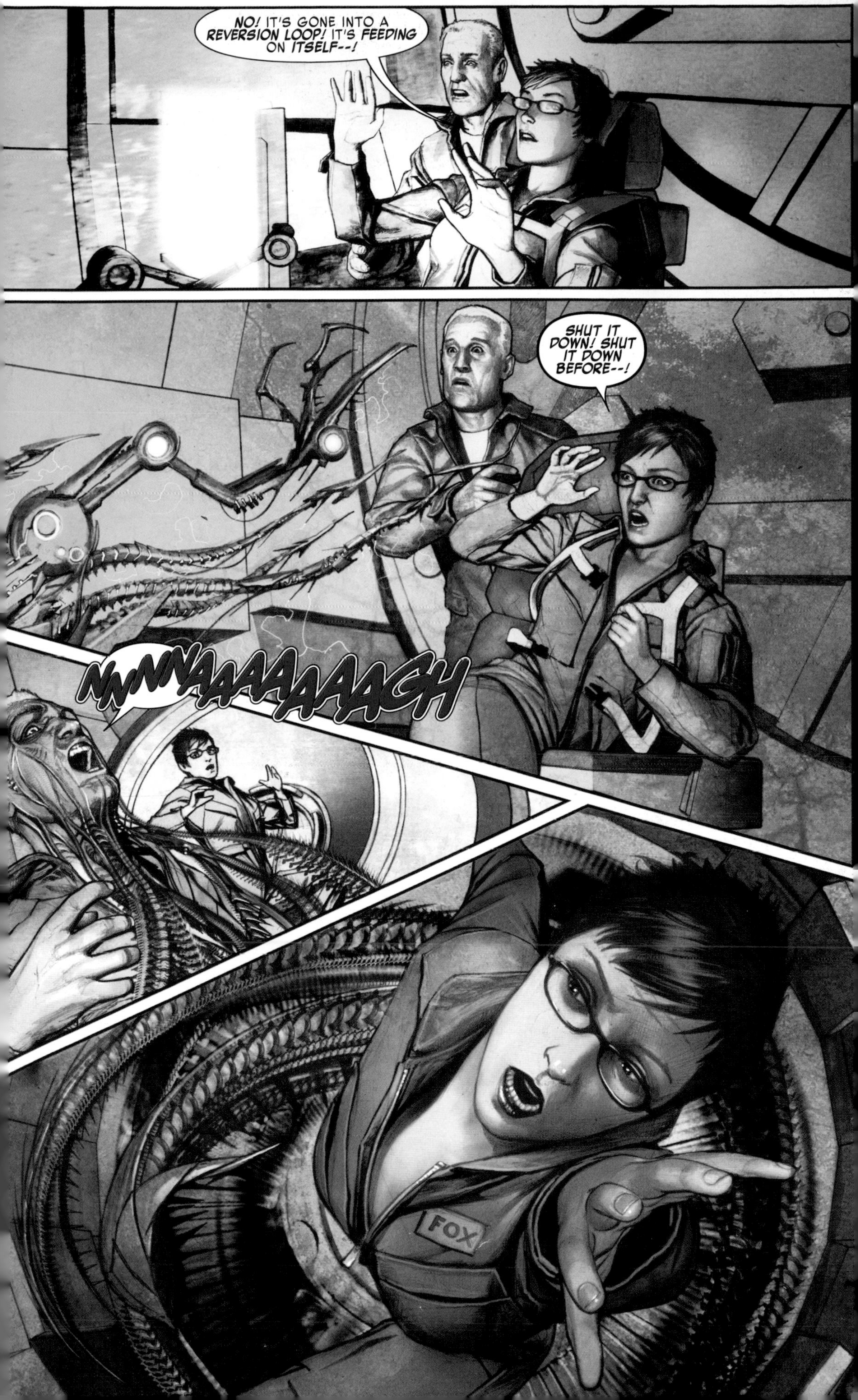
NO! IT'S GONE INTO A REVERSION LOOP! IT'S FEEDING ON ITSELF--!
SHUT IT DOWN! SHUT IT DOWN BEFORE--!
NNNNAAAAAAAAGH
FOX

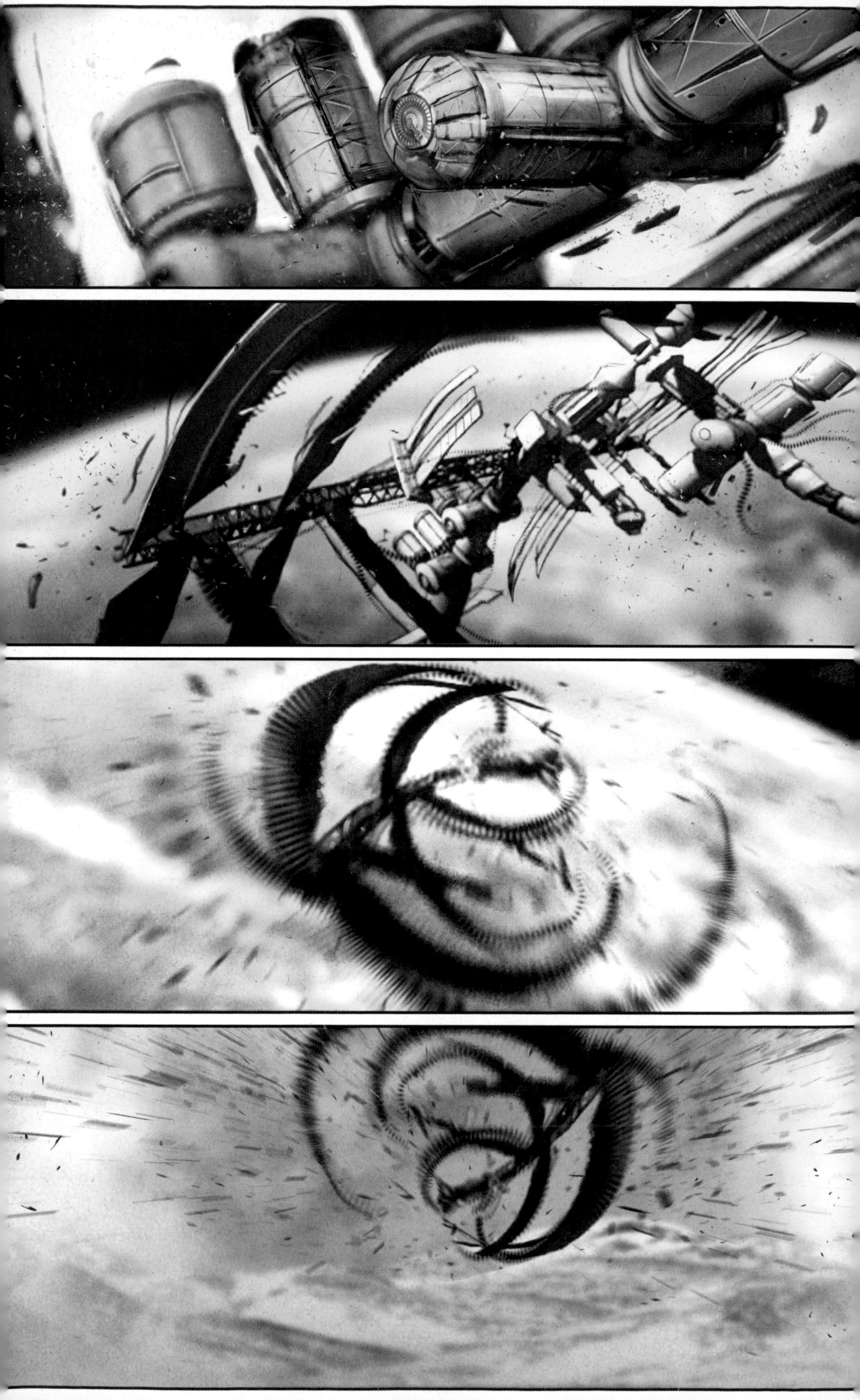

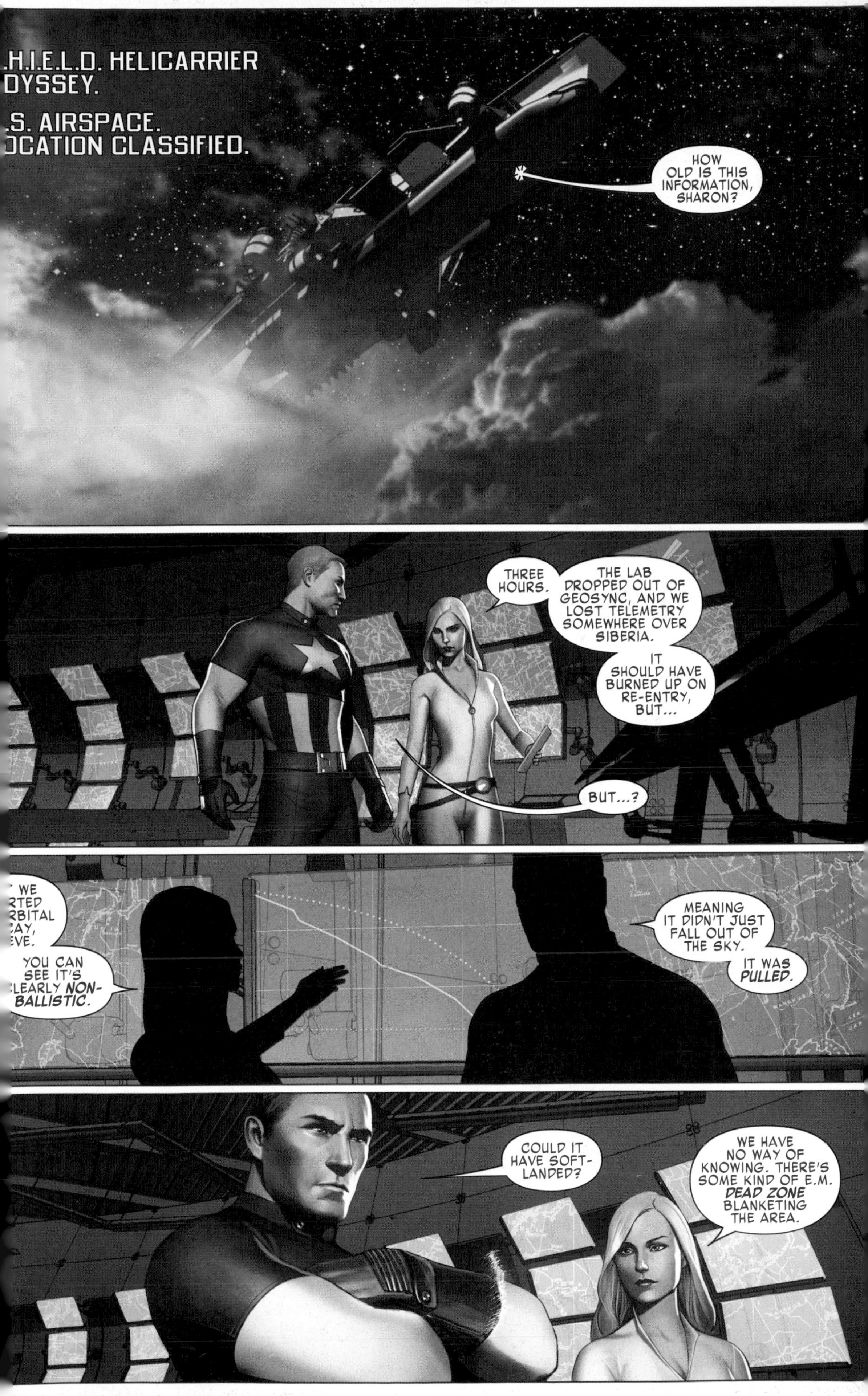
.H.I.E.L.D. HELICARRIER
DYSSEY.
.S. AIRSPACE.
OCATION CLASSIFIED.
HOW OLD IS THIS INFORMATION, SHARON?
THREE HOURS.
THE LAB DROPPED OUT OF GEOSYNC, AND WE LOST TELEMETRY SOMEWHERE OVER SIBERIA.
IT SHOULD HAVE BURNED UP ON RE-ENTRY, BUT...
BUT...?
T WE RTED RBITAL CAY, EVE.
YOU CAN SEE IT'S CLEARLY *NON-BALLISTIC*.
MEANING IT DIDN'T JUST FALL OUT OF THE SKY.
IT WAS *PULLED*.
COULD IT HAVE SOFT-LANDED?
WE HAVE NO WAY OF KNOWING. THERE'S SOME KIND OF E.M. *DEAD ZONE* BLANKETING THE AREA.

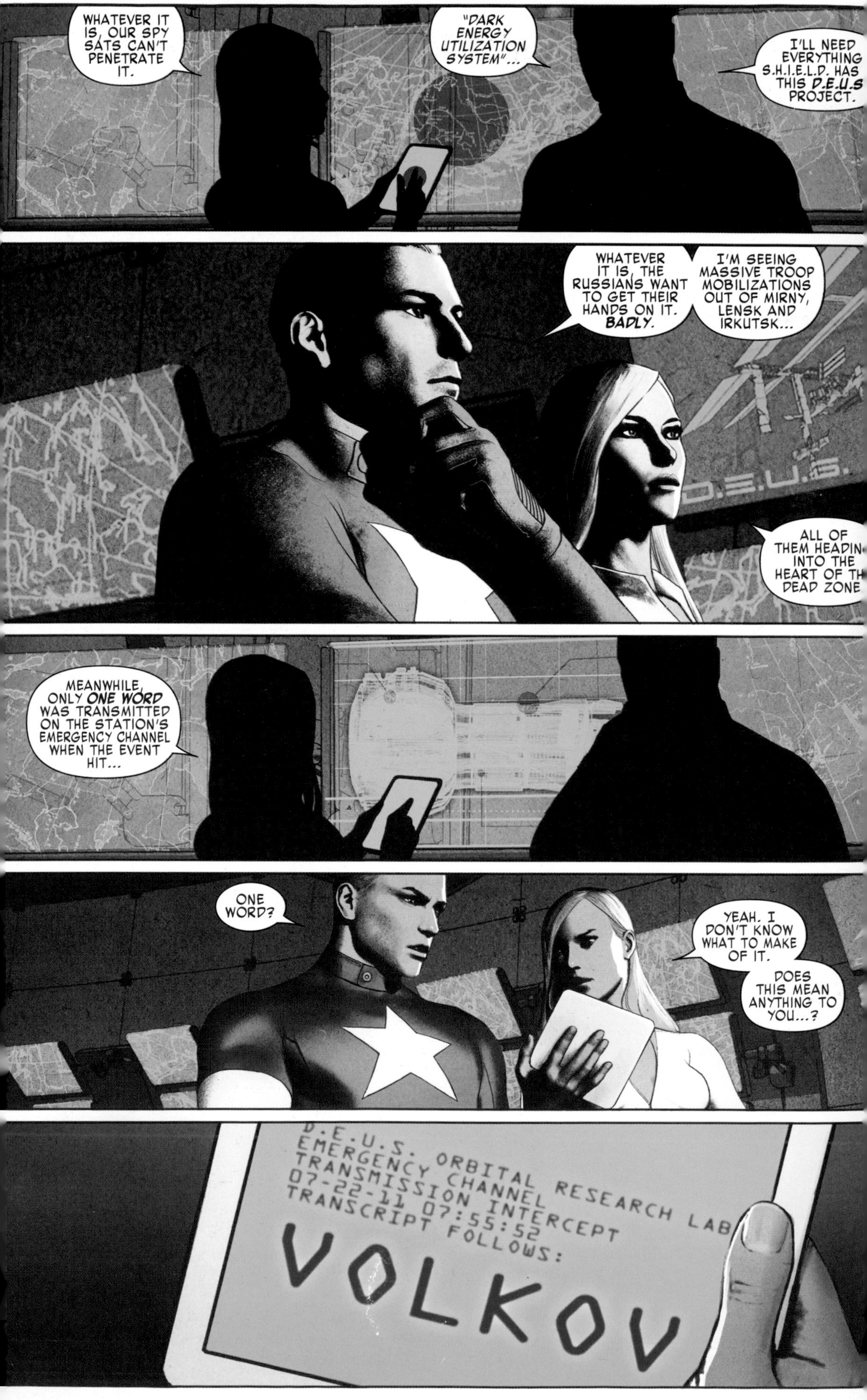
WHATEVER IT IS, OUR SPY SATS CAN'T PENETRATE IT.
"DARK ENERGY UTILIZATION SYSTEM"...
I'LL NEED EVERYTHING S.H.I.E.L.D. HAS THIS D.E.U.S PROJECT.
WHATEVER IT IS, THE RUSSIANS WANT TO GET THEIR HANDS ON IT. BADLY.
I'M SEEING MASSIVE TROOP MOBILIZATIONS OUT OF MIRNY, LENSK AND IRKUTSK...
D.E.U.S.
ALL OF THEM HEADIN INTO THE HEART OF TH DEAD ZONE
MEANWHILE, ONLY ONE WORD WAS TRANSMITTED ON THE STATION'S EMERGENCY CHANNEL WHEN THE EVENT HIT...
ONE WORD?
YEAH. I DON'T KNOW WHAT TO MAKE OF IT.
DOES THIS MEAN ANYTHING TO YOU...?
D.E.U.S. ORBITAL RESEARCH LAB
EMERGENCY CHANNEL
TRANSMISSION INTERCEPT
07-22-11 07:55:52
TRANSCRIPT FOLLOWS:
VOLKOV

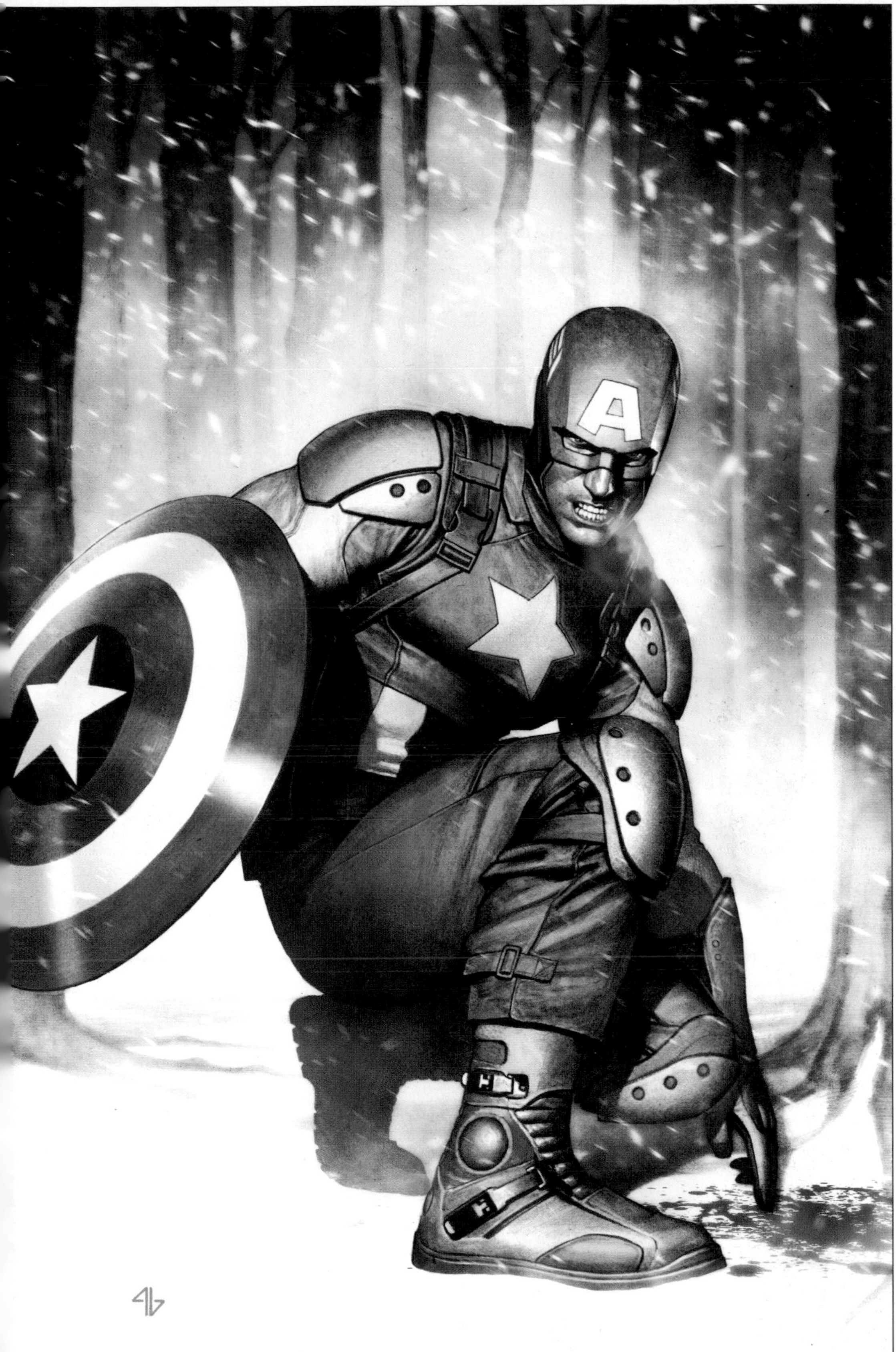

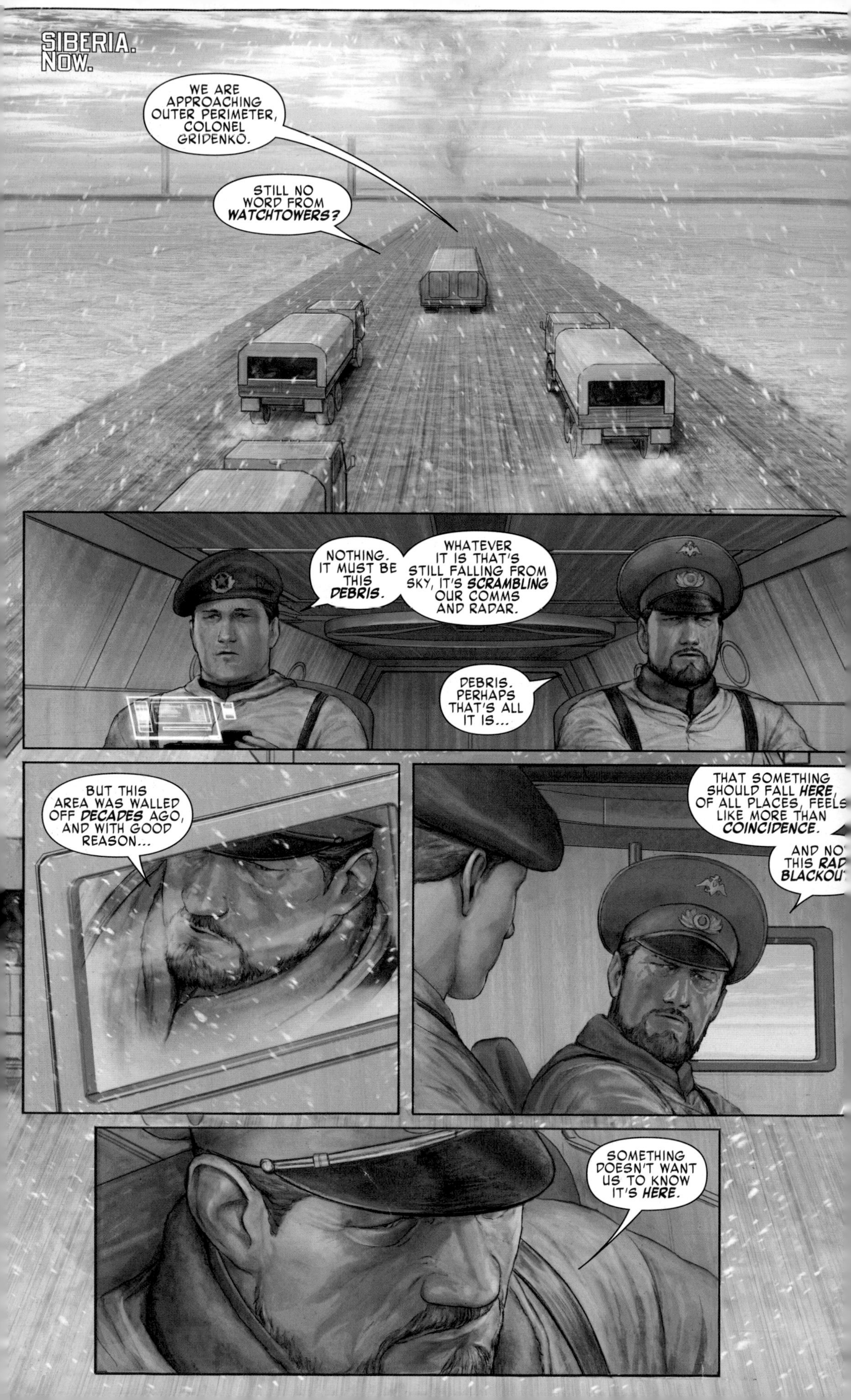
SIBERIA. NOW.
WE ARE APPROACHING OUTER PERIMETER, COLONEL GRIDENKO.
STILL NO WORD FROM WATCHTOWERS?
NOTHING. IT MUST BE THIS DEBRIS.
WHATEVER IT IS THAT'S STILL FALLING FROM SKY, IT'S SCRAMBLING OUR COMMS AND RADAR.
DEBRIS. PERHAPS THAT'S ALL IT IS...
BUT THIS AREA WAS WALLED OFF DECADES AGO, AND WITH GOOD REASON...
THAT SOMETHING SHOULD FALL HERE, OF ALL PLACES, FEELS LIKE MORE THAN COINCIDENCE.
SOMETHING DOESN'T WANT US TO KNOW IT'S HERE.

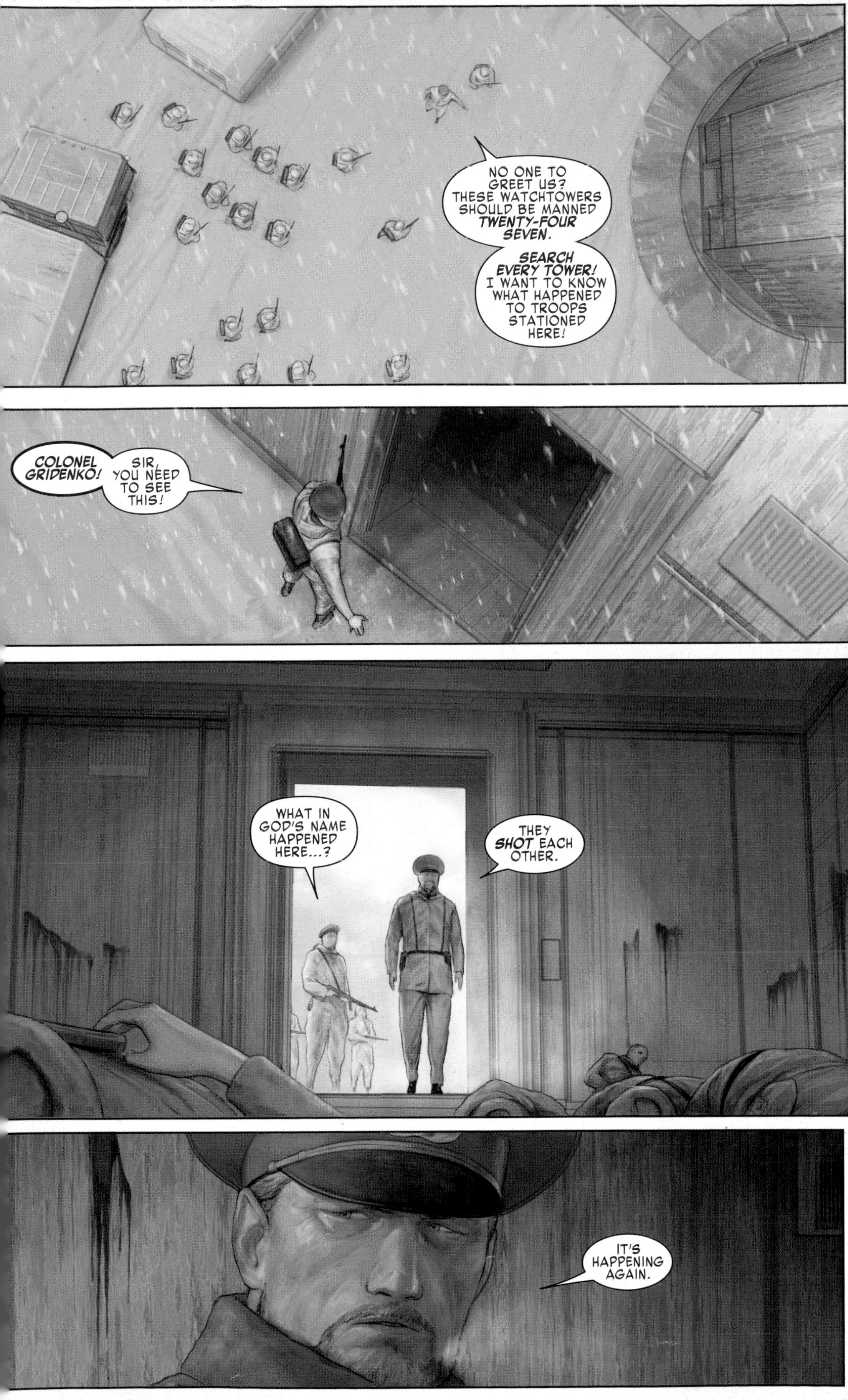
NO ONE TO GREET US? THESE WATCHTOWERS SHOULD BE MANNED TWENTY-FOUR SEVEN.
SEARCH EVERY TOWER! I WANT TO KNOW WHAT HAPPENED TO TROOPS STATIONED HERE!
COLONEL GRIDENKO!
SIR, YOU NEED TO SEE THIS!
WHAT IN GOD'S NAME HAPPENED HERE...?
THEY SHOT EACH OTHER.
IT'S HAPPENING AGAIN.

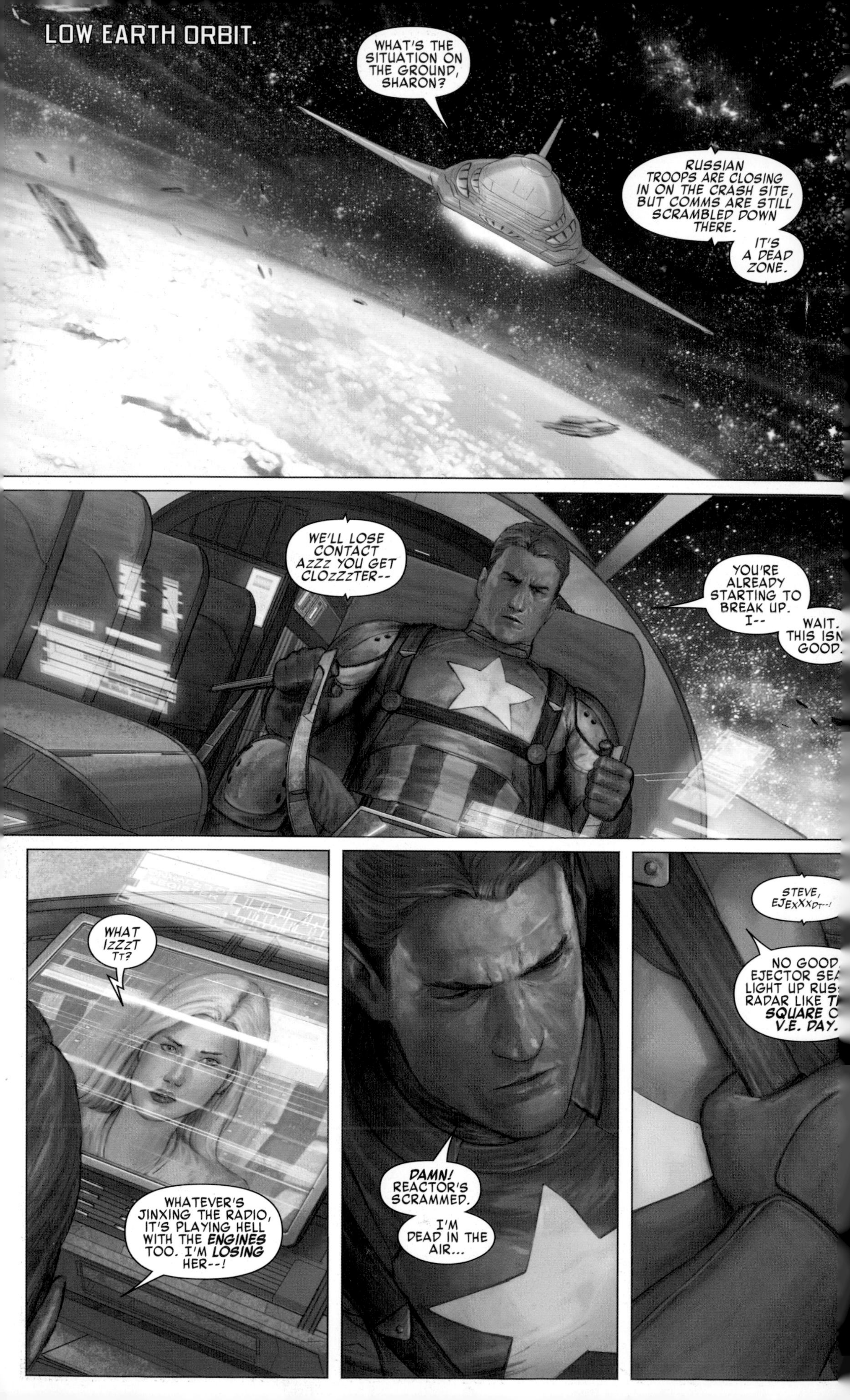
LOW EARTH ORBIT.
WHAT'S THE SITUATION ON THE GROUND, SHARON?
RUSSIAN TROOPS ARE CLOSING IN ON THE CRASH SITE, BUT COMMS ARE STILL SCRAMBLED DOWN THERE.
IT'S A DEAD ZONE.
WE'LL LOSE CONTACT AzZz YOU GET CLOzZzZTER--
YOU'RE ALREADY STARTING TO BREAK UP. I--
WAIT. THIS ISN GOOD.
WHAT IzZzT Tt?
WHATEVER'S JINXING THE RADIO, IT'S PLAYING HELL WITH THE ENGINES TOO. I'M LOSING HER--!
DAMN! REACTOR'S SCRAMMED.
I'M DEAD IN THE AIR...
STEVE, EJExXxDt--!
NO GOOD. EJECTOR SEA LIGHT UP RUS RADAR LIKE T SQUARE O V.E. DAY.

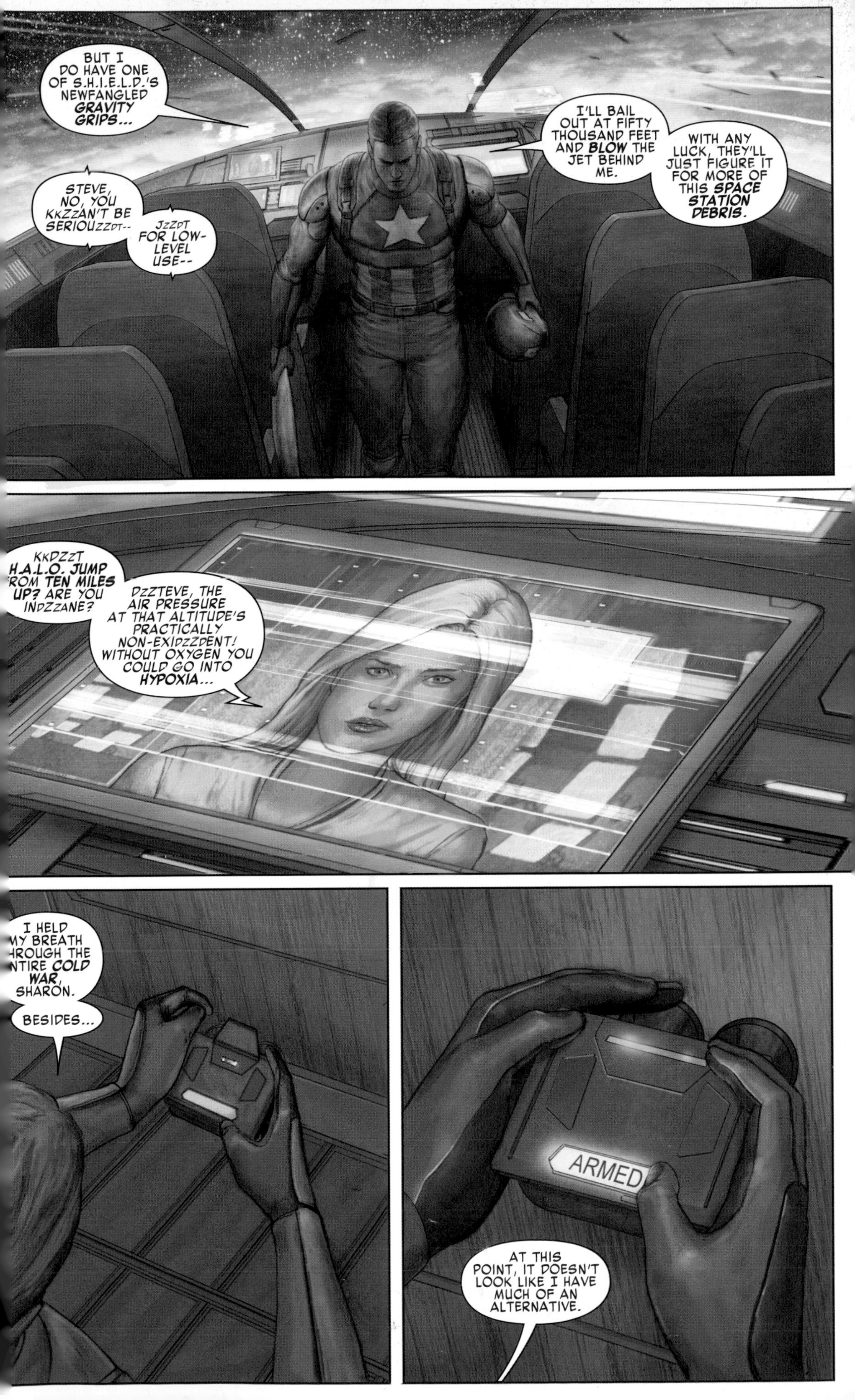
BUT I DO HAVE ONE OF S.H.I.E.L.D.'S NEWFANGLED GRAVITY GRIPS...
STEVE, NO, YOU KKZZAN'T BE SERIOUZZDT--
JZZDT FOR LOW-LEVEL USE--
I'LL BAIL OUT AT FIFTY THOUSAND FEET AND BLOW THE JET BEHIND ME.
WITH ANY LUCK, THEY'LL JUST FIGURE IT FOR MORE OF THIS SPACE STATION DEBRIS.
KKDZZT H.A.L.O. JUMP ROM TEN MILES UP? ARE YOU INDZZANE?
DZZTEVE, THE AIR PRESSURE AT THAT ALTITUDE'S PRACTICALLY NON-EXIDZZDENT! WITHOUT OXYGEN YOU COULD GO INTO HYPOXIA...
I HELD MY BREATH HROUGH THE NTIRE COLD WAR, SHARON.
BESIDES...
ARMED
AT THIS POINT, IT DOESN'T LOOK LIKE I HAVE MUCH OF AN ALTERNATIVE.

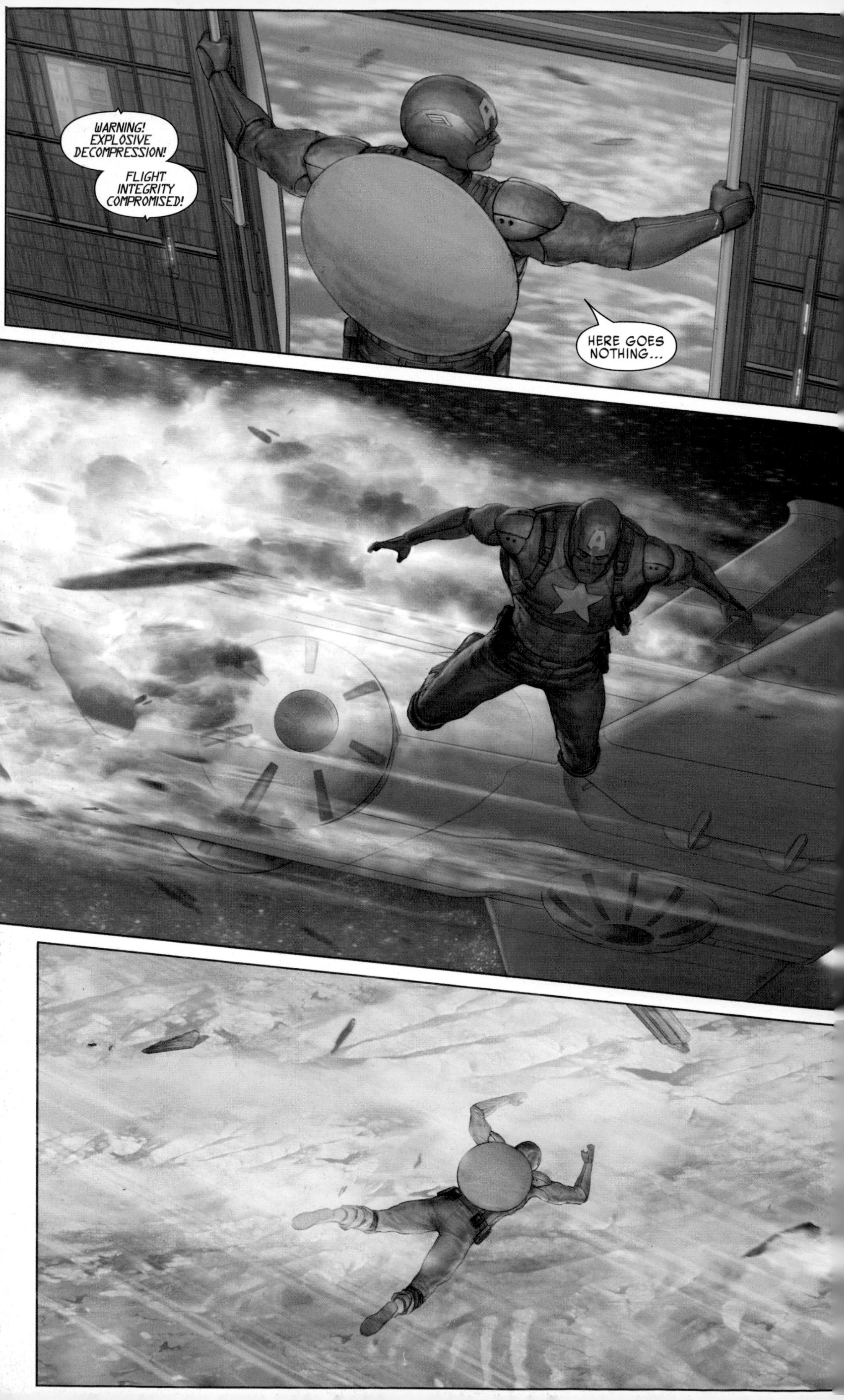
WARNING! EXPLOSIVE DECOMPRESSION!
FLIGHT INTEGRITY COMPROMISED!
HERE GOES NOTHING...

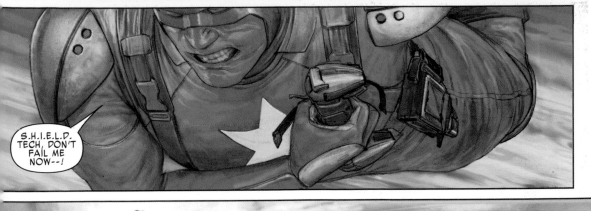

S.H.I.E.L.D. TECH, DON'T FAIL ME NOW--!

NNGH!

I'M DOWN.

SHARON, DO YOU COPY?

HELLO...?

LUNAR ORBIT.
MARCH 1968.

HELLO
DO YOU
COPY...?

NOTHING.

DARK
SIDE OF MOON,
COMRADES. NO
CONTACT WITH
NOVOSIBIRSK UNTIL WE
EMERGE FROM
SHADOW.

WE ARE
ALONE.

IF YOU ARE
CARRYING ANY DEEP,
DARK SECRETS, NOW
WOULD BE GOOD
TIME TO UNBURDEN
YOURSELF!

HAH! I WOULD TELL
YOU ABOUT TIME I
CHEATED ON MY
ILLYANA...

BUT
EVEN OUT
HERE, I FEAR
SHE WOULD
HEAR ME!

OR SMELL YOU
OUT, MORE LIKELY.
YOUR ILLYANA HAS
NOSE LIKE
SHARK!

ON
CIGAR
AND SH
YOU,

WHAT ABOUT
YOU, COMRADE
COMMANDER
VOLKOV?

WHAT
WOULD YOU
SHARE WITH US,
OUT HERE IN
DARK...?

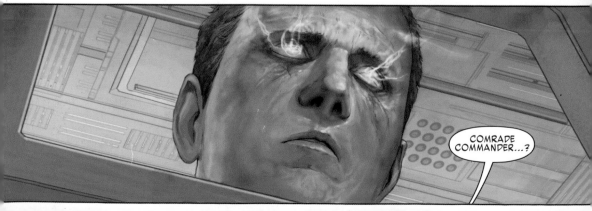

COMRADE
COMMANDER...?

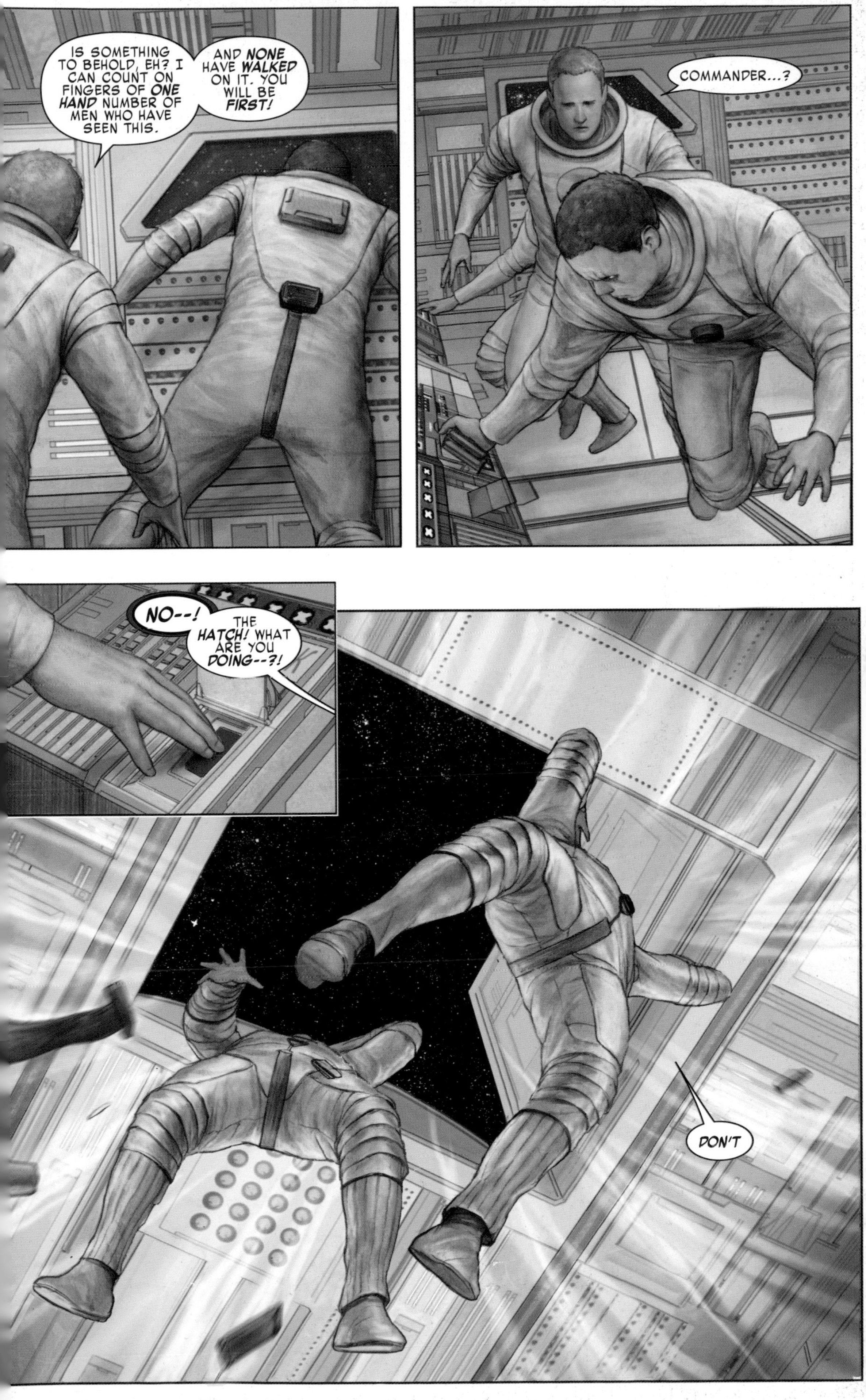
IS SOMETHING TO BEHOLD, EH? I CAN COUNT ON FINGERS OF ONE HAND NUMBER OF MEN WHO HAVE SEEN THIS.
AND NONE HAVE WALKED ON IT. YOU WILL BE FIRST!
COMMANDER...?
NO--!
THE HATCH! WHAT ARE YOU DOING--?!
DON'T

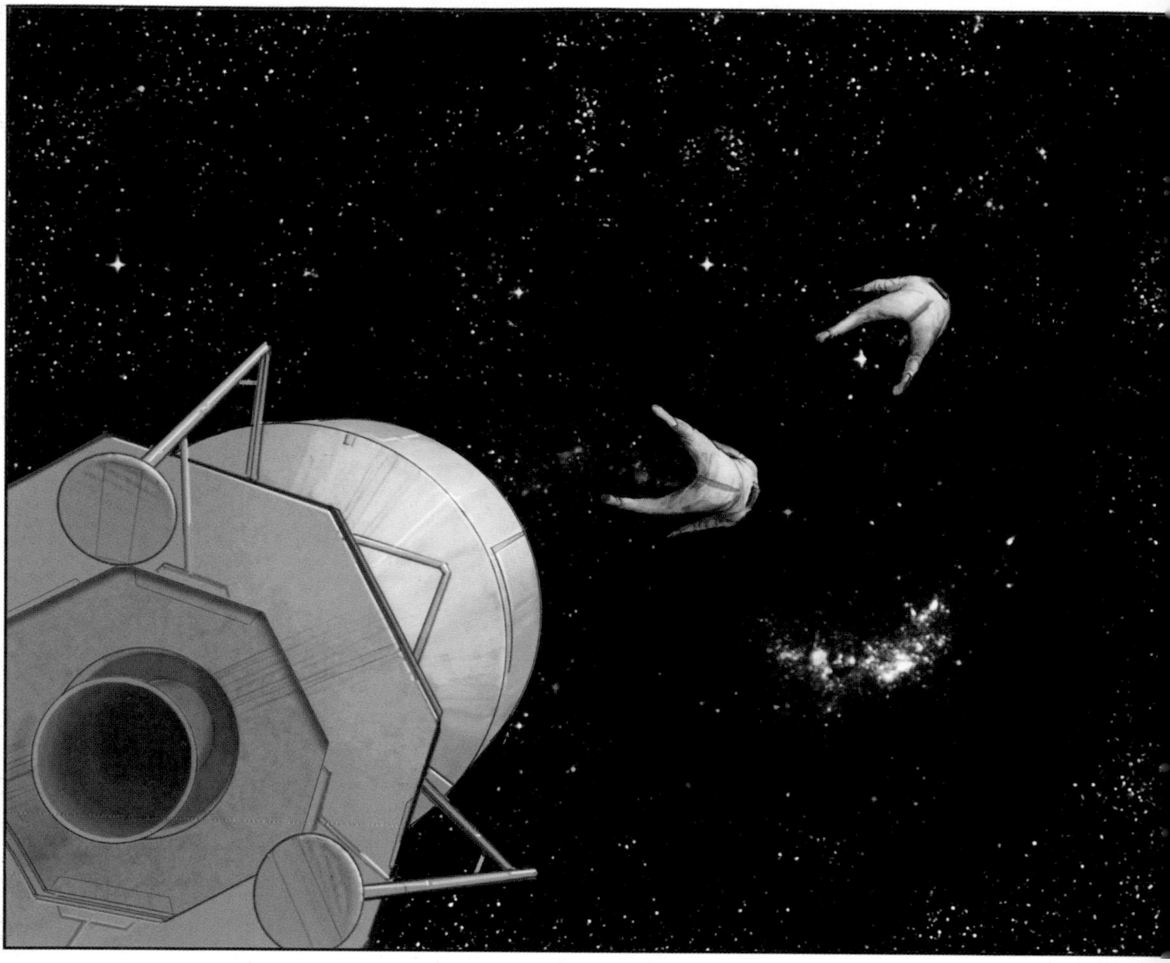

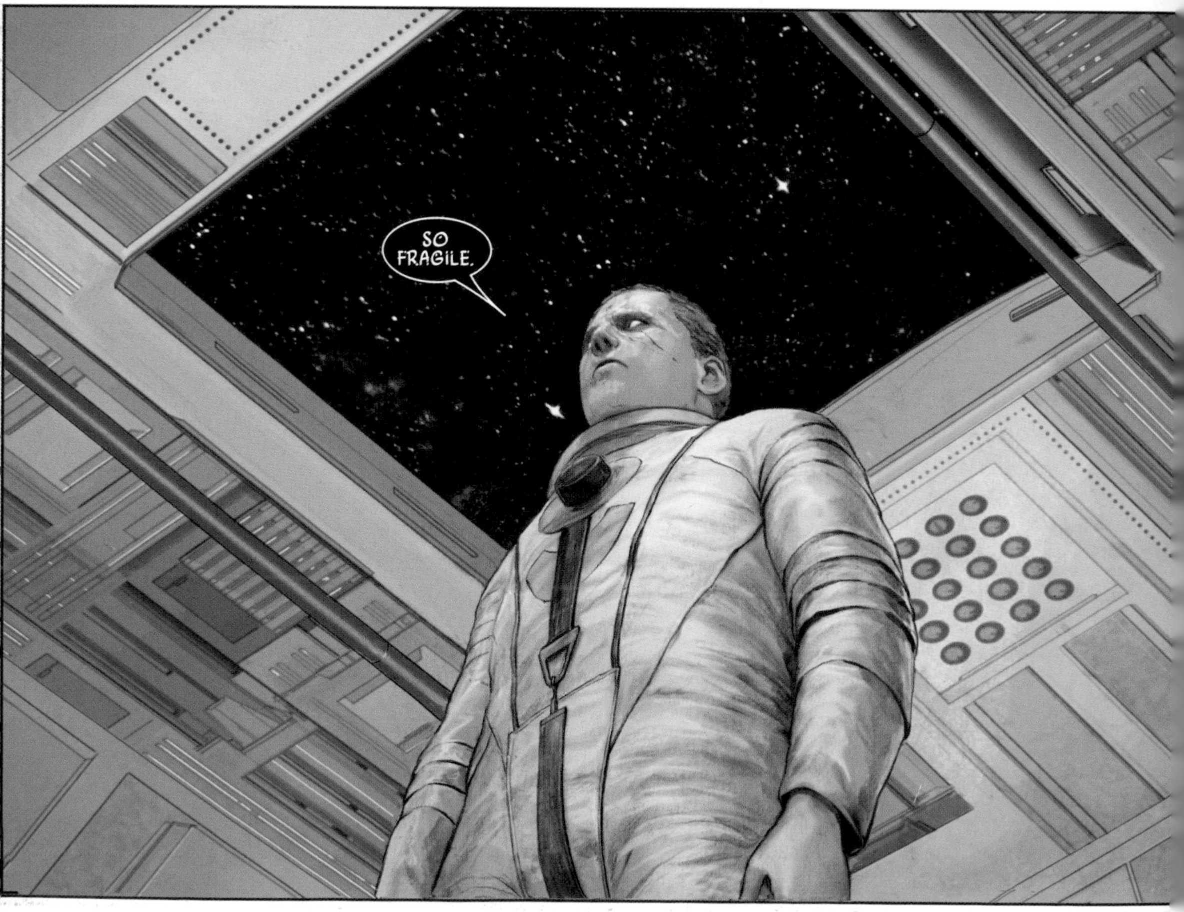
SO FRAGILE.

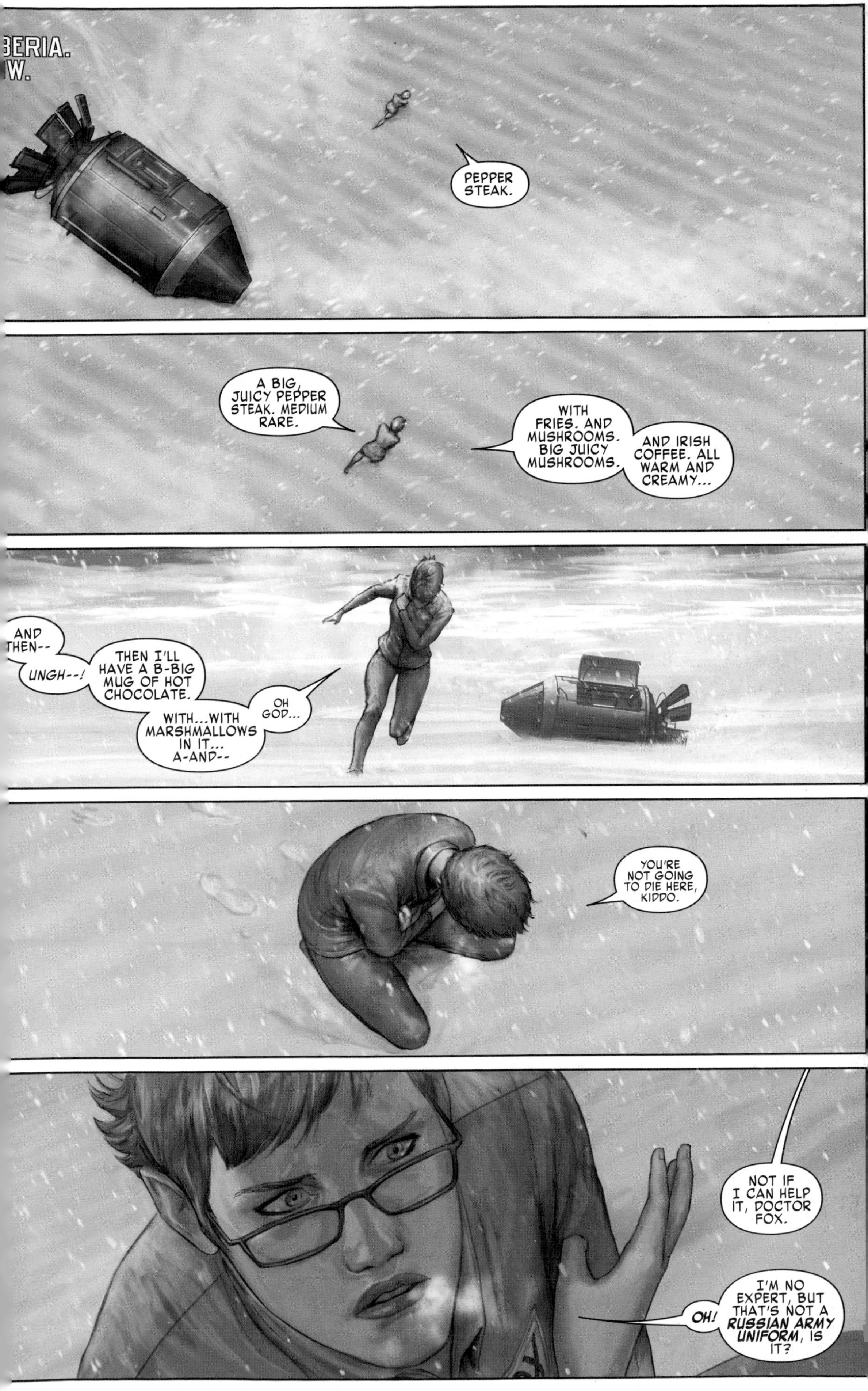
BERIA.
W.
PEPPER STEAK.
A BIG, JUICY PEPPER STEAK. MEDIUM RARE.
WITH FRIES. AND MUSHROOMS. BIG JUICY MUSHROOMS.
AND IRISH COFFEE. ALL WARM AND CREAMY...
AND THEN--
UNGH--!
THEN I'LL HAVE A B-BIG MUG OF HOT CHOCOLATE.
WITH...WITH MARSHMALLOWS IN IT... A-AND--
OH GOD...
YOU'RE NOT GOING TO DIE HERE, KIDDO.
NOT IF I CAN HELP IT, DOCTOR FOX.
OH!
I'M NO EXPERT, BUT THAT'S NOT A RUSSIAN ARMY UNIFORM, IS IT?

I'M HERE TO HELP YOU. ARE THERE ANY OTHER SURVIVORS FROM THE D.E.U.S. SPACE STATION?

I-- I DON'T THINK--

I MEAN, I HAVEN'T SEEN ANYONE. NOT SINCE I GOT TO THE ESCAPE POD...

TH STAT IT--

IT C ALIV

IT HORR

IT'S ALL RIGHT. YOU'RE SAFE NOW.

THAT'S...NOT EVEN REMOTELY TRUE, IS IT?

I W TRYING REASS

GOOD JOB.

COME ON. WE NEED TO MOVE.

FOLLOW IN MY TRACKS. AND STAY LOW.

BECAUSE IF I CAN FIND YOU, SO CAN THE RUSSIANS...

WHY?

AND IF THEY DO, YOU'LL SPEND THE REST OF YOUR LIFE IN AN INTERROGATION CELL WHILE THEY STRIP-MINE THE CONTENTS OF THAT FORMIDABLE BRAIN OF YOURS.

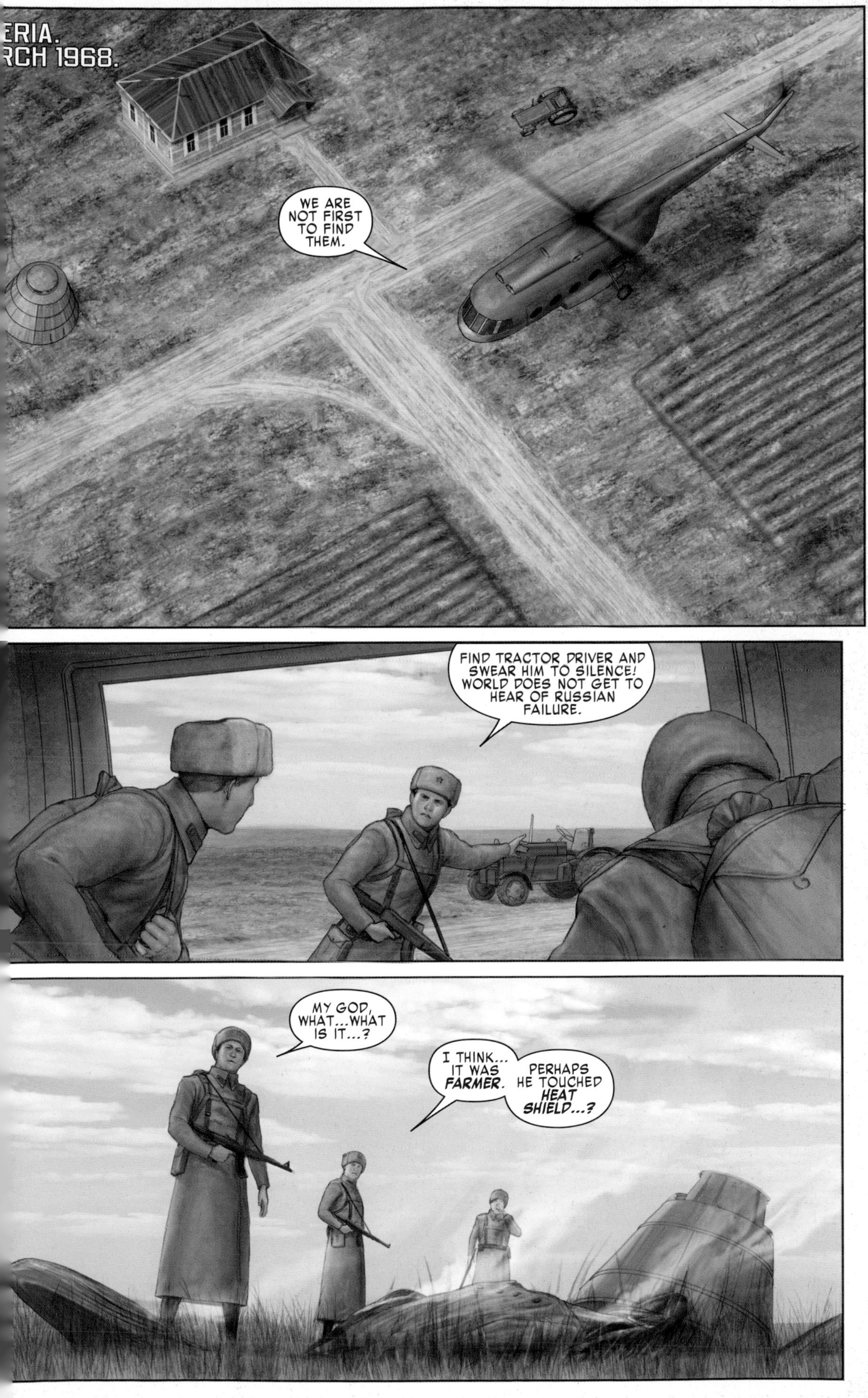
ERIA.
RCH 1968.
WE ARE NOT FIRST TO FIND THEM.
FIND TRACTOR DRIVER AND SWEAR HIM TO SILENCE! WORLD DOES NOT GET TO HEAR OF RUSSIAN FAILURE.
MY GOD, WHAT...WHAT IS IT...?
I THINK... IT WAS FARMER.
PERHAPS HE TOUCHED HEAT SHIELD...?

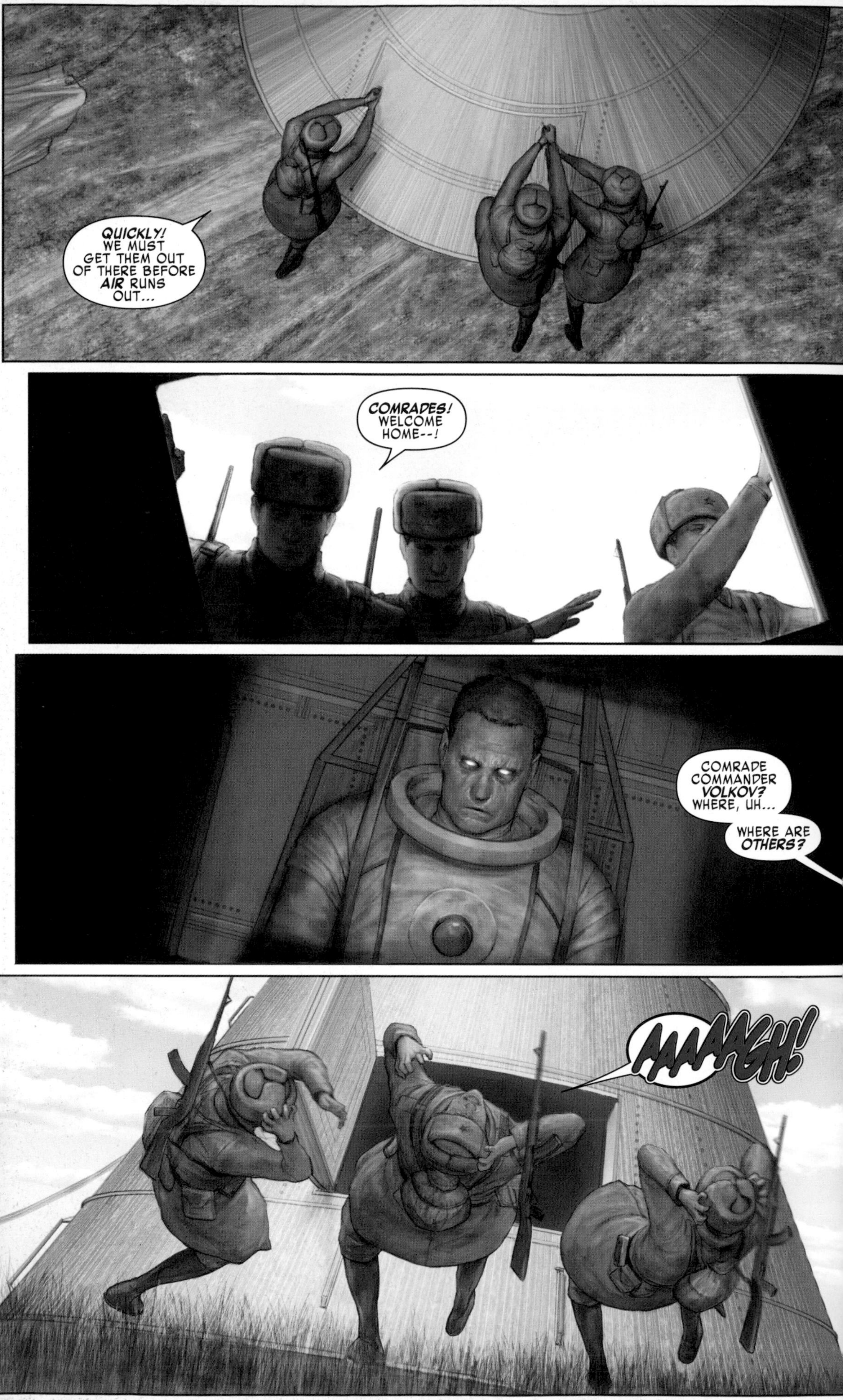
QUICKLY! WE MUST GET THEM OUT OF THERE BEFORE AIR RUNS OUT...
COMRADES! WELCOME HOME--!
COMRADE COMMANDER VOLKOV? WHERE, UH...
WHERE ARE OTHERS?
AAAAAGH!

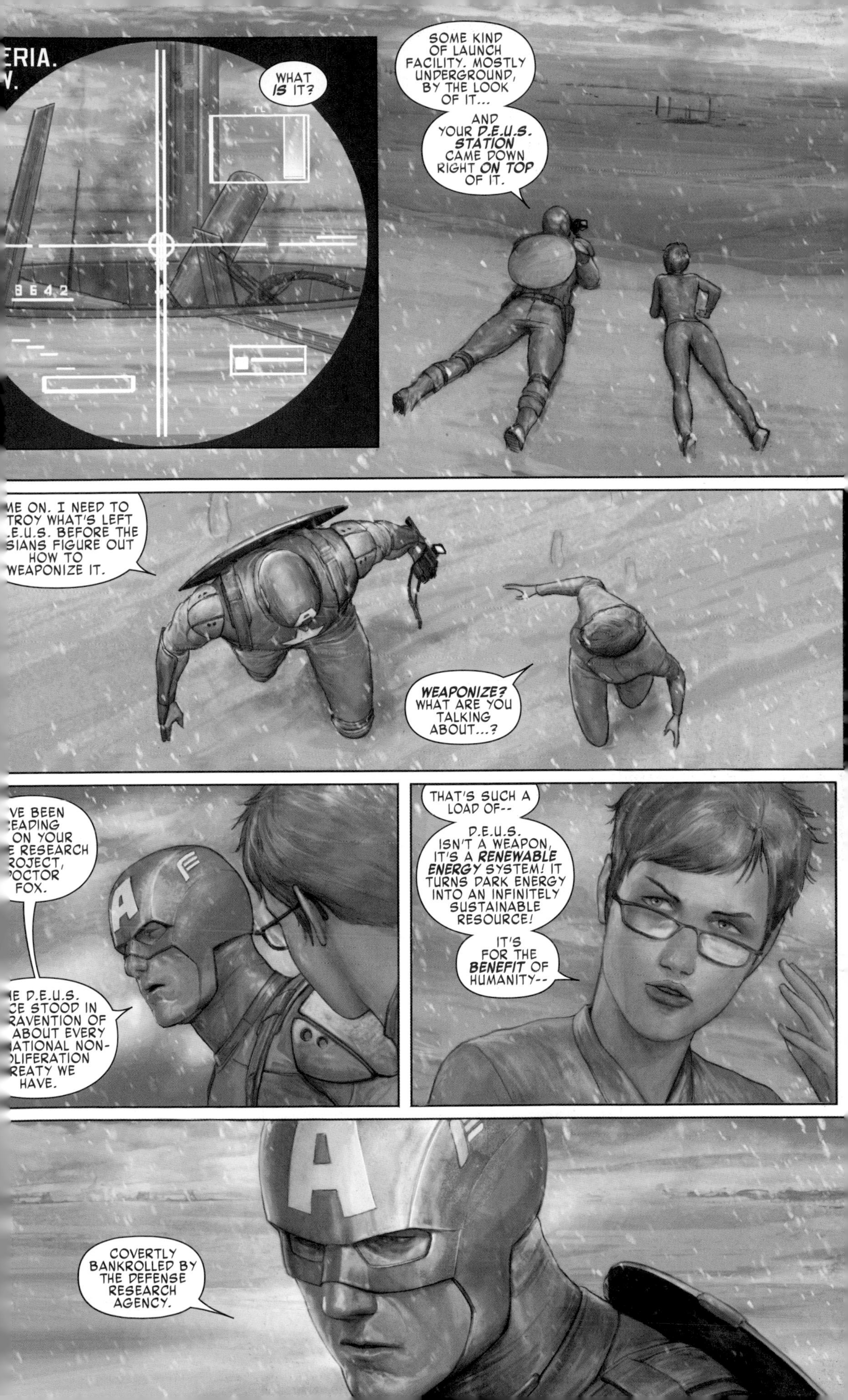
ERIA.
V.
WHAT IS IT?
8642
SOME KIND OF LAUNCH FACILITY. MOSTLY UNDERGROUND, BY THE LOOK OF IT...
AND YOUR D.E.U.S. STATION CAME DOWN RIGHT ON TOP OF IT.
ME ON. I NEED TO TROY WHAT'S LEFT D.E.U.S. BEFORE THE SIANS FIGURE OUT HOW TO WEAPONIZE IT.
WEAPONIZE? WHAT ARE YOU TALKING ABOUT...?
VE BEEN EADING ON YOUR E RESEARCH ROJECT, DOCTOR FOX.
HE D.E.U.S. CE STOOD IN RAVENTION OF ABOUT EVERY NATIONAL NON- OLIFERATION REATY WE HAVE.
THAT'S SUCH A LOAD OF--
D.E.U.S. ISN'T A WEAPON, IT'S A RENEWABLE ENERGY SYSTEM! IT TURNS DARK ENERGY INTO AN INFINITELY SUSTAINABLE RESOURCE!
IT'S FOR THE BENEFIT OF HUMANITY--
COVERTLY BANKROLLED BY THE DEFENSE RESEARCH AGENCY.

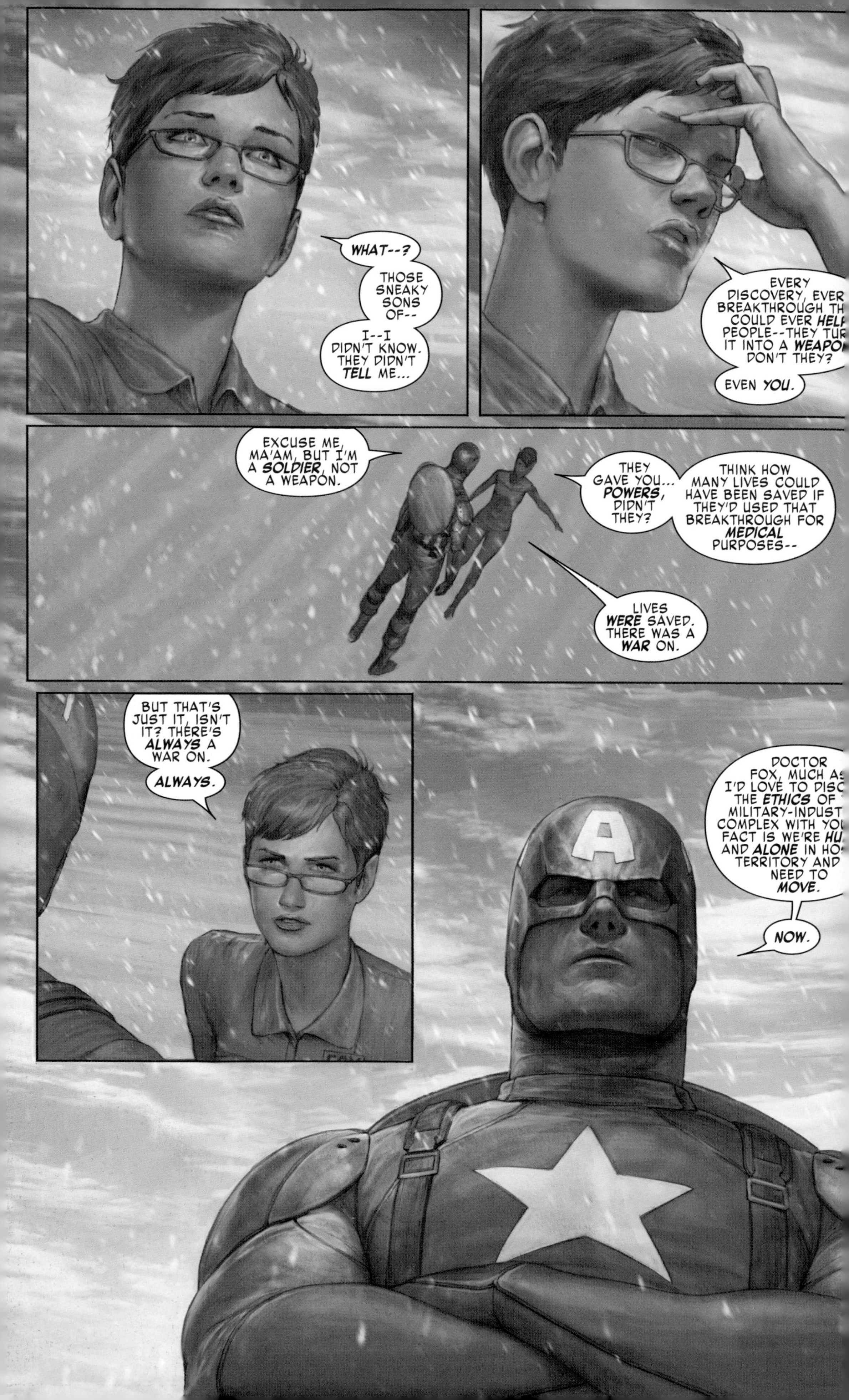
WHAT--?
THOSE SNEAKY SONS OF--
I--I DIDN'T KNOW. THEY DIDN'T TELL ME...
EVERY DISCOVERY, EVER BREAKTHROUGH TH COULD EVER HELP PEOPLE--THEY TUR IT INTO A WEAPON DON'T THEY?
EVEN YOU.
EXCUSE ME, MA'AM, BUT I'M A SOLDIER, NOT A WEAPON.
THEY GAVE YOU... POWERS, DIDN'T THEY?
THINK HOW MANY LIVES COULD HAVE BEEN SAVED IF THEY'D USED THAT BREAKTHROUGH FOR MEDICAL PURPOSES--
LIVES WERE SAVED. THERE WAS A WAR ON.
BUT THAT'S JUST IT, ISN'T IT? THERE'S ALWAYS A WAR ON.
ALWAYS.
DOCTOR FOX, MUCH AS I'D LOVE TO DISC THE ETHICS OF MILITARY-INDUST COMPLEX WITH YOU FACT IS WE'RE HU AND ALONE IN HO TERRITORY AND NEED TO MOVE.
NOW.

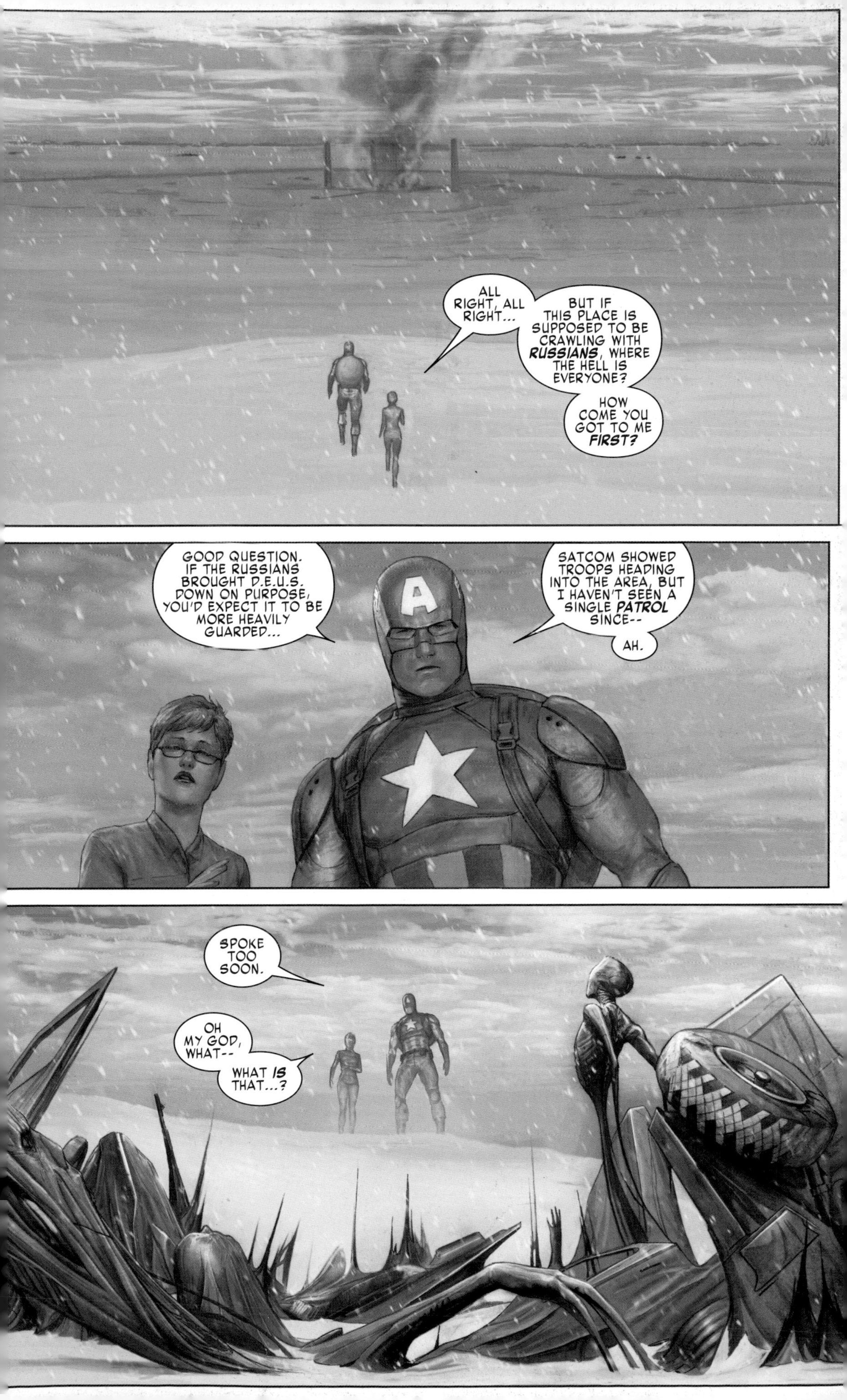
ALL RIGHT, ALL RIGHT...
BUT IF THIS PLACE IS SUPPOSED TO BE CRAWLING WITH RUSSIANS, WHERE THE HELL IS EVERYONE?
HOW COME YOU GOT TO ME FIRST?
GOOD QUESTION. IF THE RUSSIANS BROUGHT D.E.U.S. DOWN ON PURPOSE, YOU'D EXPECT IT TO BE MORE HEAVILY GUARDED...
SATCOM SHOWED TROOPS HEADING INTO THE AREA, BUT I HAVEN'T SEEN A SINGLE PATROL SINCE--
AH.
SPOKE TOO SOON.
OH MY GOD, WHAT--
WHAT IS THAT...?

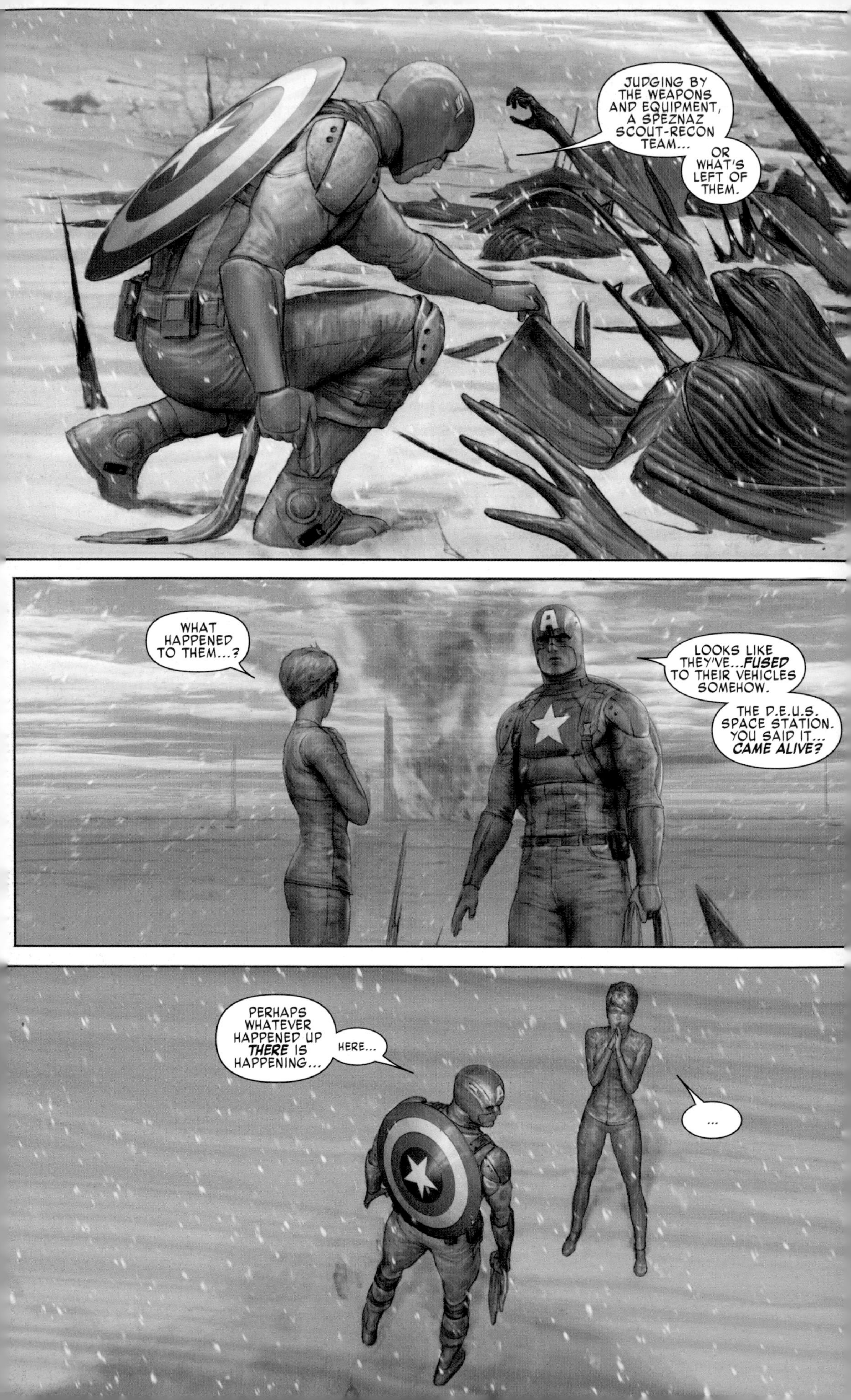
JUDGING BY THE WEAPONS AND EQUIPMENT, A SPEZNAZ SCOUT-RECON TEAM...
OR WHAT'S LEFT OF THEM.
WHAT HAPPENED TO THEM...?
LOOKS LIKE THEY'VE...FUSED TO THEIR VEHICLES SOMEHOW.
THE D.E.U.S. SPACE STATION. YOU SAID IT... CAME ALIVE?
PERHAPS WHATEVER HAPPENED UP THERE IS HAPPENING...
HERE...
...

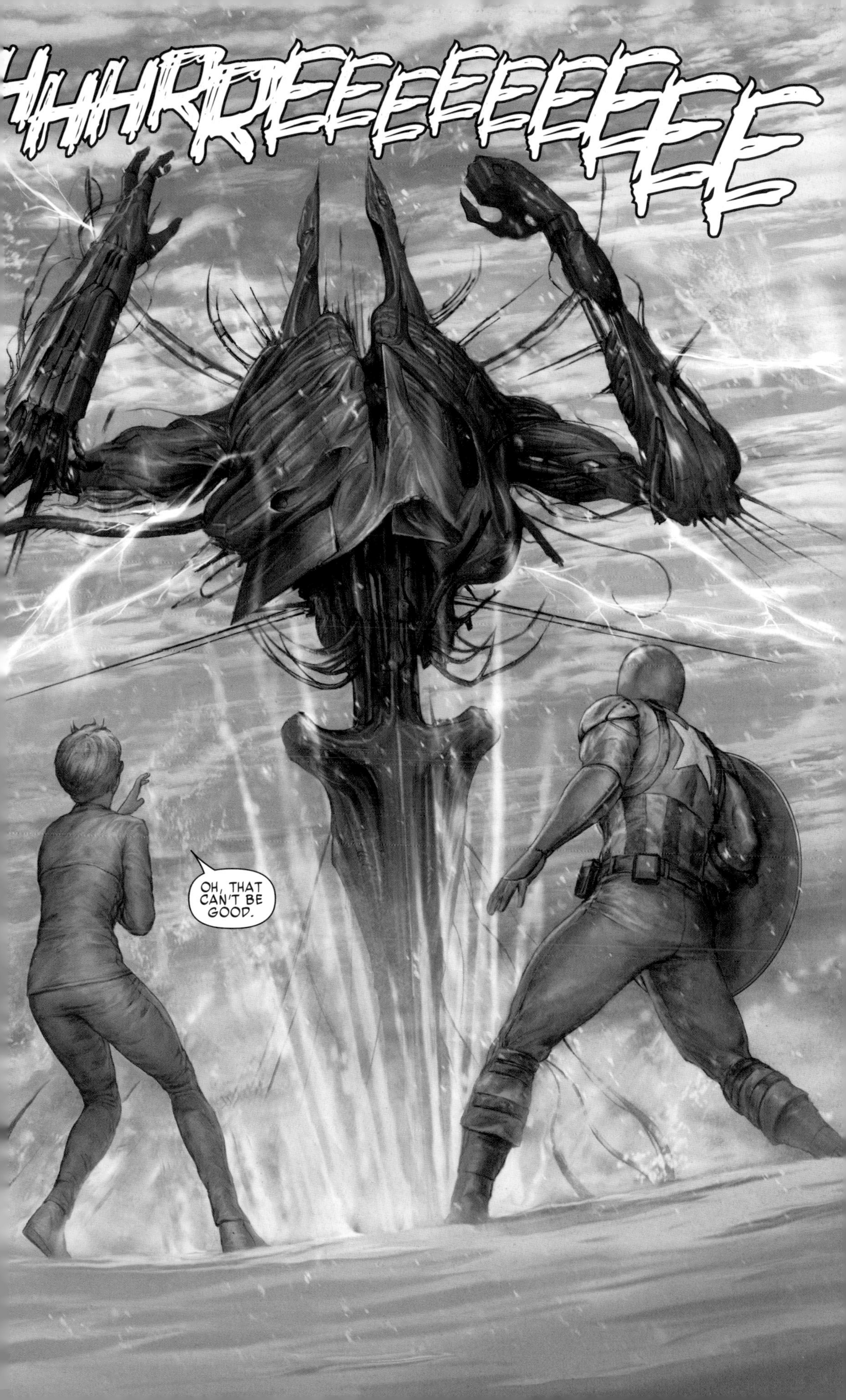
HHHREEEEEEEEEEEEE
OH, THAT CAN'T BE GOOD.

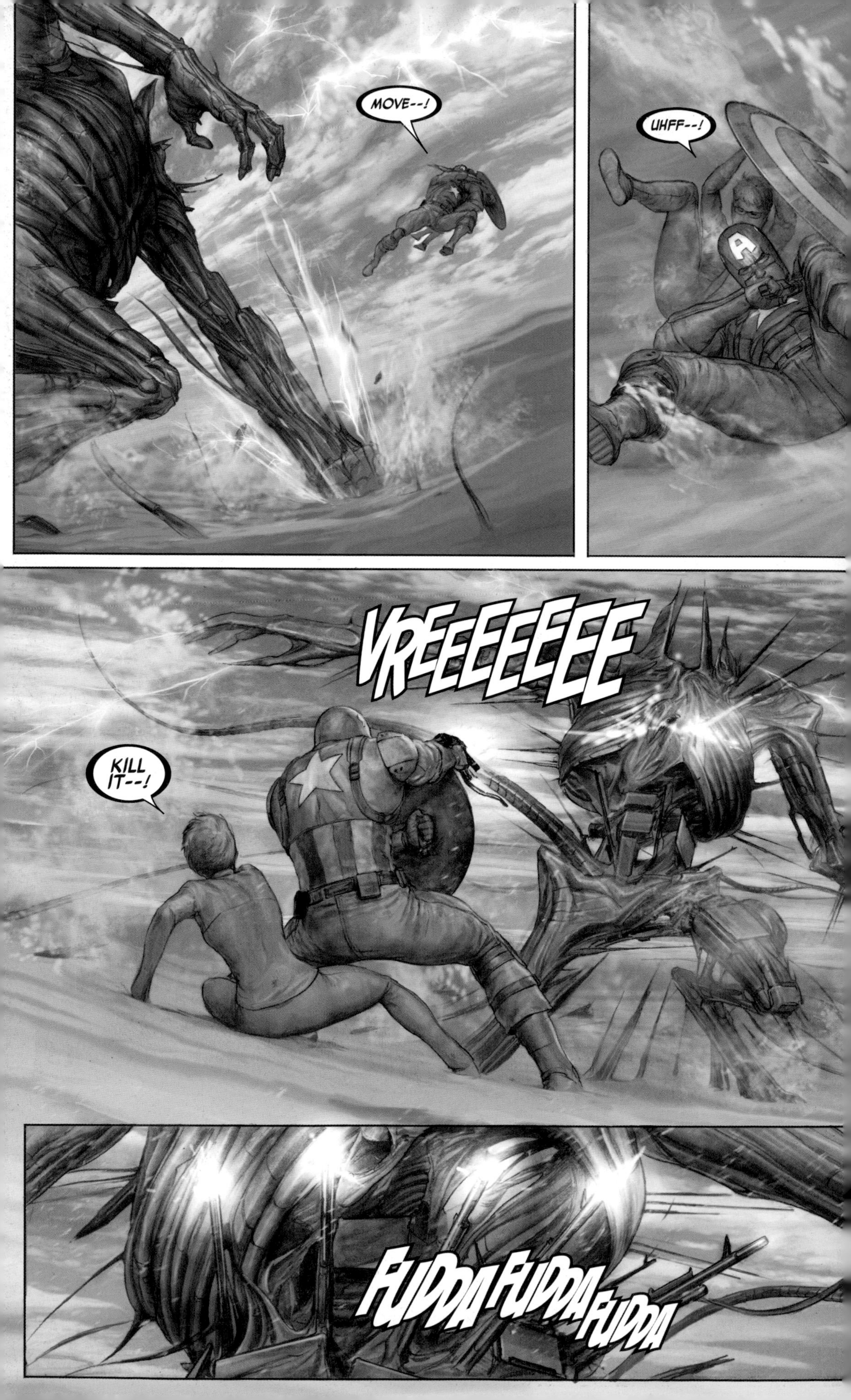
MOVE--!
UHFF--!
VREEEEEEE
KILL IT--!
FUDDA FUDDA FUDDA

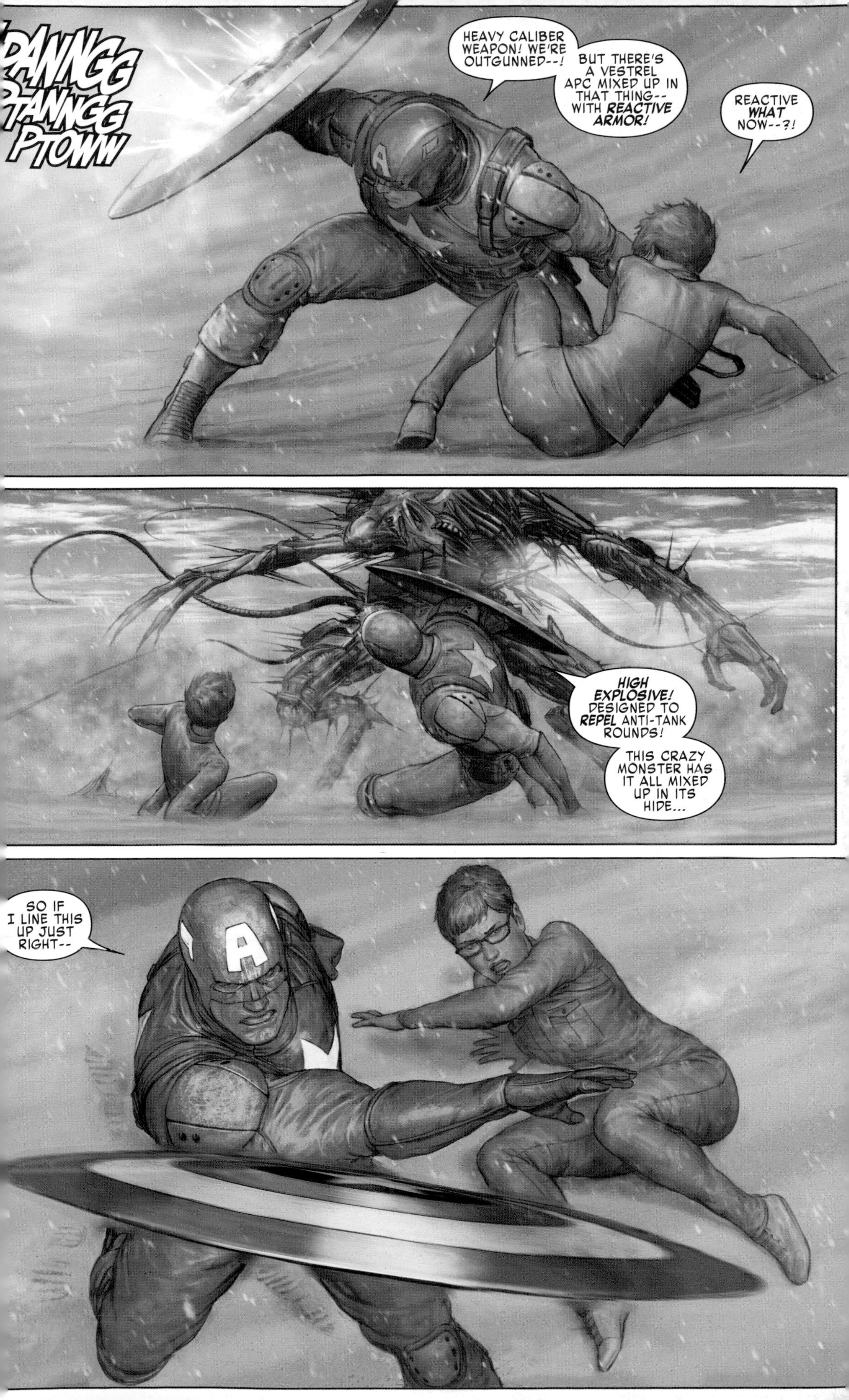
DANNGG
TANNGG
PTOWW
HEAVY CALIBER WEAPON! WE'RE OUTGUNNED--!
BUT THERE'S A VESTREL APC MIXED UP IN THAT THING-- WITH **REACTIVE ARMOR!**
REACTIVE **WHAT** NOW--?!
HIGH EXPLOSIVE! DESIGNED TO ***REPEL*** ANTI-TANK ROUNDS!
THIS CRAZY MONSTER HAS IT ALL MIXED UP IN ITS HIDE...
SO IF I LINE THIS UP JUST RIGHT--

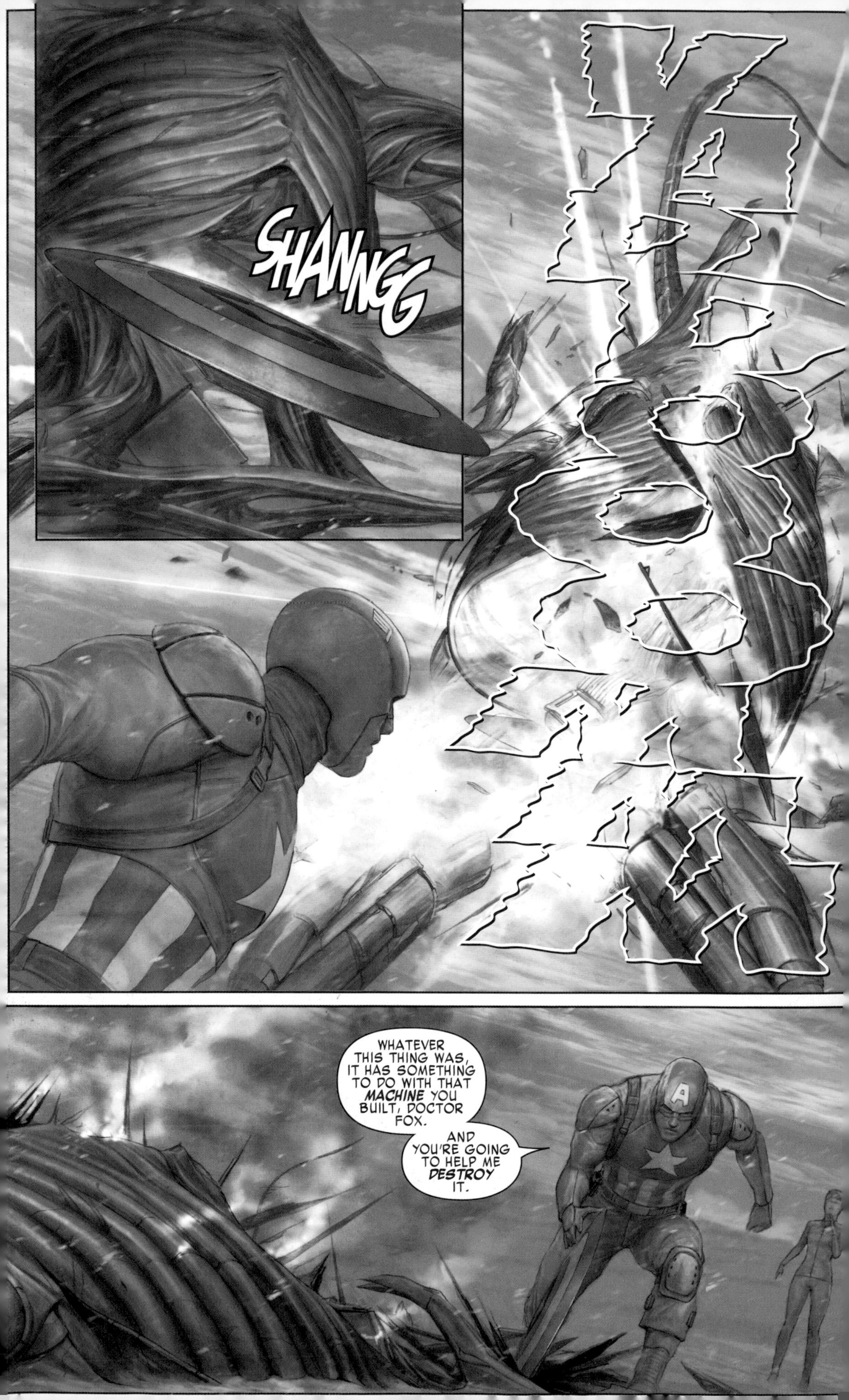
SHANNGG
WHATEVER THIS THING WAS, IT HAS SOMETHING TO DO WITH THAT *MACHINE* YOU BUILT, DOCTOR FOX.
AND YOU'RE GOING TO HELP ME *DESTROY* IT.

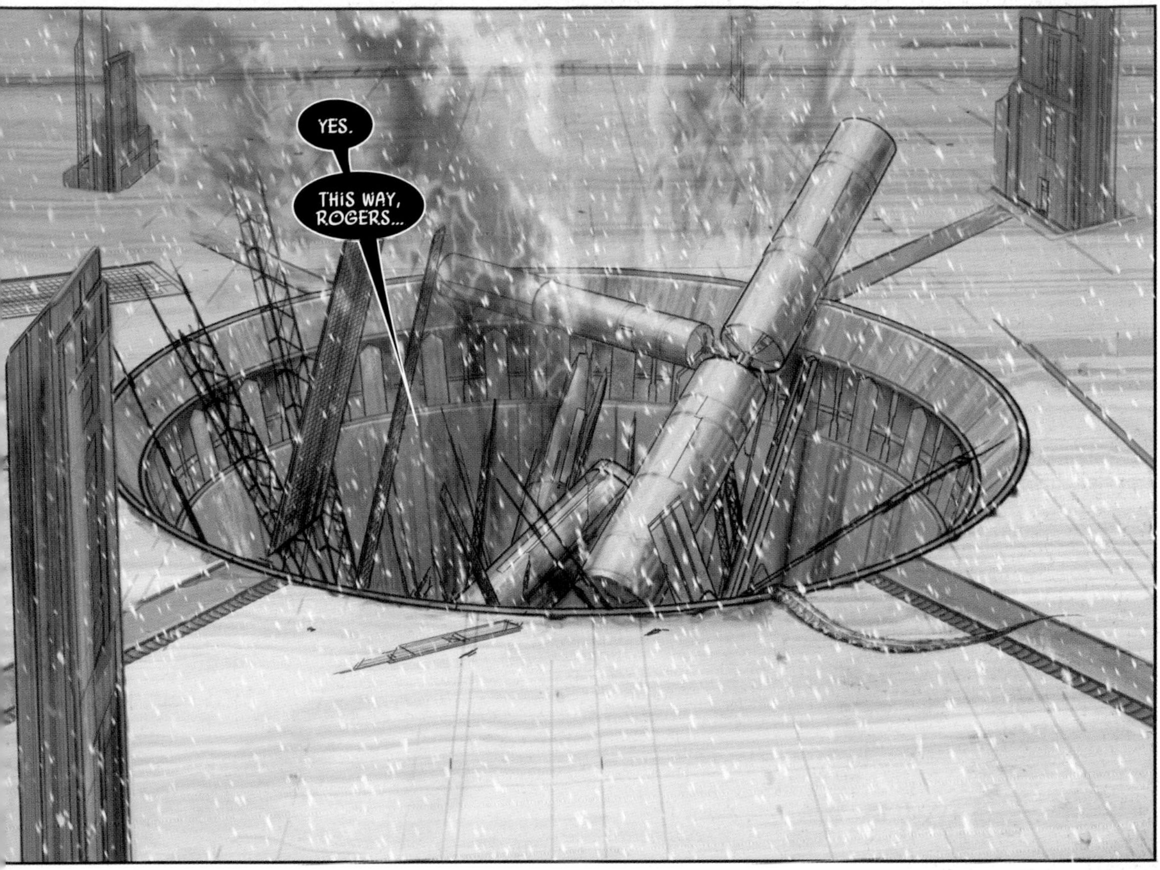
YES.
THIS WAY, ROGERS...

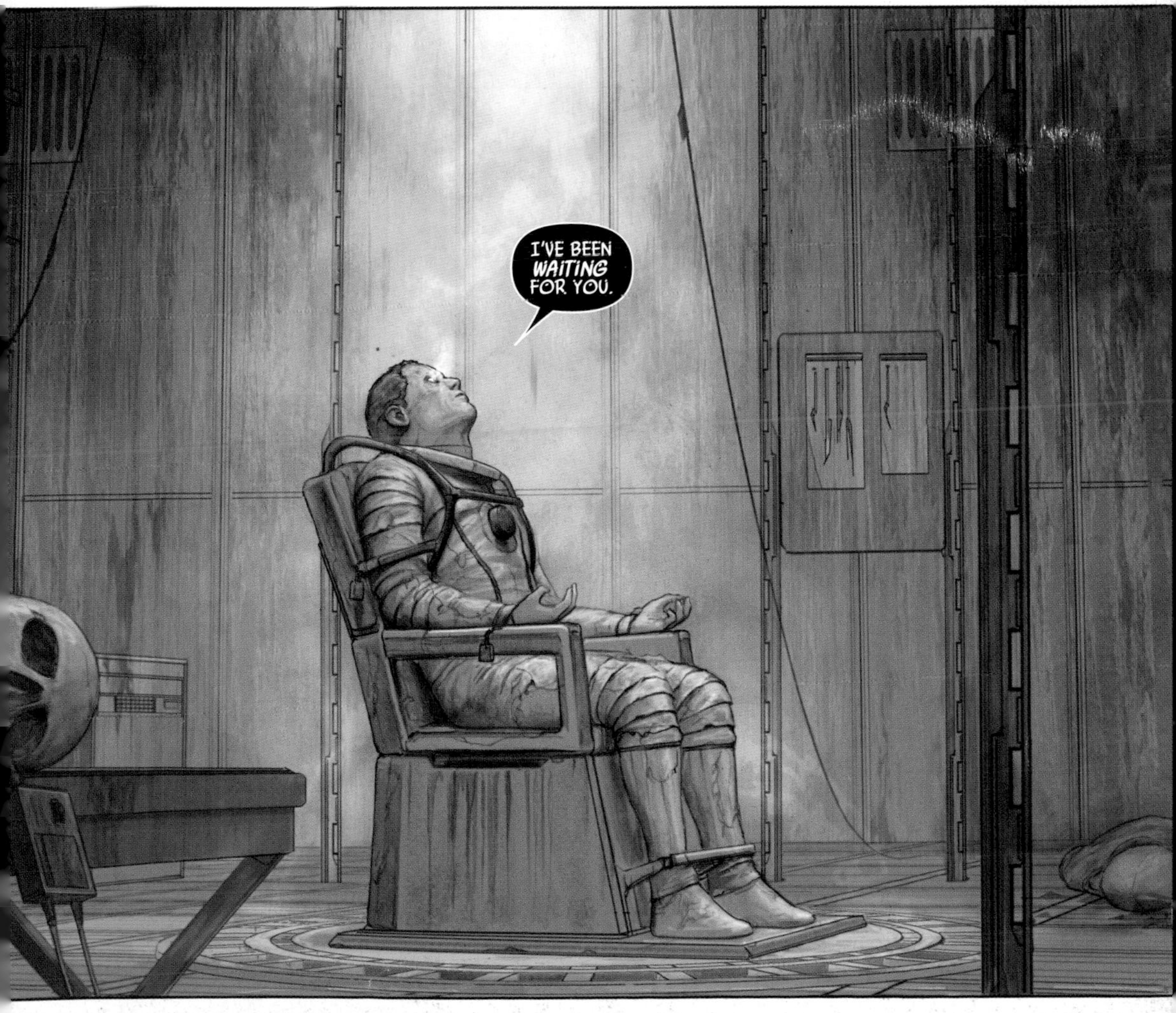
I'VE BEEN WAITING FOR YOU.

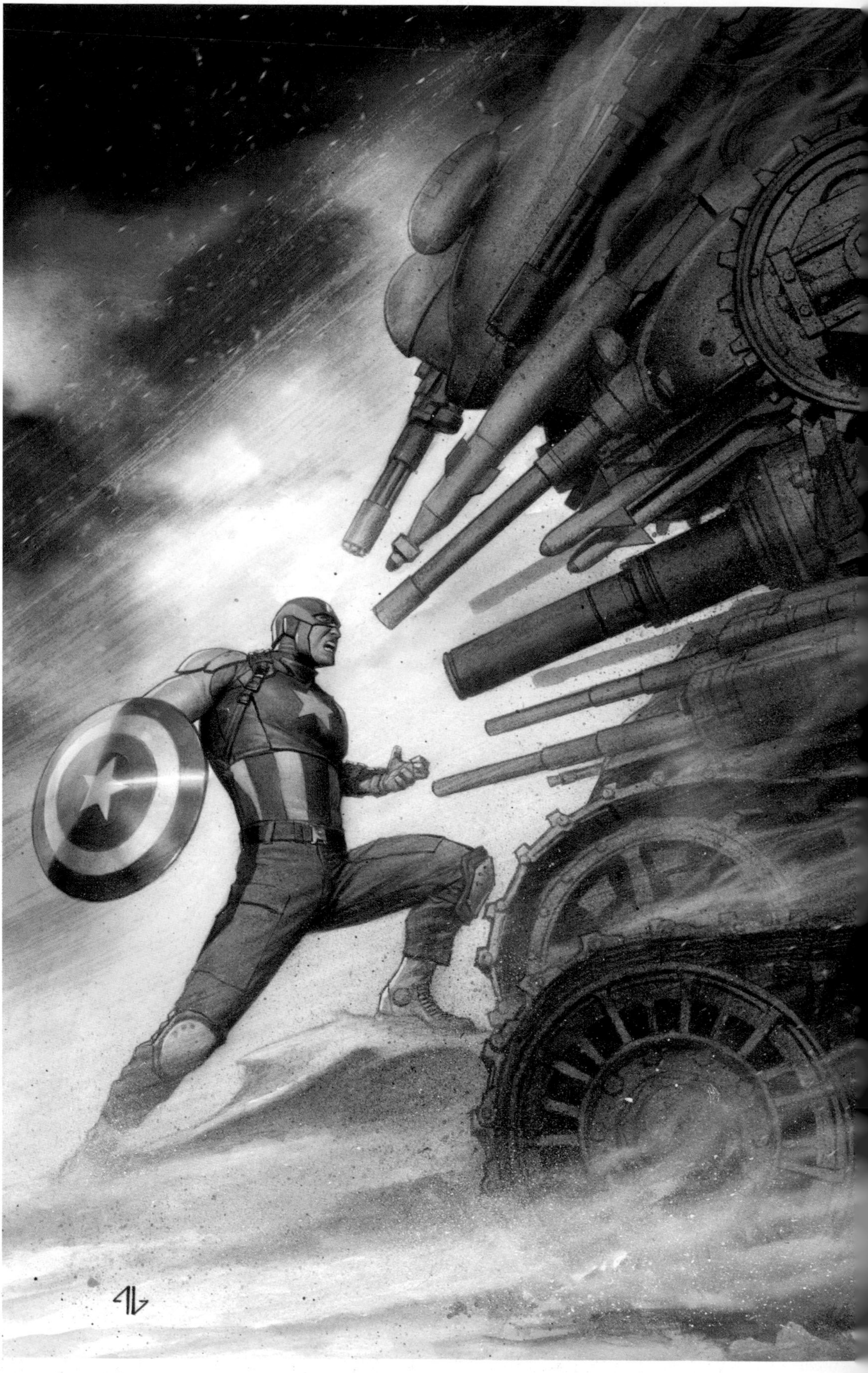

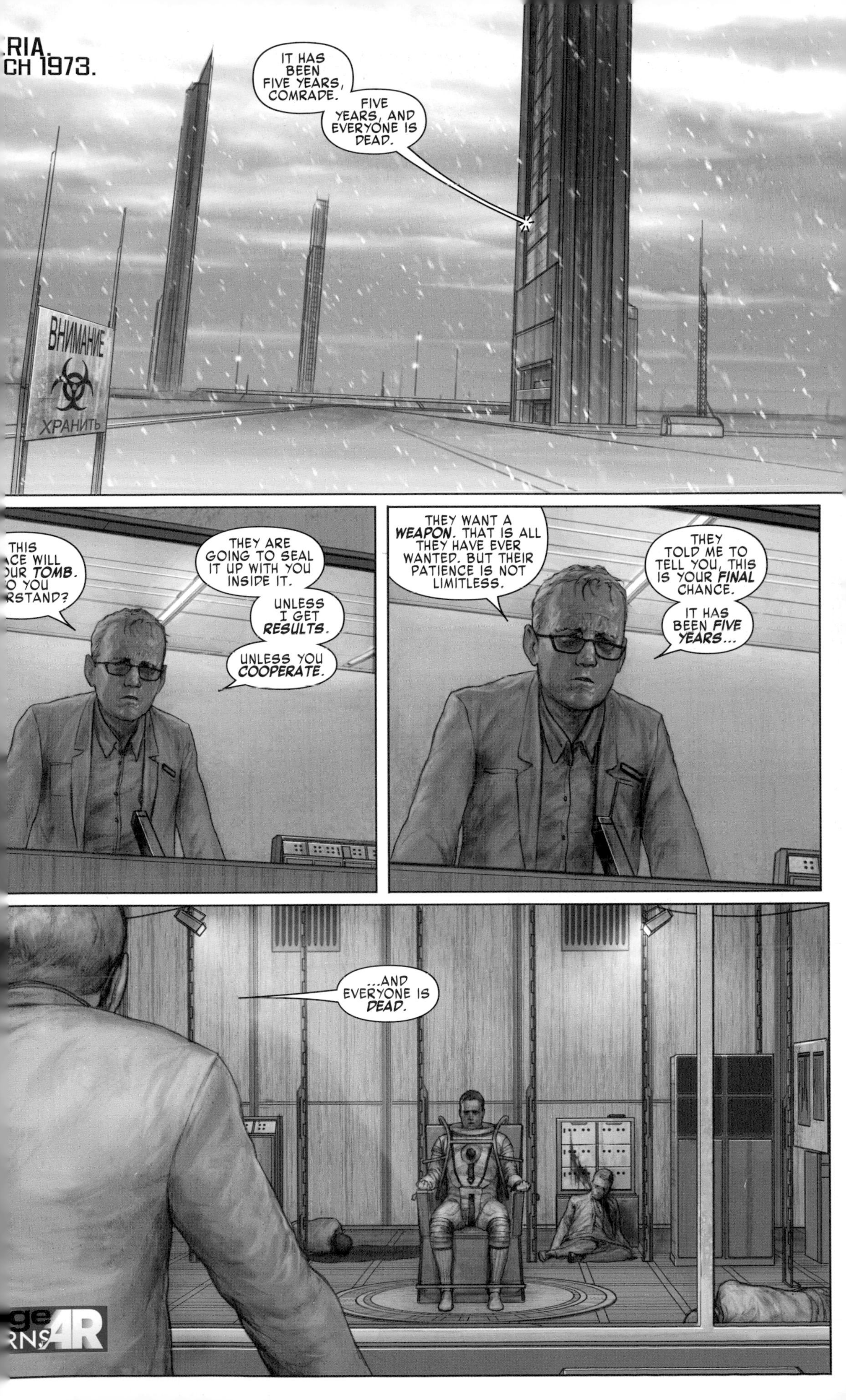

.RIA.
CH 1973.
IT HAS BEEN FIVE YEARS, COMRADE.
FIVE YEARS, AND EVERYONE IS DEAD.
ВНИМАНИЕ
ХРАНИТЬ
THIS
ACE WILL
UR TOMB.
O YOU
RSTAND?
THEY ARE GOING TO SEAL IT UP WITH YOU INSIDE IT.
UNLESS I GET RESULTS.
UNLESS YOU COOPERATE.
THEY WANT A WEAPON. THAT IS ALL THEY HAVE EVER WANTED. BUT THEIR PATIENCE IS NOT LIMITLESS.
THEY TOLD ME TO TELL YOU, THIS IS YOUR FINAL CHANCE.
IT HAS BEEN FIVE YEARS...
...AND EVERYONE IS DEAD.

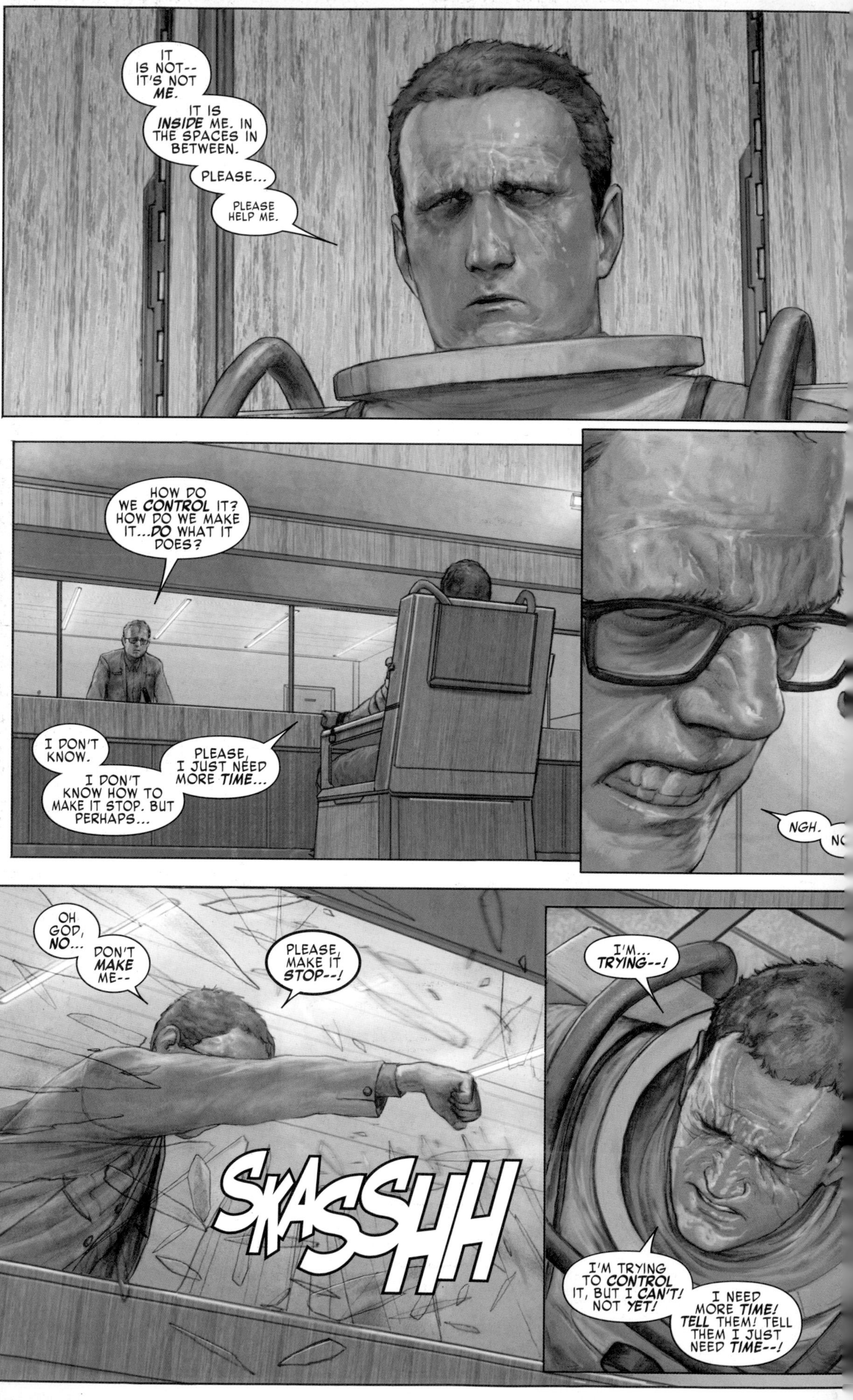
IT IS NOT-- IT'S NOT ME.
IT IS INSIDE ME. IN THE SPACES IN BETWEEN.
PLEASE...
PLEASE HELP ME.
HOW DO WE CONTROL IT? HOW DO WE MAKE IT...DO WHAT IT DOES?
I DON'T KNOW.
I DON'T KNOW HOW TO MAKE IT STOP. BUT PERHAPS...
PLEASE, I JUST NEED MORE TIME...
NGH.
OH GOD, NO...
DON'T MAKE ME--
PLEASE, MAKE IT STOP--!
SKASSHH
I'M... TRYING--!
I'M TRYING TO CONTROL IT, BUT I CAN'T! NOT YET!
I NEED MORE TIME! TELL THEM! TELL THEM I JUST NEED TIME--!

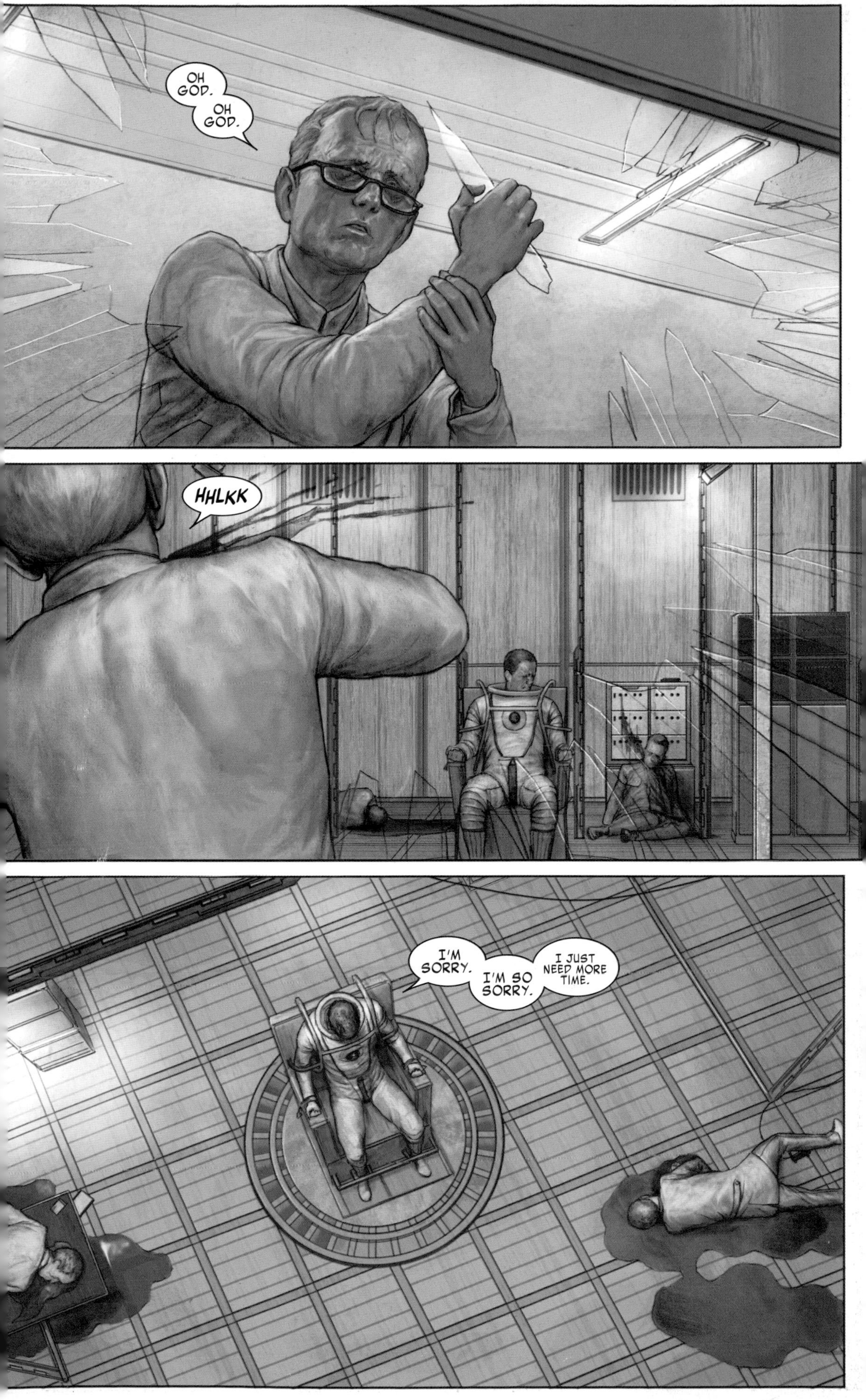
OH GOD.
OH GOD.
HHLKK
I'M SORRY.
I'M SO SORRY.
I JUST NEED MORE TIME.

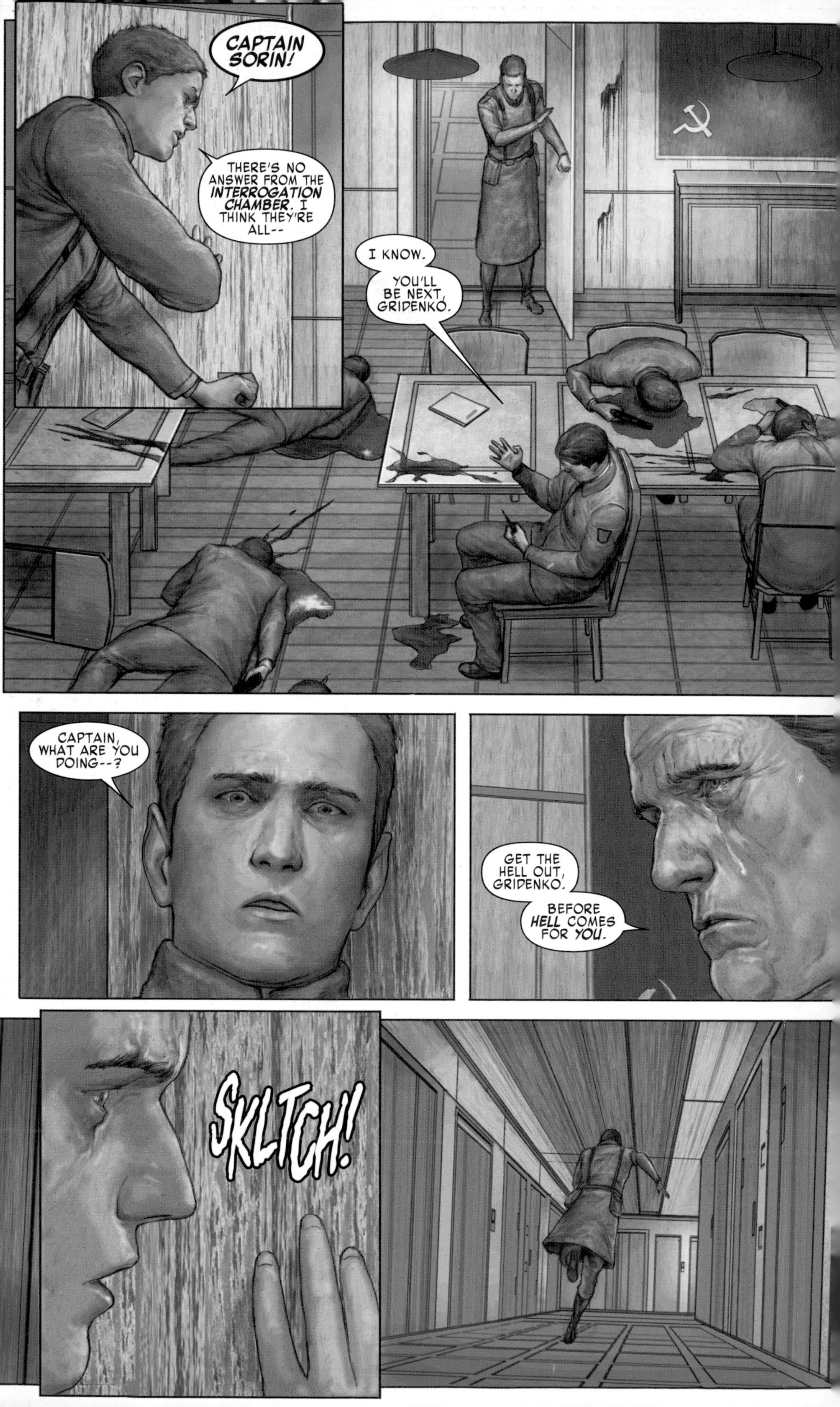
CAPTAIN SORIN!
THERE'S NO ANSWER FROM THE INTERROGATION CHAMBER. I THINK THEY'RE ALL--
I KNOW.
YOU'LL BE NEXT, GRIDENKO.
CAPTAIN, WHAT ARE YOU DOING--?
GET THE HELL OUT, GRIDENKO.
BEFORE HELL COMES FOR YOU.
SKLTCH!

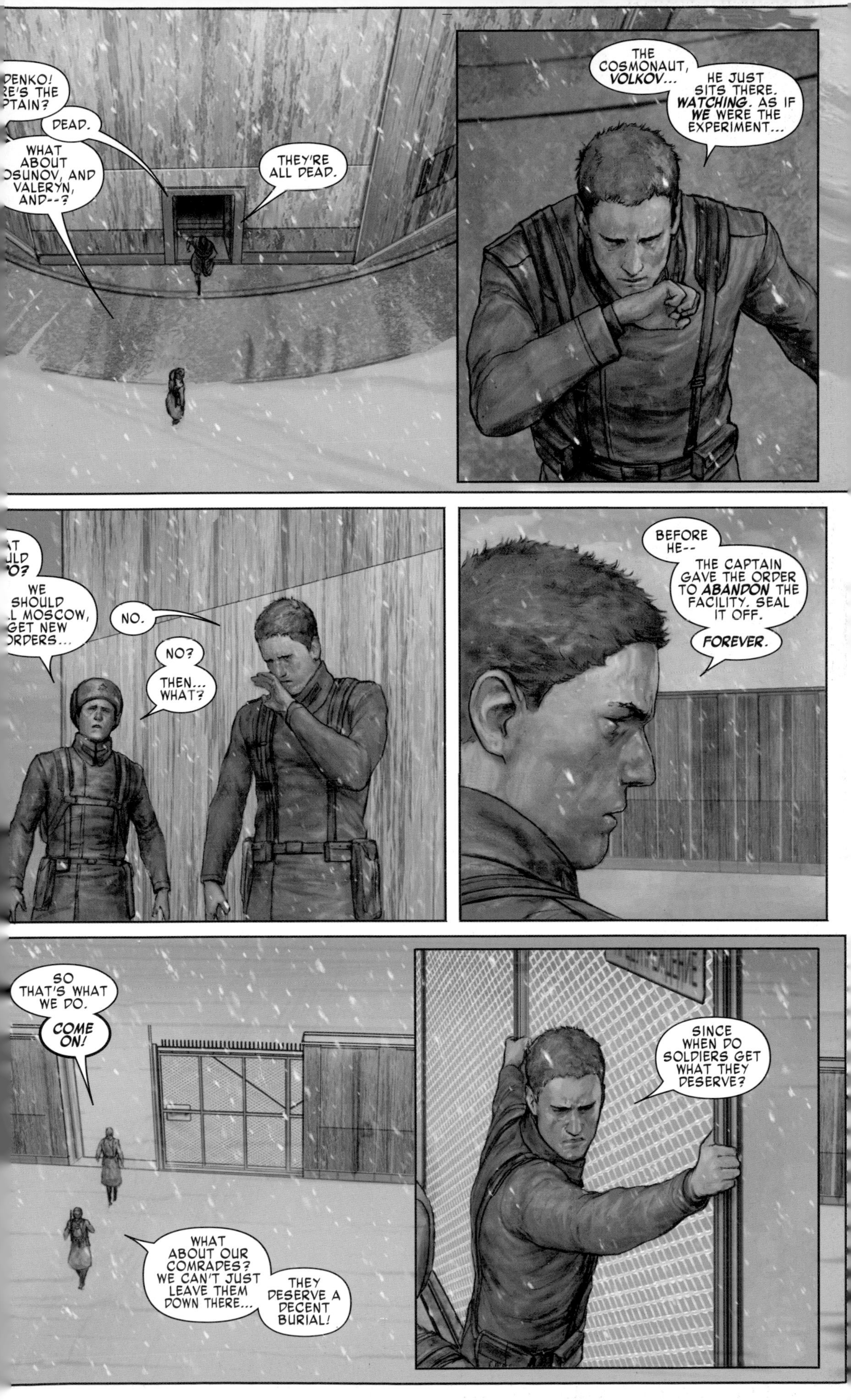
DENKO! RE'S THE PTAIN?
DEAD.
WHAT ABOUT OSUNOV, AND VALERYN, AND--?
THEY'RE ALL DEAD.
THE COSMONAUT, VOLKOV...
HE JUST SITS THERE. WATCHING. AS IF WE WERE THE EXPERIMENT...
AT ULD O?
WE SHOULD L MOSCOW, GET NEW ORDERS...
NO.
NO?
THEN... WHAT?
BEFORE HE--
THE CAPTAIN GAVE THE ORDER TO ABANDON THE FACILITY. SEAL IT OFF.
FOREVER.
SO THAT'S WHAT WE DO.
COME ON!
WHAT ABOUT OUR COMRADES? WE CAN'T JUST LEAVE THEM DOWN THERE...
THEY DESERVE A DECENT BURIAL!
SINCE WHEN DO SOLDIERS GET WHAT THEY DESERVE?

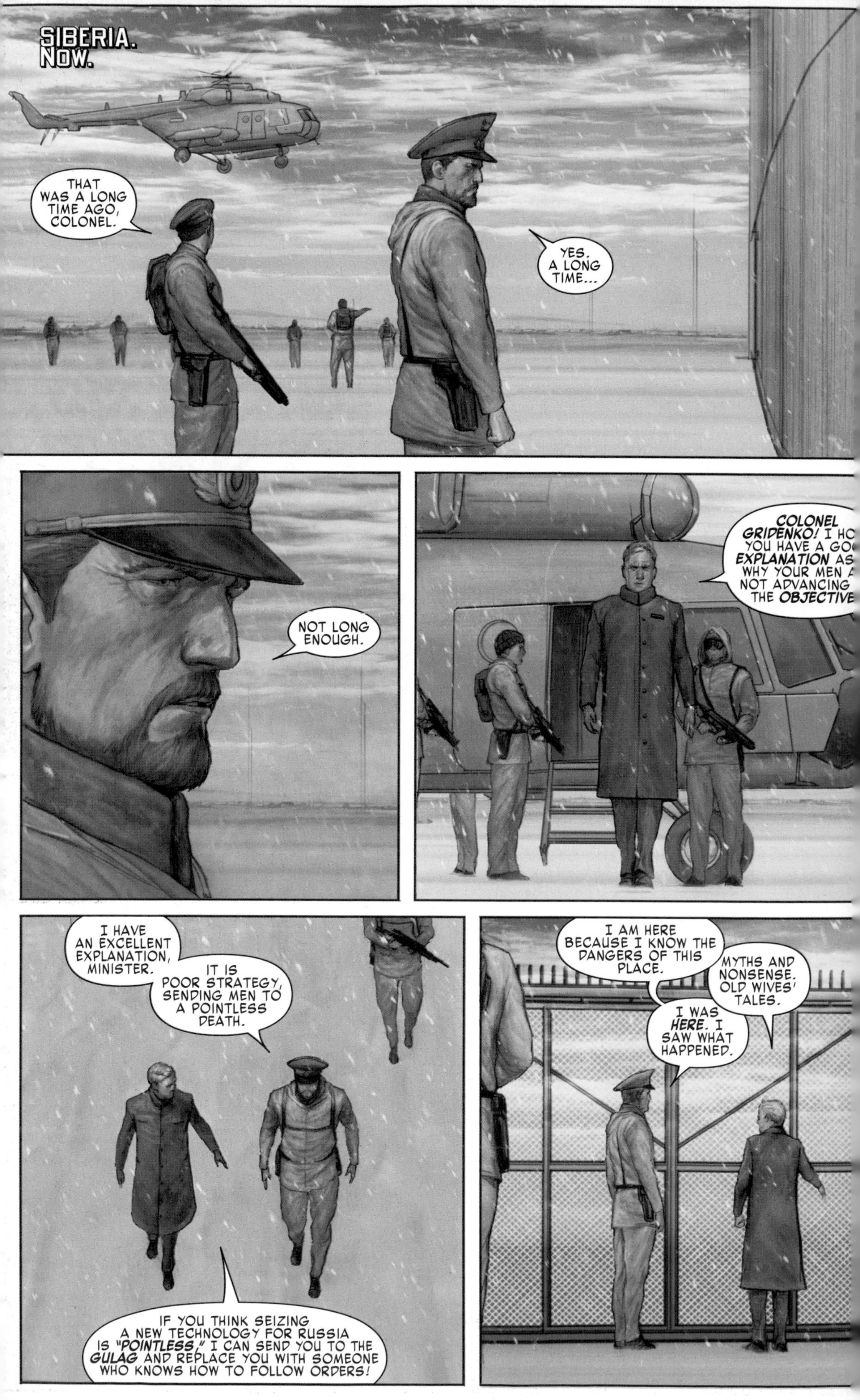
SIBERIA. NOW.
THAT WAS A LONG TIME AGO, COLONEL.
YES. A LONG TIME...
NOT LONG ENOUGH.
COLONEL GRIDENKO! I HO YOU HAVE A GO EXPLANATION AS WHY YOUR MEN A NOT ADVANCING THE OBJECTIVE
I HAVE AN EXCELLENT EXPLANATION, MINISTER.
IT IS POOR STRATEGY, SENDING MEN TO A POINTLESS DEATH.
IF YOU THINK SEIZING A NEW TECHNOLOGY FOR RUSSIA IS "POINTLESS," I CAN SEND YOU TO THE GULAG AND REPLACE YOU WITH SOMEONE WHO KNOWS HOW TO FOLLOW ORDERS!
I AM HERE BECAUSE I KNOW THE DANGERS OF THIS PLACE.
I WAS HERE. I SAW WHAT HAPPENED.
MYTHS AND NONSENSE. OLD WIVES' TALES.

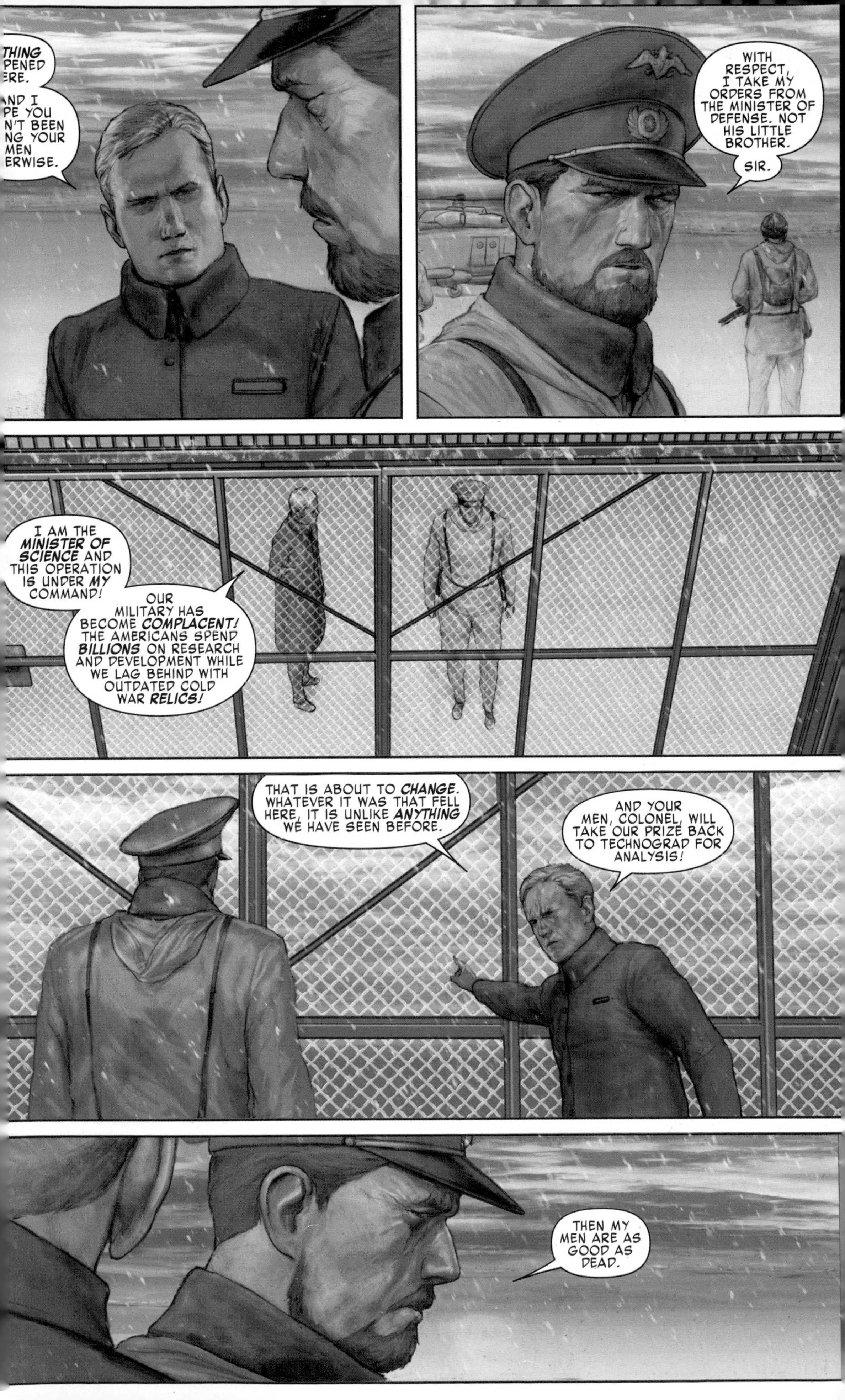
THING PENED ERE.
ND I PE YOU N'T BEEN NG YOUR MEN ERWISE.
WITH RESPECT, I TAKE MY ORDERS FROM THE MINISTER OF DEFENSE. NOT HIS LITTLE BROTHER.
SIR.
I AM THE MINISTER OF SCIENCE AND THIS OPERATION IS UNDER MY COMMAND!
OUR MILITARY HAS BECOME COMPLACENT! THE AMERICANS SPEND BILLIONS ON RESEARCH AND DEVELOPMENT WHILE WE LAG BEHIND WITH OUTDATED COLD WAR RELICS!
THAT IS ABOUT TO CHANGE. WHATEVER IT WAS THAT FELL HERE, IT IS UNLIKE ANYTHING WE HAVE SEEN BEFORE.
AND YOUR MEN, COLONEL, WILL TAKE OUR PRIZE BACK TO TECHNOGRAD FOR ANALYSIS!
THEN MY MEN ARE AS GOOD AS DEAD.

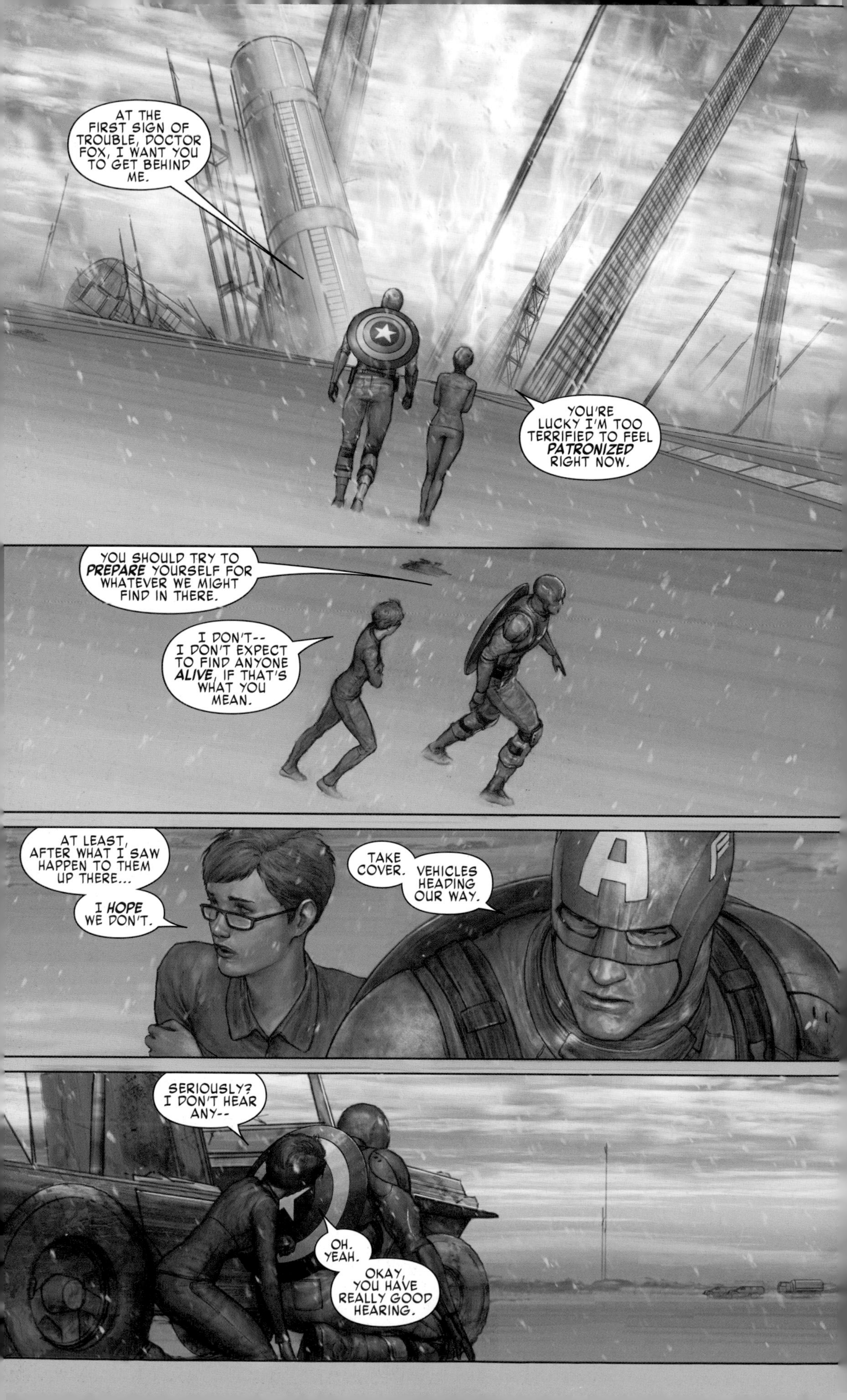
AT THE FIRST SIGN OF TROUBLE, DOCTOR FOX, I WANT YOU TO GET BEHIND ME.
YOU'RE LUCKY I'M TOO TERRIFIED TO FEEL PATRONIZED RIGHT NOW.
YOU SHOULD TRY TO PREPARE YOURSELF FOR WHATEVER WE MIGHT FIND IN THERE.
I DON'T-- I DON'T EXPECT TO FIND ANYONE ALIVE, IF THAT'S WHAT YOU MEAN.
AT LEAST, AFTER WHAT I SAW HAPPEN TO THEM UP THERE...
I HOPE WE DON'T.
TAKE COVER.
VEHICLES HEADING OUR WAY.
SERIOUSLY? I DON'T HEAR ANY--
OH. YEAH.
OKAY, YOU HAVE REALLY GOOD HEARING.

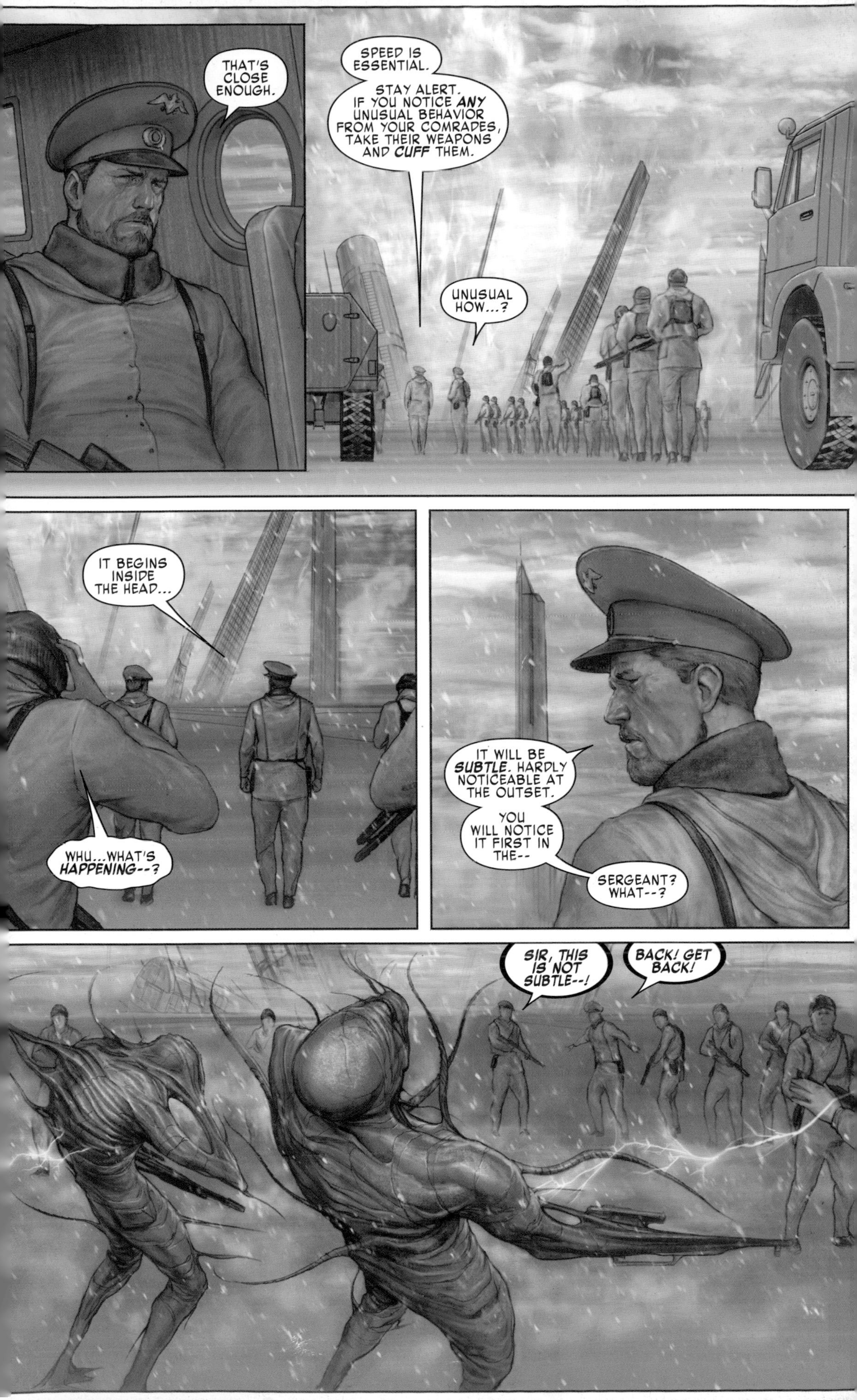

THAT'S CLOSE ENOUGH.
SPEED IS ESSENTIAL.
STAY ALERT. IF YOU NOTICE ANY UNUSUAL BEHAVIOR FROM YOUR COMRADES, TAKE THEIR WEAPONS AND CUFF THEM.
UNUSUAL HOW...?
IT BEGINS INSIDE THE HEAD...
WHU...WHAT'S HAPPENING--?
IT WILL BE SUBTLE. HARDLY NOTICEABLE AT THE OUTSET.
YOU WILL NOTICE IT FIRST IN THE--
SERGEANT? WHAT--?
SIR, THIS IS NOT SUBTLE--!
BACK! GET BACK!

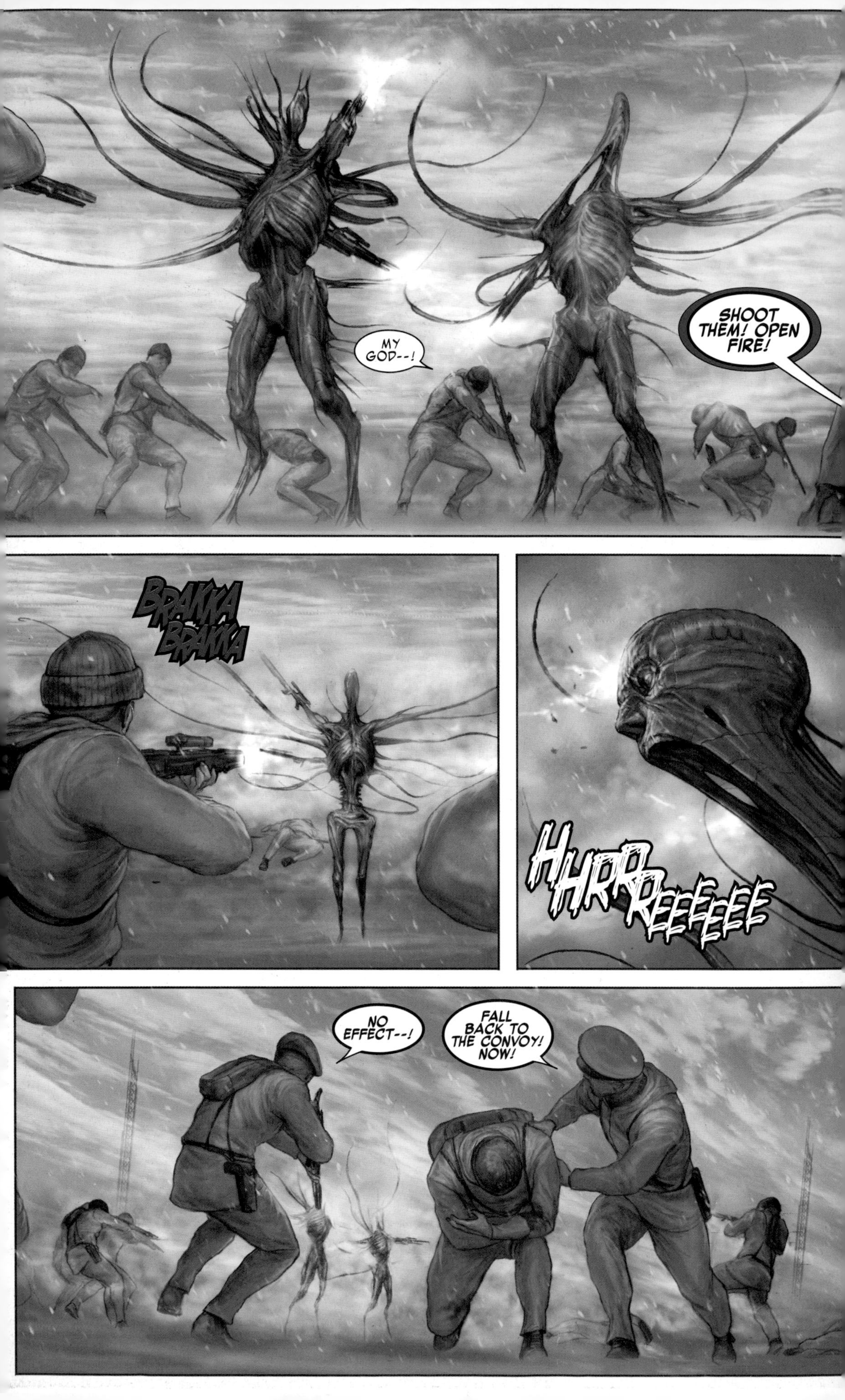
MY GOD--!
SHOOT THEM! OPEN FIRE!
BRAKKA BRAKKA
HHRRREEEEEE
NO EFFECT--!
FALL BACK TO THE CONVOY! NOW!

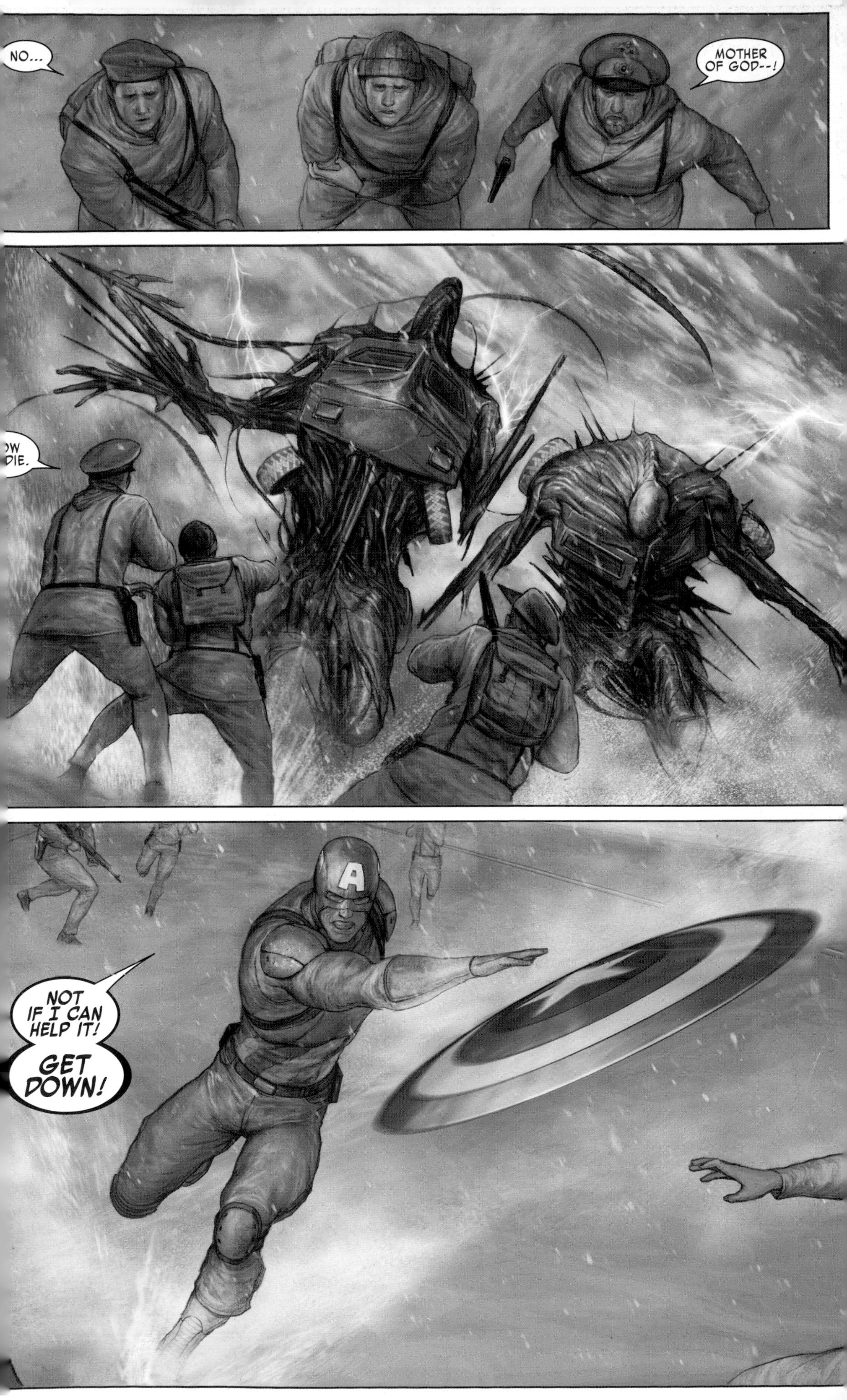
NO...
MOTHER OF GOD--!
NOT IF I CAN HELP IT!
GET DOWN!

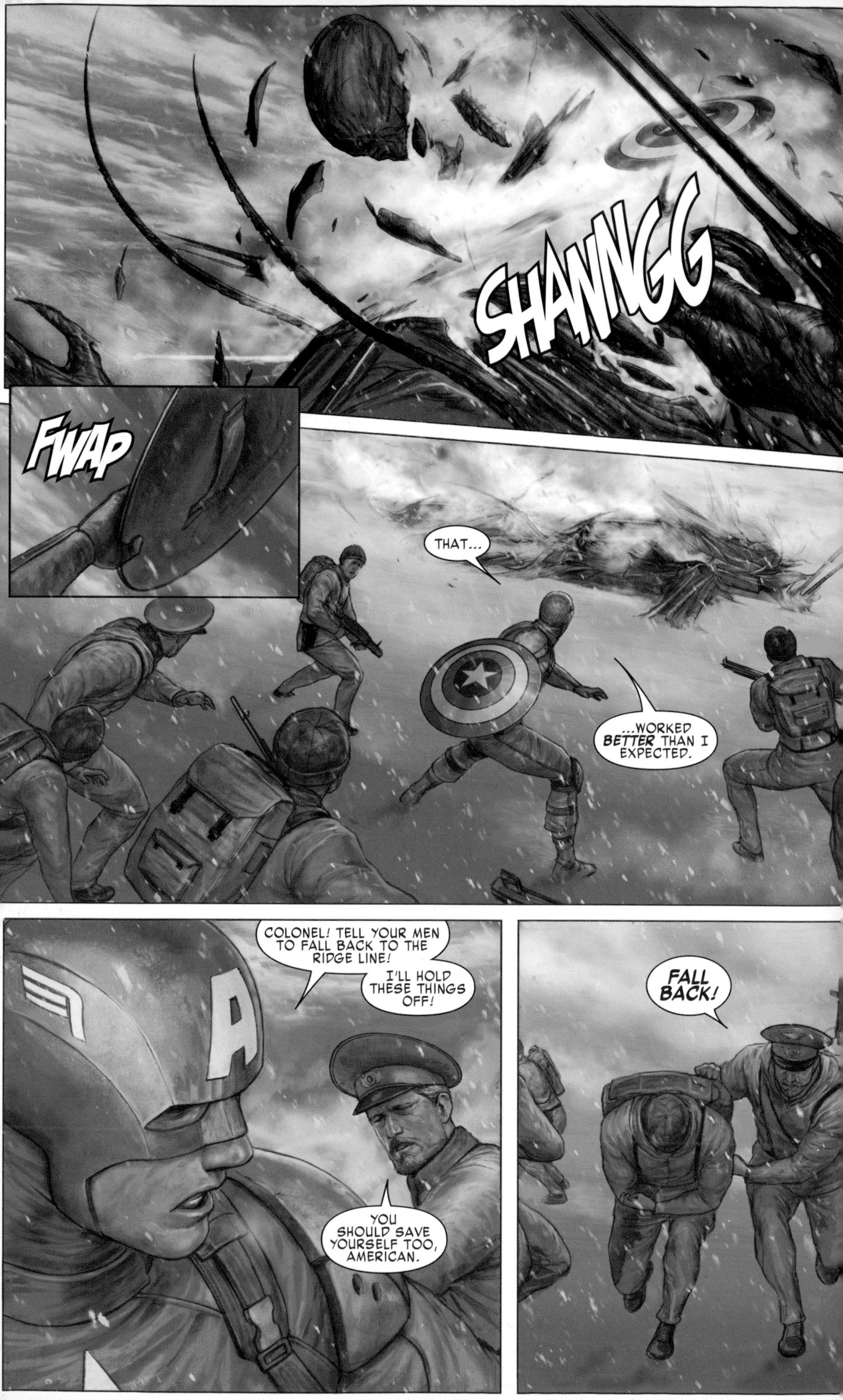
SHANNGG
FWAP
THAT...
...WORKED BETTER THAN I EXPECTED.
COLONEL! TELL YOUR MEN TO FALL BACK TO THE RIDGE LINE!
I'LL HOLD THESE THINGS OFF!
YOU SHOULD SAVE YOURSELF TOO, AMERICAN.
FALL BACK!

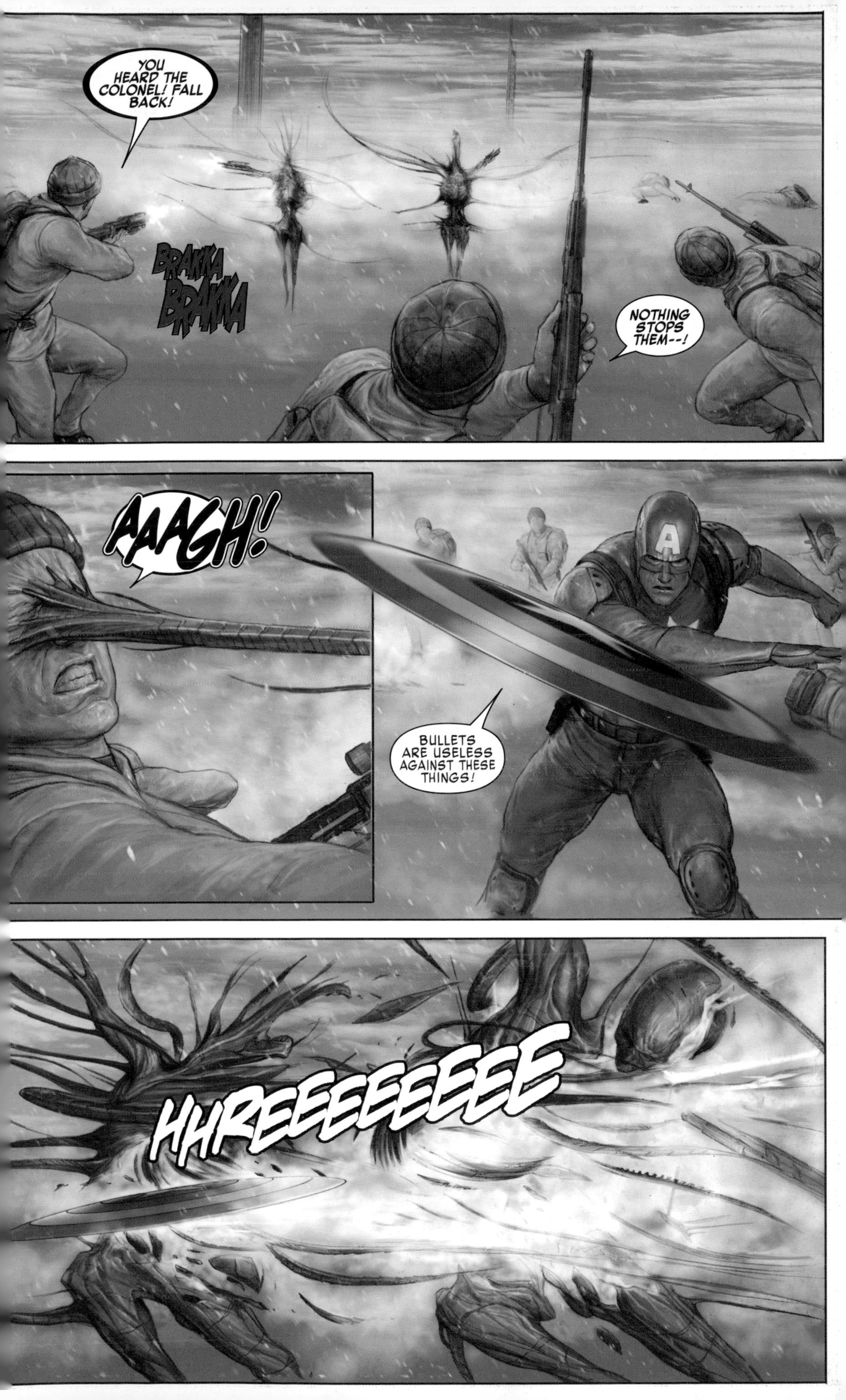
YOU HEARD THE COLONEL! FALL BACK!
BRAKKA BRAKKA
NOTHING STOPS THEM--!
AAAGH!
BULLETS ARE USELESS AGAINST THESE THINGS!
HHREEEEEEEEEE

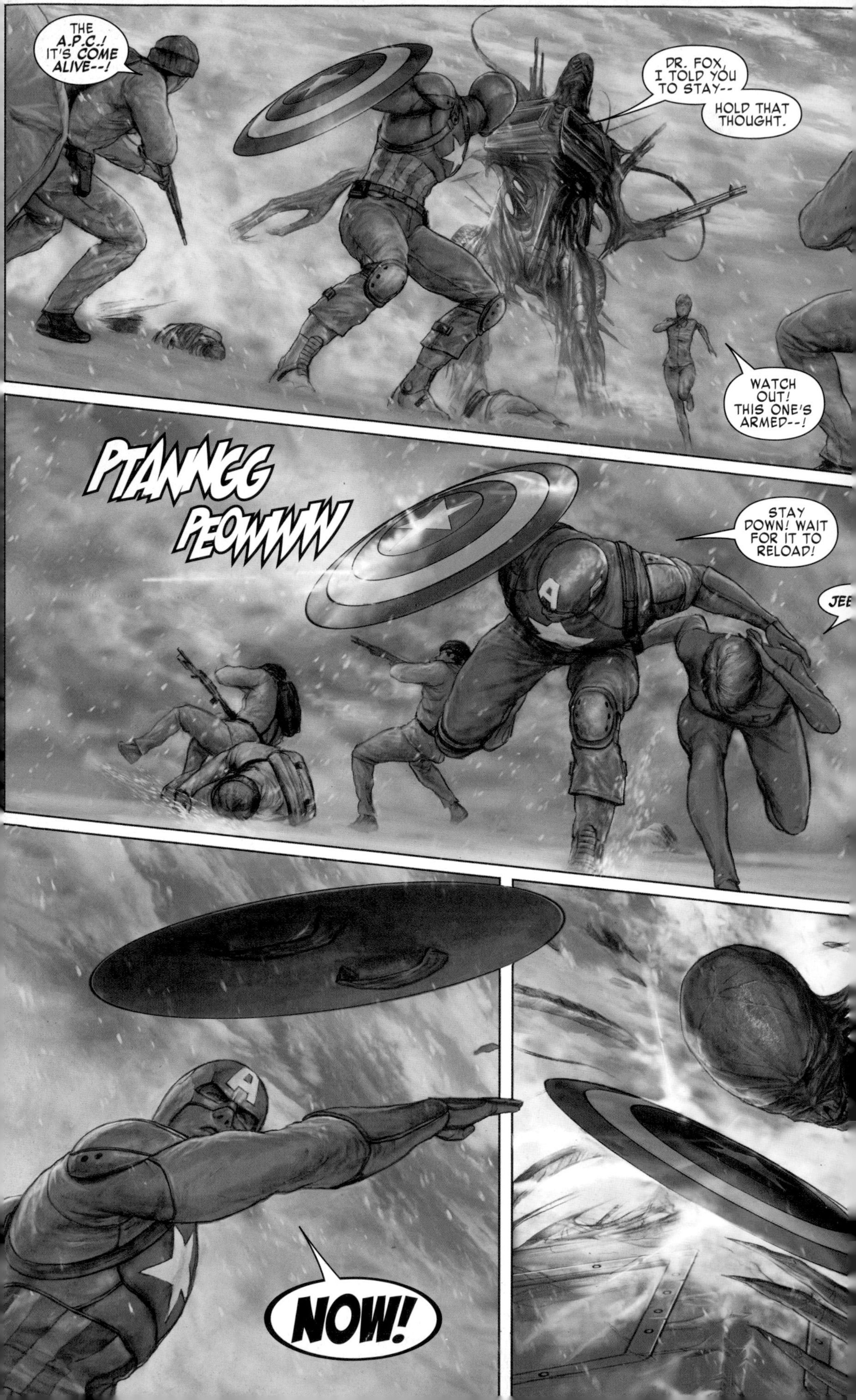
THE A.P.C.! IT'S COME ALIVE--!
DR. FOX, I TOLD YOU TO STAY--
HOLD THAT THOUGHT.
WATCH OUT! THIS ONE'S ARMED--!
PTANNGG
PEOWWW
STAY DOWN! WAIT FOR IT TO RELOAD!
NOW!

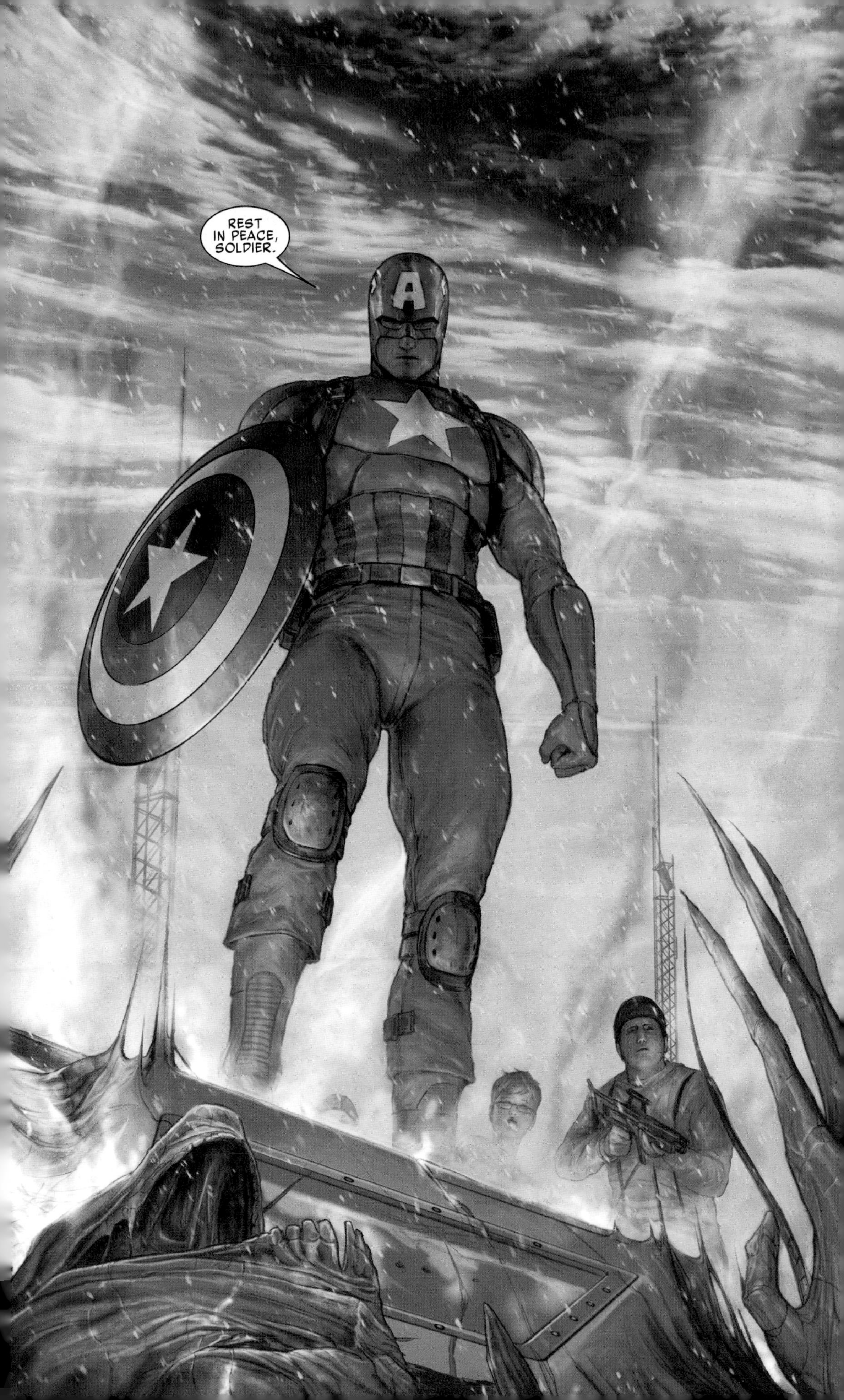
REST IN PEACE, SOLDIER.

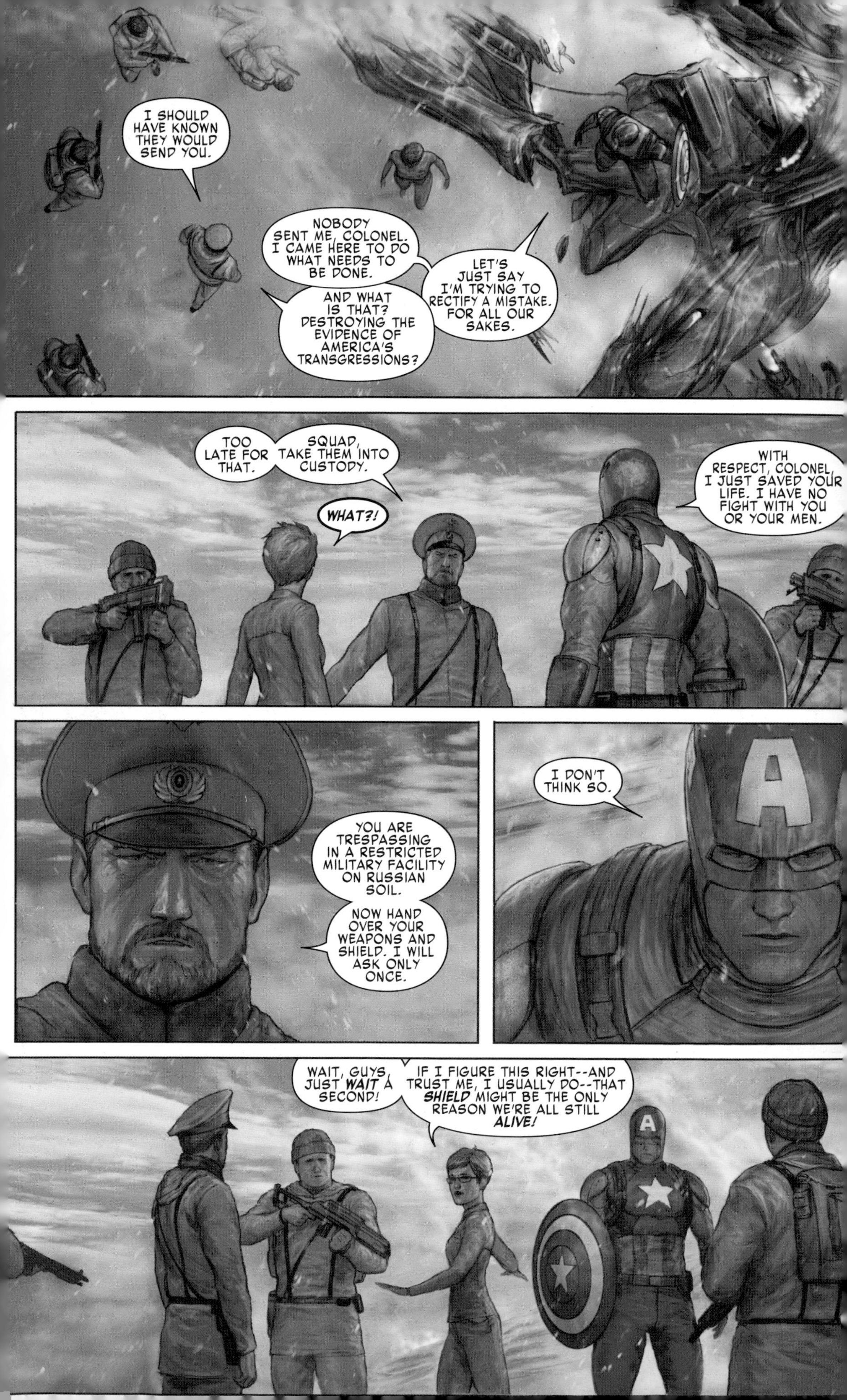
I SHOULD HAVE KNOWN THEY WOULD SEND YOU.
NOBODY SENT ME, COLONEL. I CAME HERE TO DO WHAT NEEDS TO BE DONE.
AND WHAT IS THAT? DESTROYING THE EVIDENCE OF AMERICA'S TRANSGRESSIONS?
LET'S JUST SAY I'M TRYING TO RECTIFY A MISTAKE. FOR ALL OUR SAKES.
TOO LATE FOR THAT.
SQUAD, TAKE THEM INTO CUSTODY.
WHAT?!
WITH RESPECT, COLONEL, I JUST SAVED YOUR LIFE. I HAVE NO FIGHT WITH YOU OR YOUR MEN.
YOU ARE TRESPASSING IN A RESTRICTED MILITARY FACILITY ON RUSSIAN SOIL.
NOW HAND OVER YOUR WEAPONS AND SHIELD. I WILL ASK ONLY ONCE.
I DON'T THINK SO.
WAIT, GUYS, JUST WAIT A SECOND!
IF I FIGURE THIS RIGHT--AND TRUST ME, I USUALLY DO--THAT SHIELD MIGHT BE THE ONLY REASON WE'RE ALL STILL ALIVE!

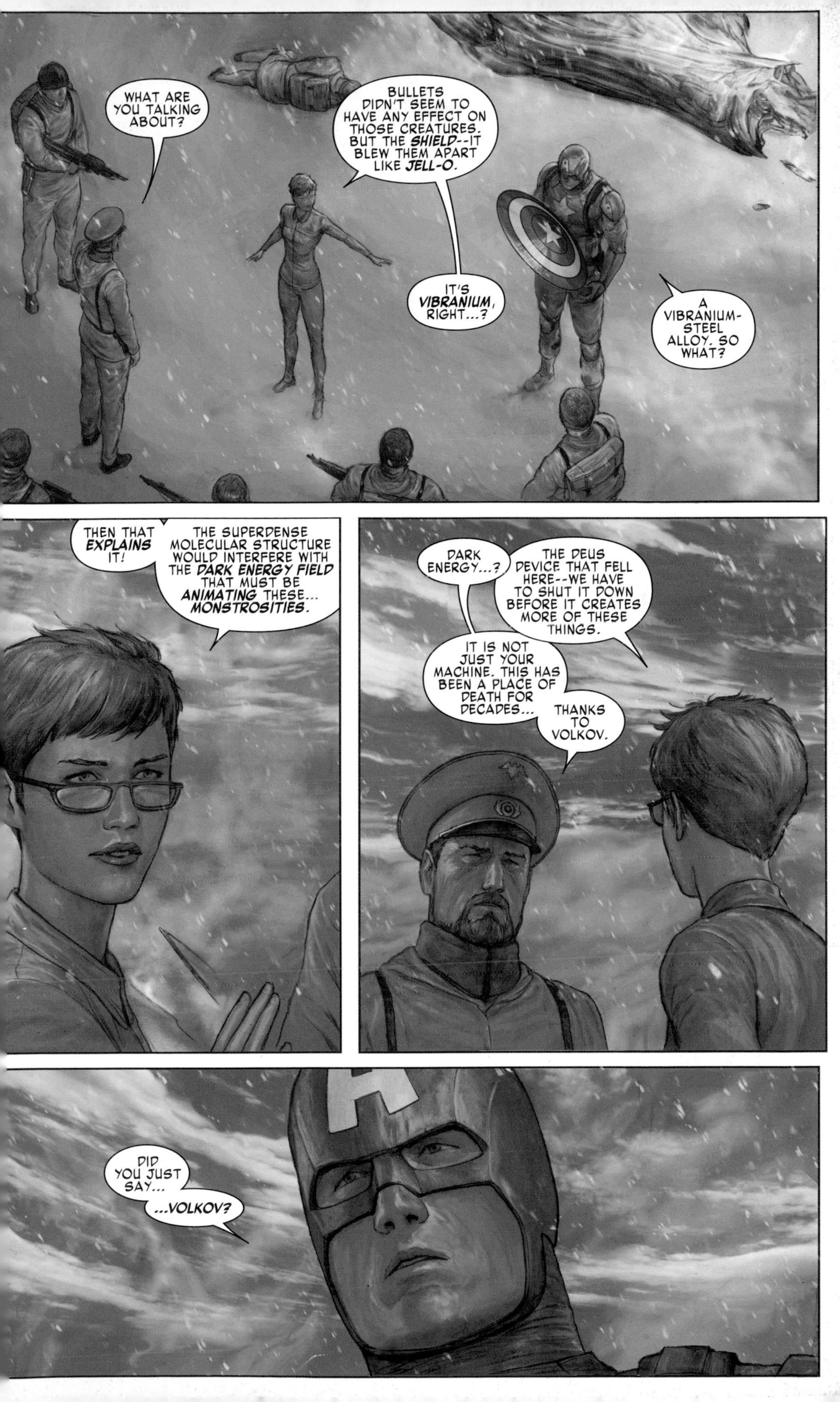
WHAT ARE YOU TALKING ABOUT?
BULLETS DIDN'T SEEM TO HAVE ANY EFFECT ON THOSE CREATURES. BUT THE SHIELD--IT BLEW THEM APART LIKE JELL-O.
IT'S VIBRANIUM, RIGHT...?
A VIBRANIUM-STEEL ALLOY. SO WHAT?
THEN THAT EXPLAINS IT!
THE SUPERDENSE MOLECULAR STRUCTURE WOULD INTERFERE WITH THE DARK ENERGY FIELD THAT MUST BE ANIMATING THESE... MONSTROSITIES.
DARK ENERGY...?
THE DEUS DEVICE THAT FELL HERE--WE HAVE TO SHUT IT DOWN BEFORE IT CREATES MORE OF THESE THINGS.
IT IS NOT JUST YOUR MACHINE. THIS HAS BEEN A PLACE OF DEATH FOR DECADES...
THANKS TO VOLKOV.
DID YOU JUST SAY...
...VOLKOV?

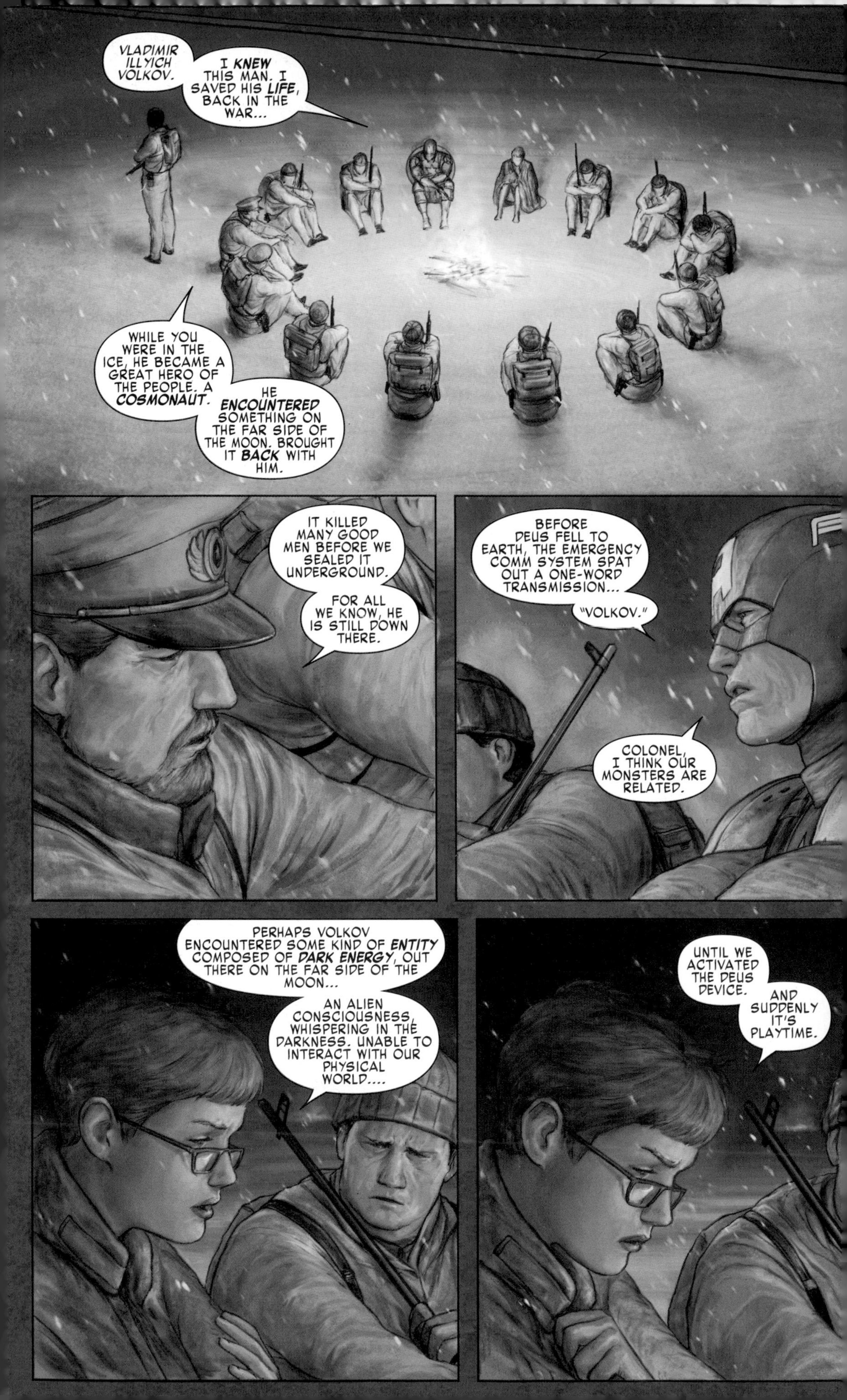
VLADIMIR ILLYICH VOLKOV.
I KNEW THIS MAN. I SAVED HIS LIFE, BACK IN THE WAR...
WHILE YOU WERE IN THE ICE, HE BECAME A GREAT HERO OF THE PEOPLE. A COSMONAUT.
HE ENCOUNTERED SOMETHING ON THE FAR SIDE OF THE MOON. BROUGHT IT BACK WITH HIM.
IT KILLED MANY GOOD MEN BEFORE WE SEALED IT UNDERGROUND.
FOR ALL WE KNOW, HE IS STILL DOWN THERE.
BEFORE DEUS FELL TO EARTH, THE EMERGENCY COMM SYSTEM SPAT OUT A ONE-WORD TRANSMISSION...
"VOLKOV."
COLONEL, I THINK OUR MONSTERS ARE RELATED.
PERHAPS VOLKOV ENCOUNTERED SOME KIND OF ENTITY COMPOSED OF DARK ENERGY, OUT THERE ON THE FAR SIDE OF THE MOON...
AN ALIEN CONSCIOUSNESS, WHISPERING IN THE DARKNESS. UNABLE TO INTERACT WITH OUR PHYSICAL WORLD....
UNTIL WE ACTIVATED THE DEUS DEVICE.
AND SUDDENLY IT'S PLAYTIME.

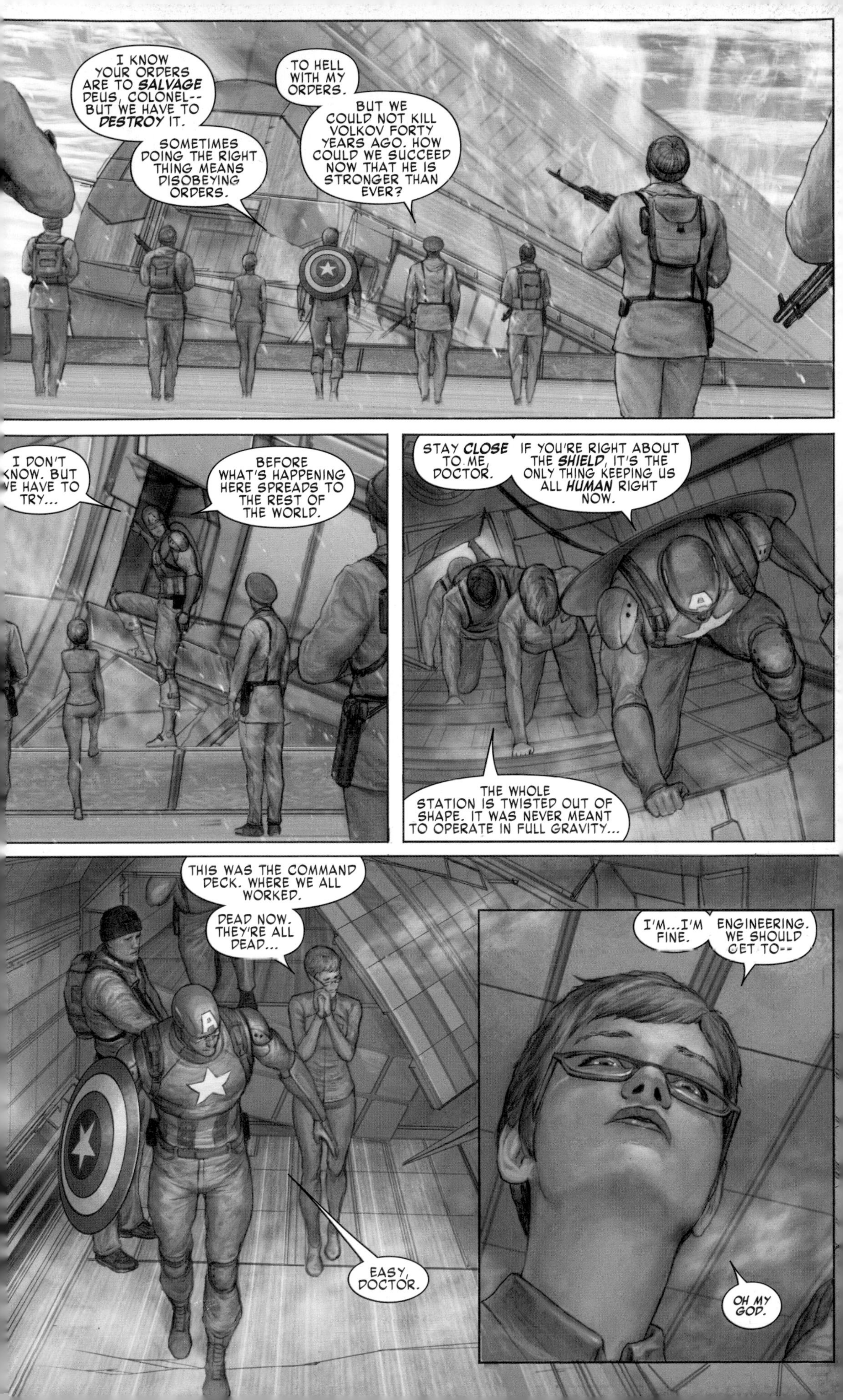
I KNOW YOUR ORDERS ARE TO SALVAGE DEUS, COLONEL-- BUT WE HAVE TO DESTROY IT.
SOMETIMES DOING THE RIGHT THING MEANS DISOBEYING ORDERS.
TO HELL WITH MY ORDERS.
BUT WE COULD NOT KILL VOLKOV FORTY YEARS AGO. HOW COULD WE SUCCEED NOW THAT HE IS STRONGER THAN EVER?
I DON'T KNOW. BUT WE HAVE TO TRY...
BEFORE WHAT'S HAPPENING HERE SPREADS TO THE REST OF THE WORLD.
STAY CLOSE TO ME, DOCTOR.
IF YOU'RE RIGHT ABOUT THE SHIELD, IT'S THE ONLY THING KEEPING US ALL HUMAN RIGHT NOW.
THE WHOLE STATION IS TWISTED OUT OF SHAPE. IT WAS NEVER MEANT TO OPERATE IN FULL GRAVITY...
THIS WAS THE COMMAND DECK. WHERE WE ALL WORKED.
DEAD NOW. THEY'RE ALL DEAD...
EASY, DOCTOR.
I'M...I'M FINE.
ENGINEERING. WE SHOULD GET TO--
OH MY GOD.

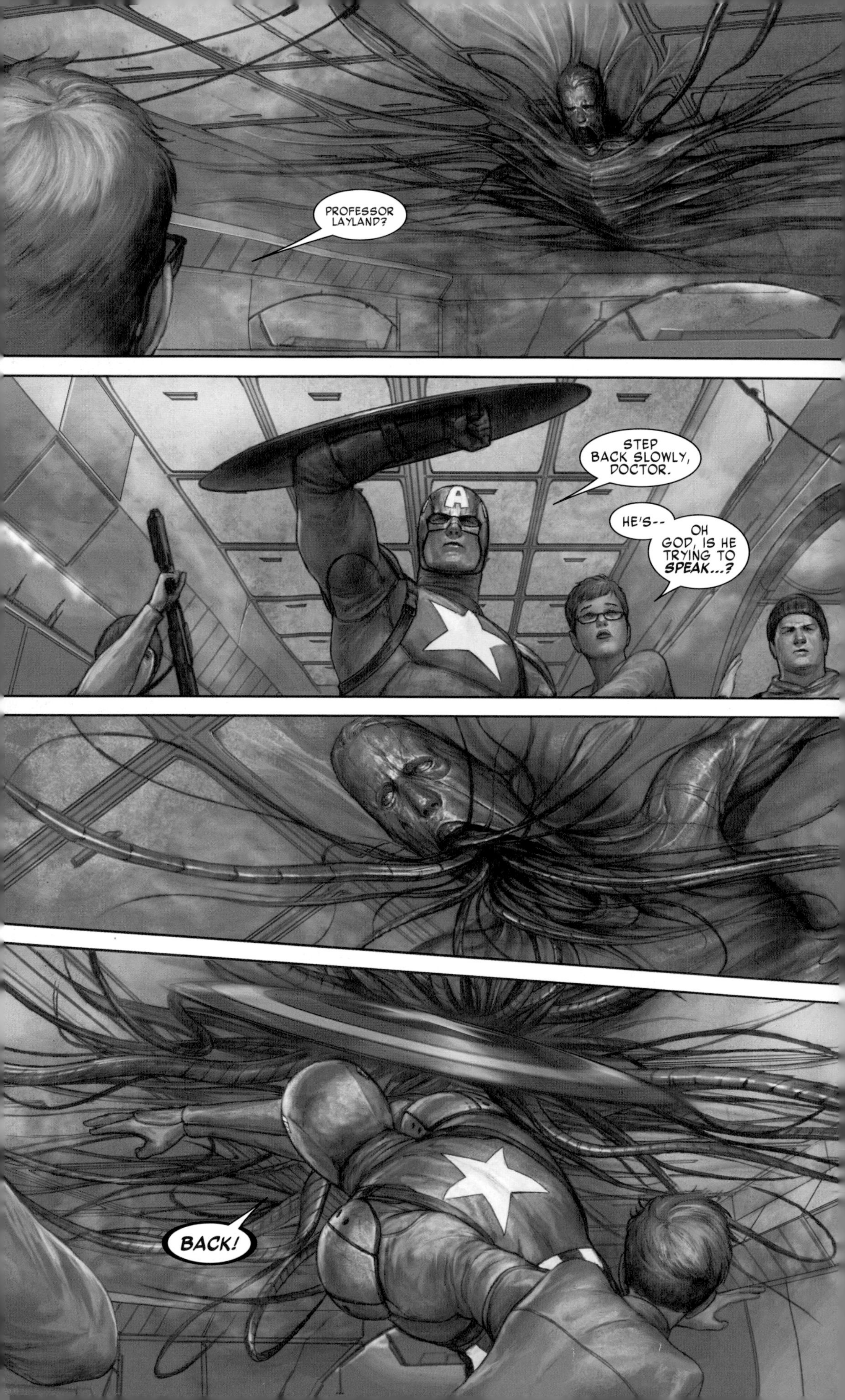
PROFESSOR LAYLAND?
STEP BACK SLOWLY, DOCTOR.
HE'S--
OH GOD, IS HE TRYING TO SPEAK...?
BACK!

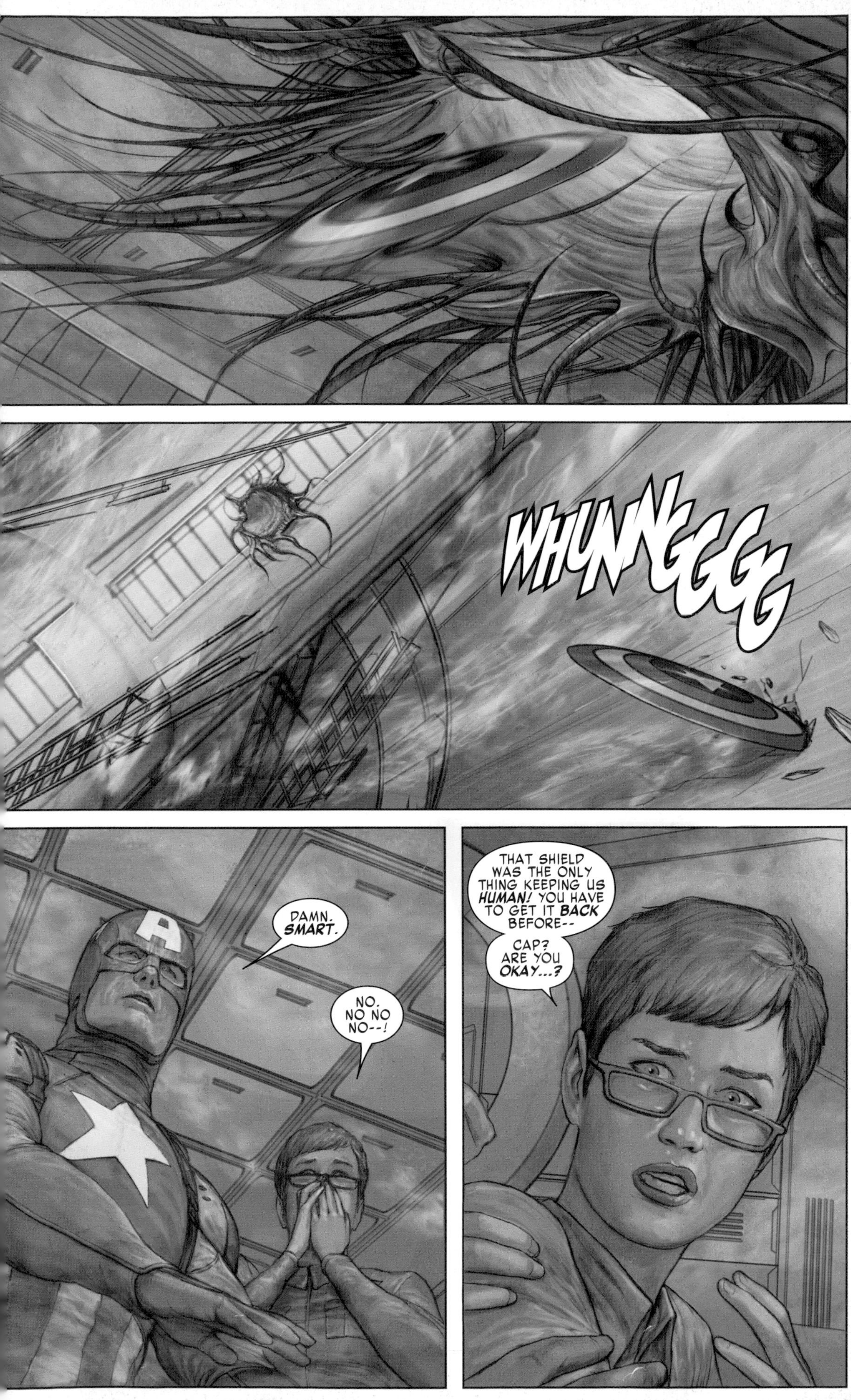
WHUNNGGGG
DAMN. SMART.
NO. NO NO NO--!
THAT SHIELD WAS THE ONLY THING KEEPING US HUMAN! YOU HAVE TO GET IT BACK BEFORE--
CAP? ARE YOU OKAY...?

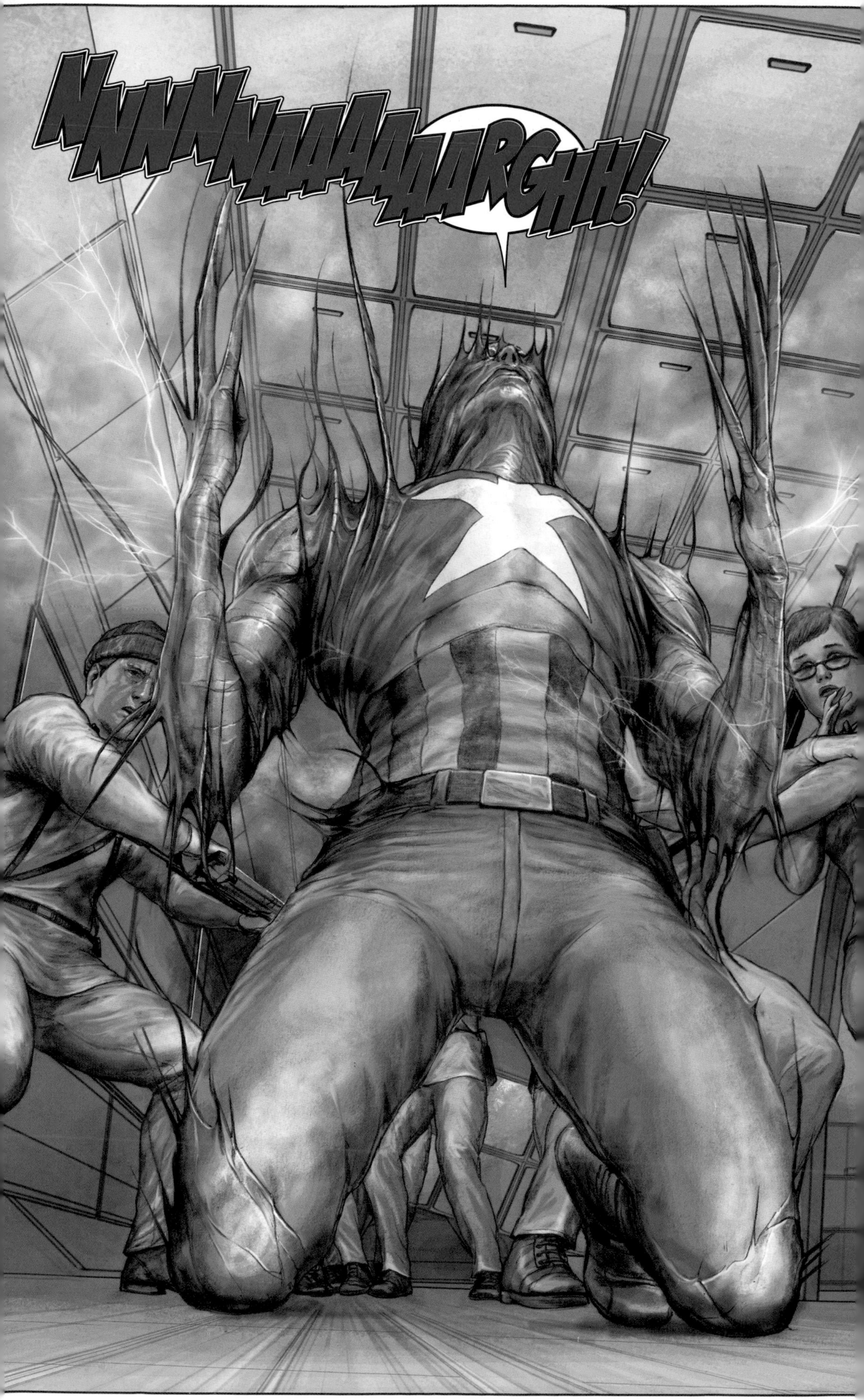
NNNNNAAAAAAARGHH!

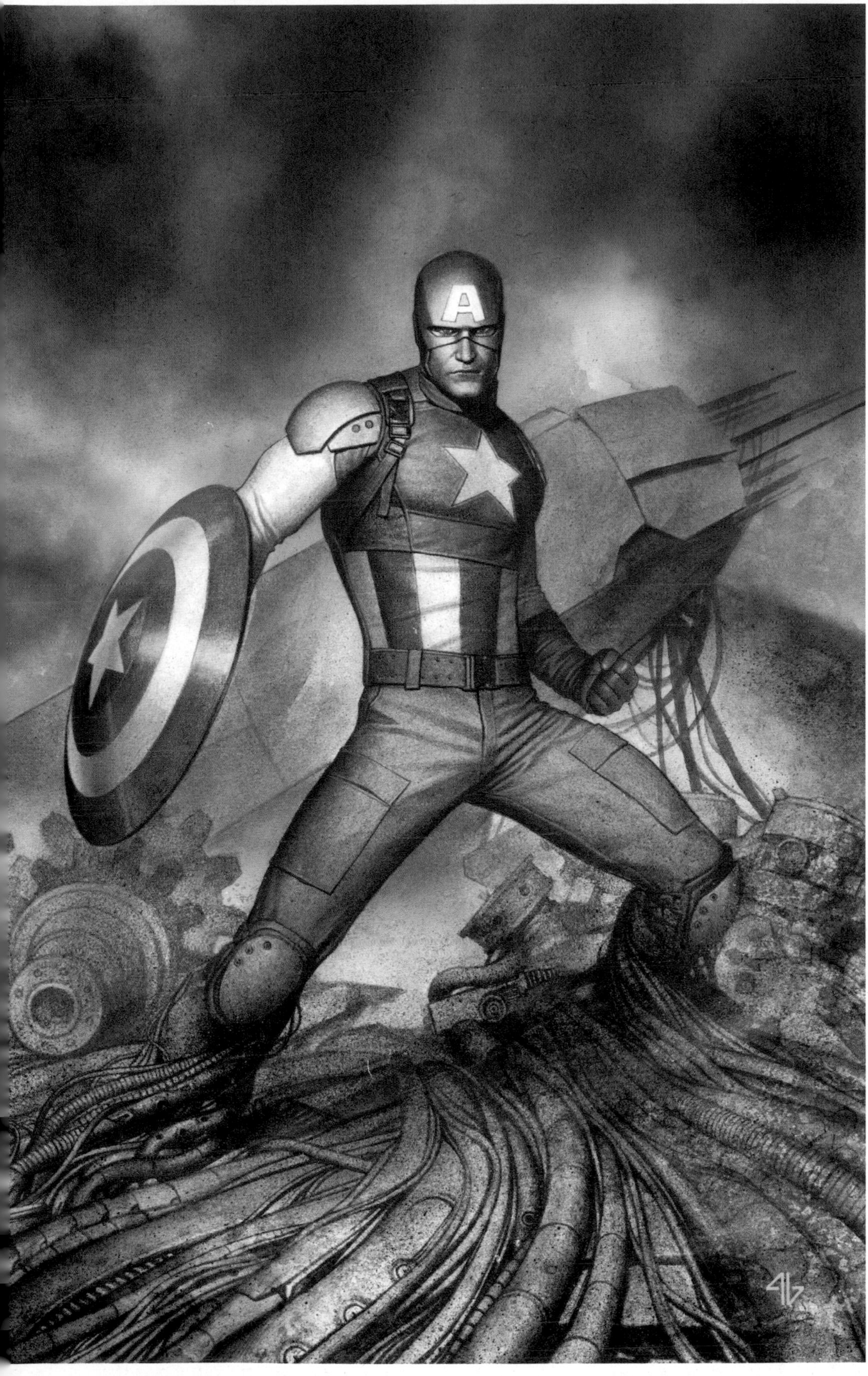

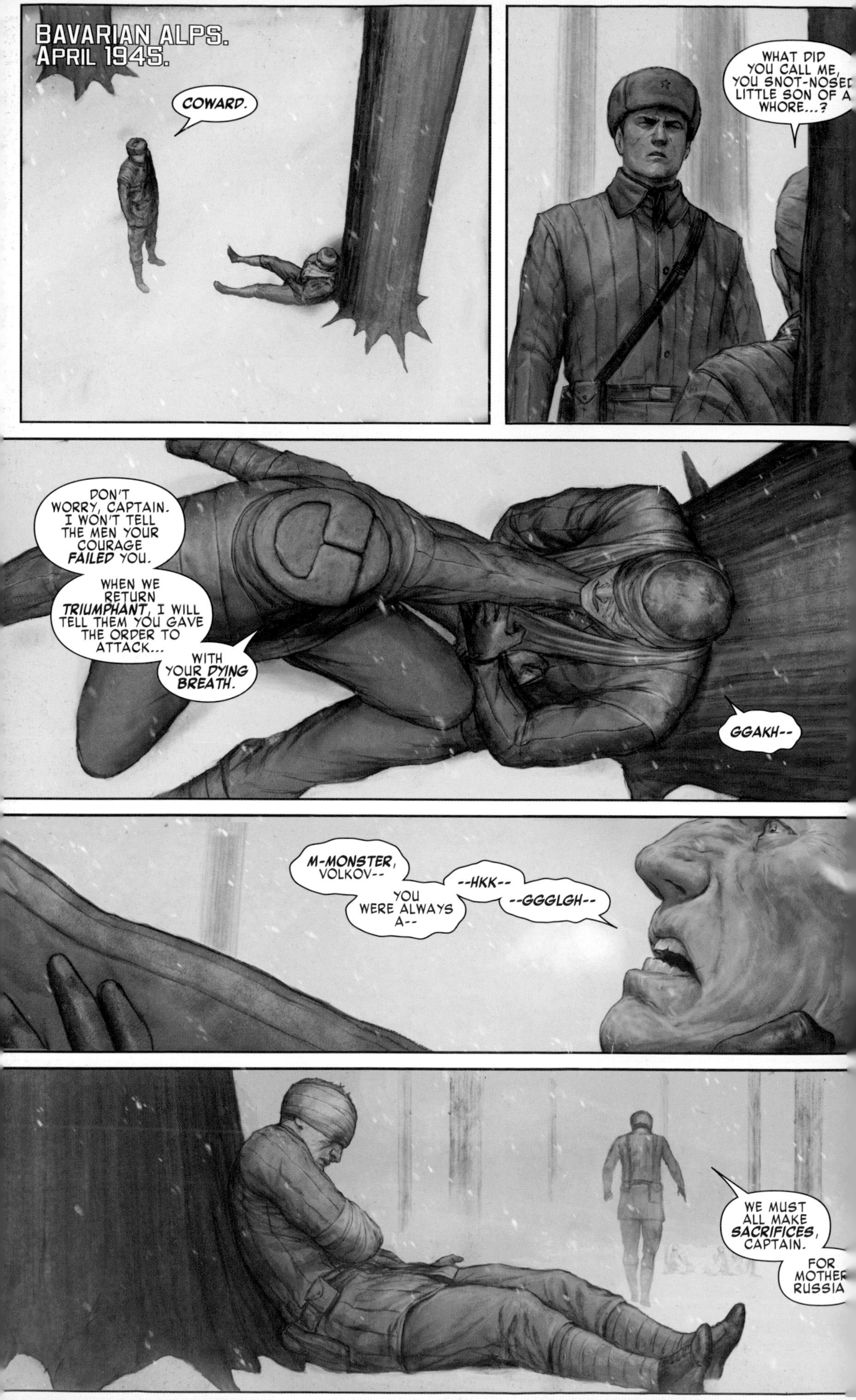
BAVARIAN ALPS.
APRIL 1945.
COWARD.
WHAT DID YOU CALL ME, YOU SNOT-NOSED LITTLE SON OF A WHORE...?
DON'T WORRY, CAPTAIN. I WON'T TELL THE MEN YOUR COURAGE FAILED YOU.
WHEN WE RETURN TRIUMPHANT, I WILL TELL THEM YOU GAVE THE ORDER TO ATTACK...
WITH YOUR DYING BREATH.
GGAKH--
M-MONSTER, VOLKOV--
YOU WERE ALWAYS A--
--HKK--
--GGGLGH--
WE MUST ALL MAKE SACRIFICES, CAPTAIN.
FOR MOTHER RUSSIA

NNNNNNG--

GET BACK! KEEP AWAY FROM HIM--!

NNNNUUUUUGGHH!

WITHOUT HIS *SHIELD*, HE'S BECOMING *ONE* OF THEM!

DESTROY HIM!

NO--!

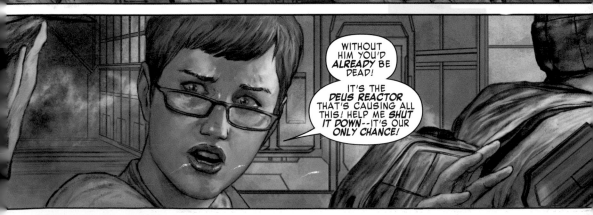

WITHOUT HIM YOU'D *ALREADY* BE DEAD!

IT'S THE *DEUS REACTOR* THAT'S CAUSING ALL THIS! HELP ME *SHUT IT DOWN*--IT'S OUR ONLY CHANCE!

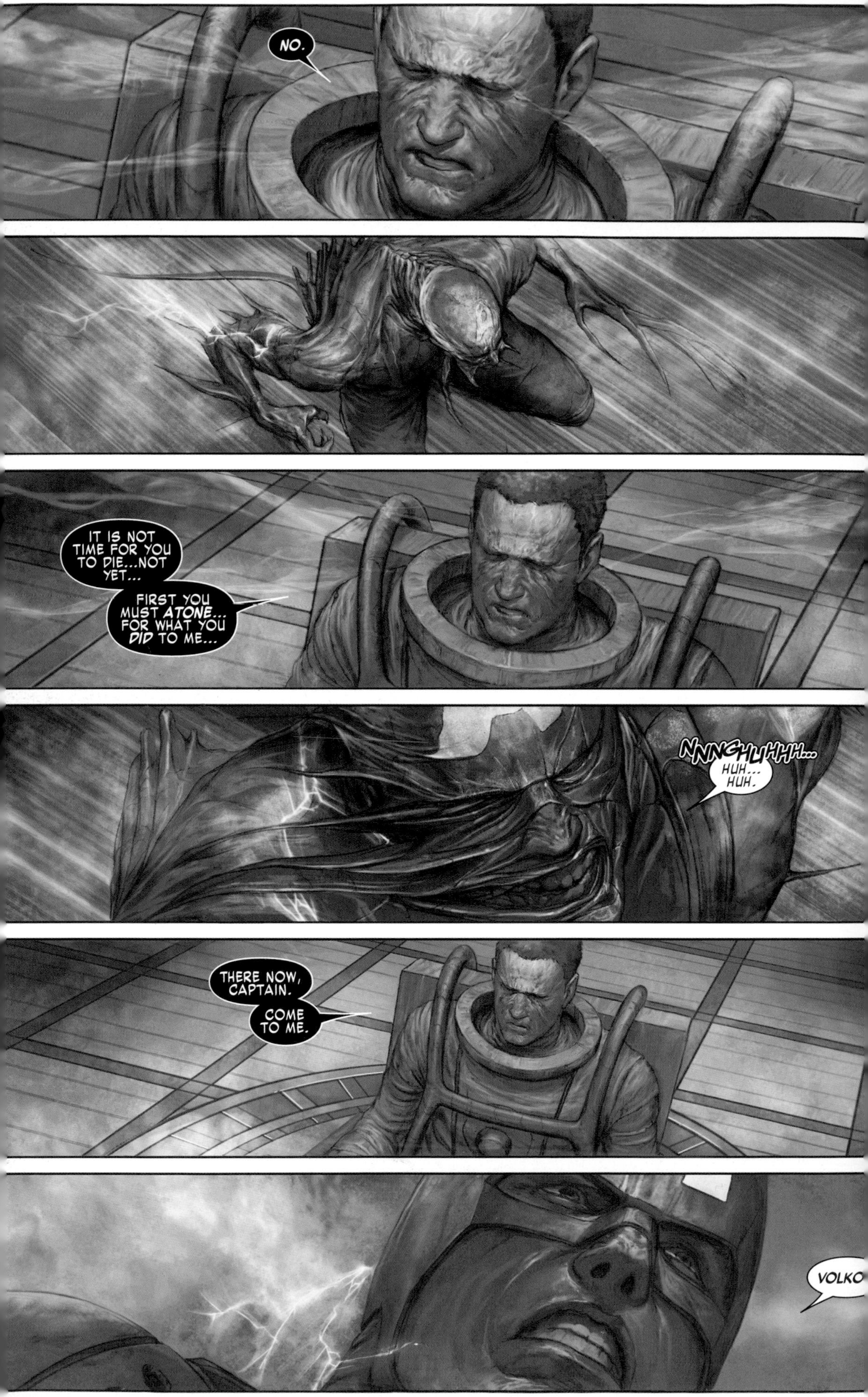
NO.
IT IS NOT TIME FOR YOU TO DIE...NOT YET...
FIRST YOU MUST ATONE... FOR WHAT YOU DID TO ME...
NNNGHUHHH...
HUH... HUH.
THERE NOW, CAPTAIN.
COME TO ME.
VOLKO

IT WAS... VOLKOV...HE WAS IN MY HEAD...

HE *SAVED* ME SOMEHOW... PULLED ME BACK...FROM THE *BRINK*...

THEN GOD HELP YOU, CAPTAIN.

I CAN ONLY IMAGINE HE HAS AN EVEN *WORSE* FATE IN MIND FOR YOU.

HE SAID I HAD TO *ATONE*. BUT FOR *WHAT?*

I SAVED HIS *LIFE*, ALL THOSE YEARS AGO...

NO TIME TO SPECULATE! *HEADS UP!*

...UH, SO TO SPEAK.

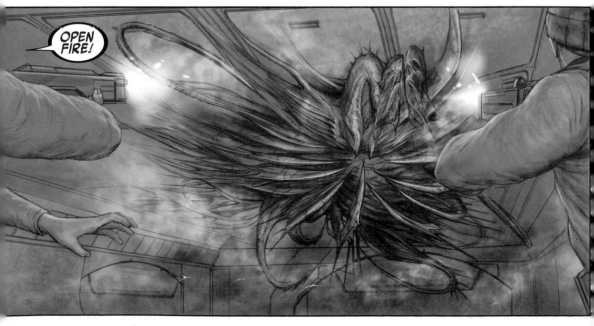

OPEN *FIRE!*

YOU'RE WASTING YOUR TIME! *BULLETS* CAN'T KILL IT!

JUST KEEP IT AT BAY FOR AS LONG AS YOU CAN--!

CAP, WHERE ARE YOU GOING...?

CAP--!

I DO BELIEV HE LE IN HE

...A LEFT TO

THIS WAY! THE MAINTENANCE LOCKERS!

PLEA LET T STILL BE PLEAS

NO GOOD! FALL BACK--!

YES!

WHAT IN THE NAME OF GOD'S TEETH IS THAT?

WELDING LASER! WE USED 'EM FOR HULL REPAIRS!

ARE THEY STILL *FUNCTIONAL*...?

AFFIRMATIVE.

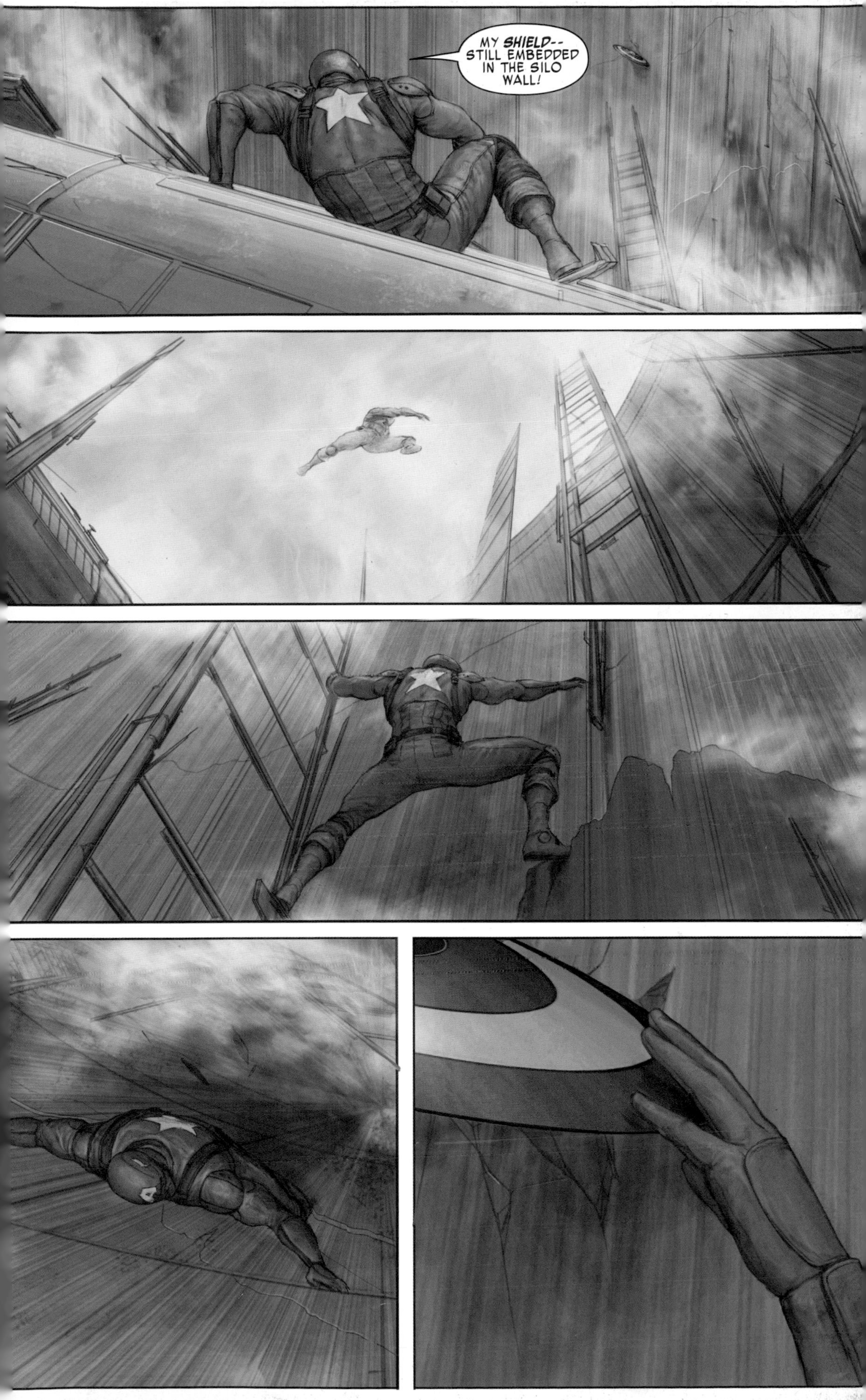
MY SHIELD-- STILL EMBEDDED IN THE SILO WALL!

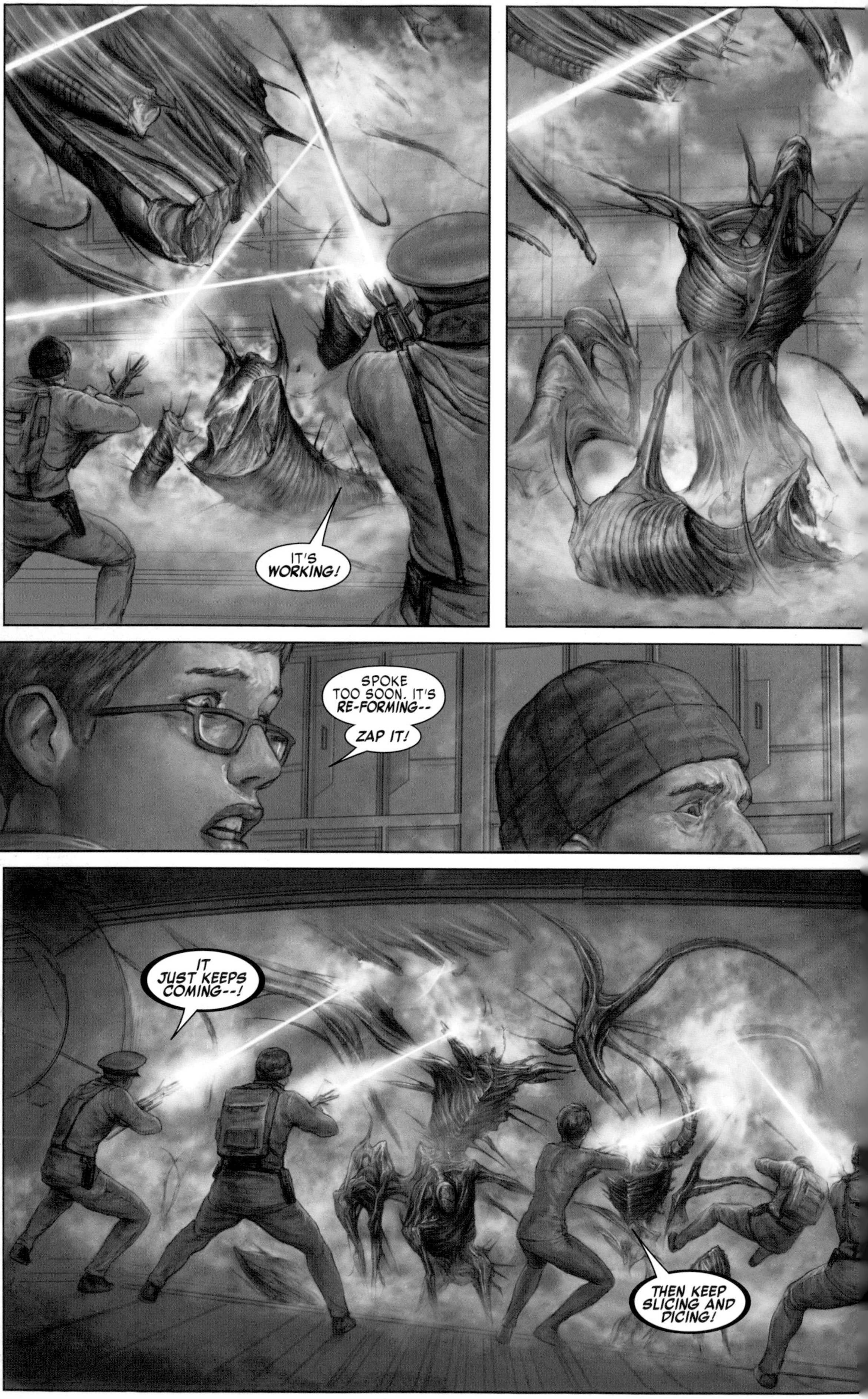
IT'S WORKING!
SPOKE TOO SOON. IT'S RE-FORMING--
ZAP IT!
IT JUST KEEPS COMING--!
THEN KEEP SLICING AND DICING!

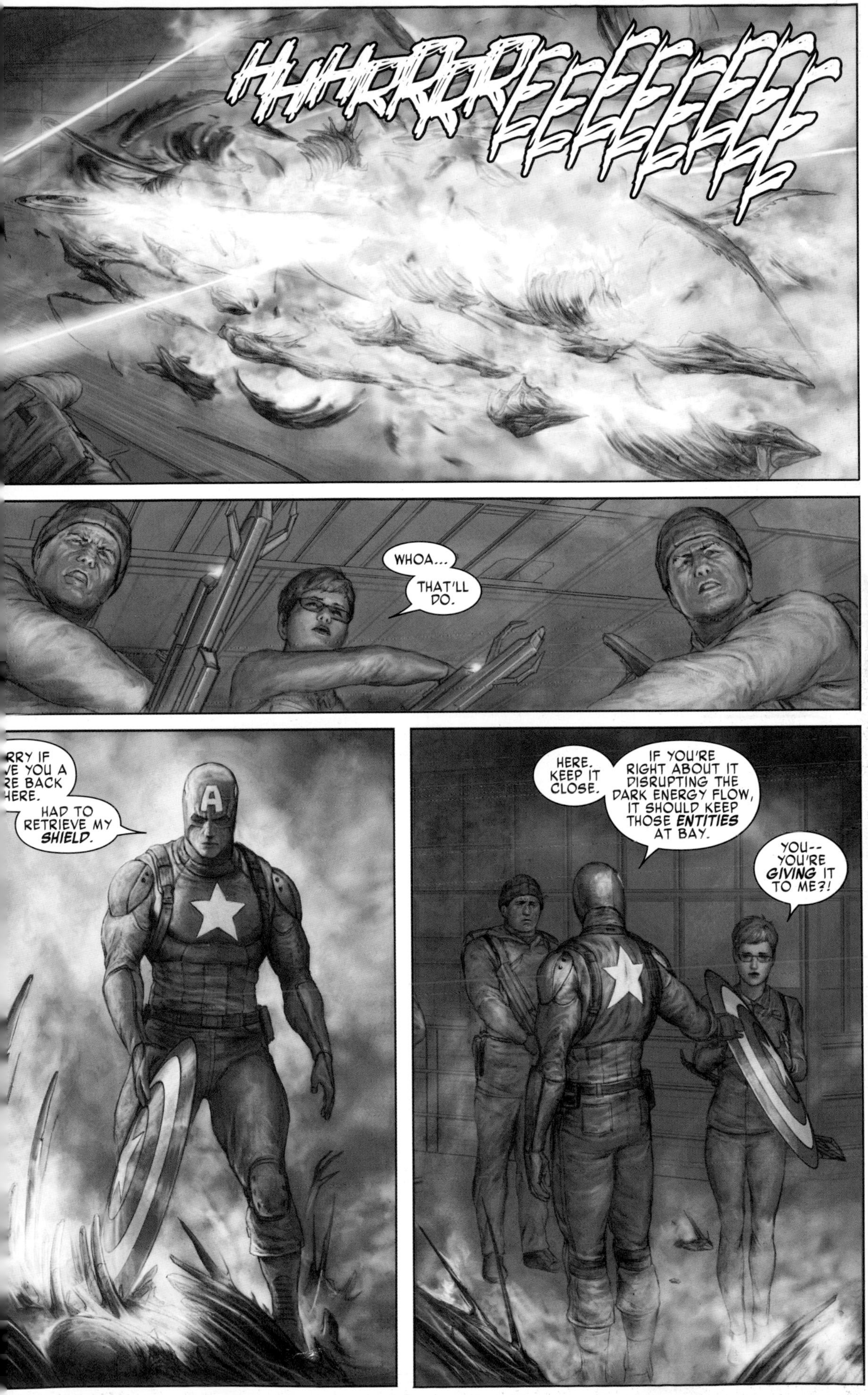
HHHRRRRREEEEEEEEEE
WHOA... THAT'LL DO.
RRY IF VE YOU A RE BACK HERE.
HAD TO RETRIEVE MY SHIELD.
HERE. KEEP IT CLOSE.
IF YOU'RE RIGHT ABOUT IT DISRUPTING THE DARK ENERGY FLOW, IT SHOULD KEEP THOSE ENTITIES AT BAY.
YOU-- YOU'RE GIVING IT TO ME?!

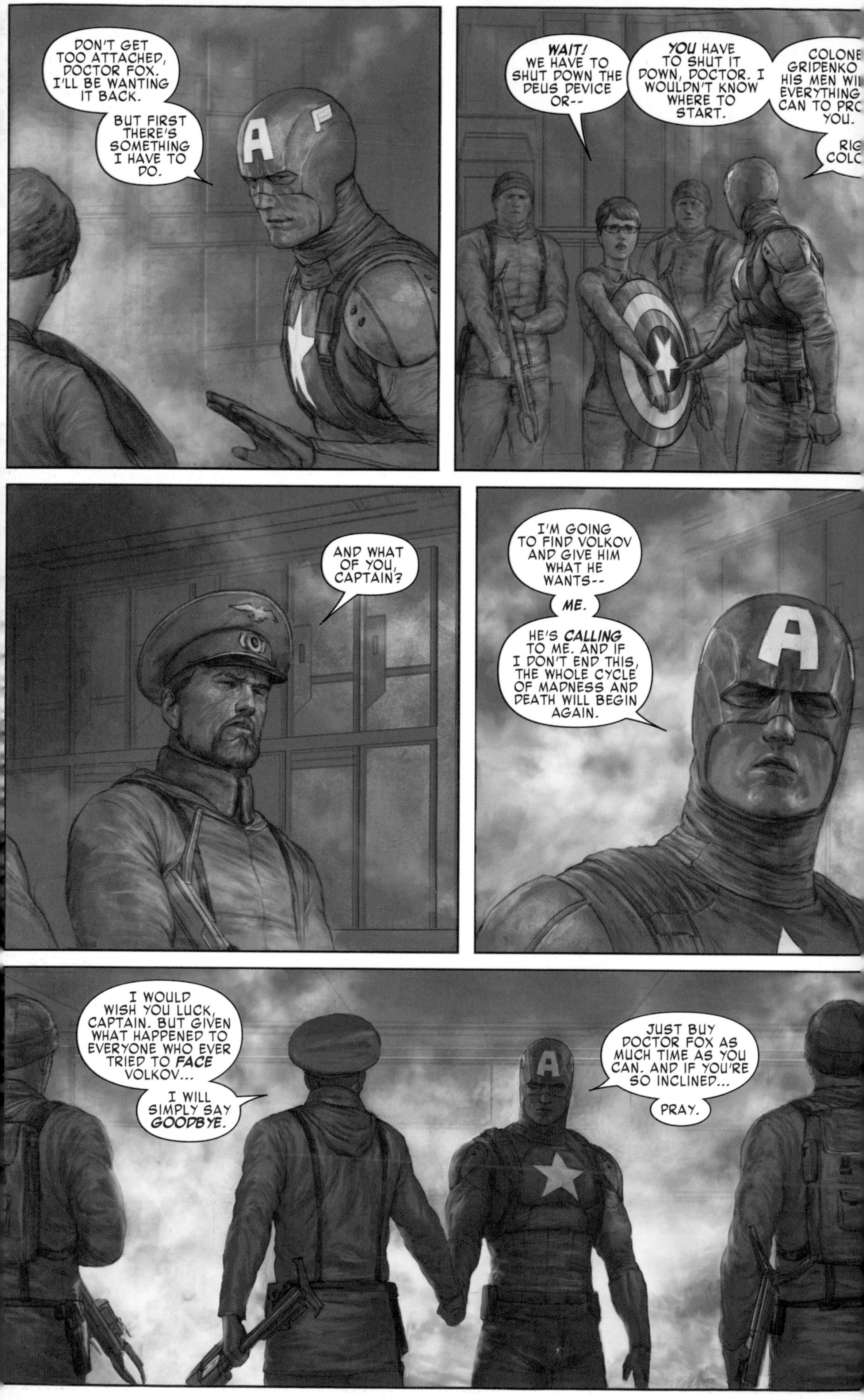

DON'T GET TOO ATTACHED, DOCTOR FOX. I'LL BE WANTING IT BACK.
BUT FIRST THERE'S SOMETHING I HAVE TO DO.
WAIT! WE HAVE TO SHUT DOWN THE DEUS DEVICE OR--
YOU HAVE TO SHUT IT DOWN, DOCTOR. I WOULDN'T KNOW WHERE TO START.
COLONE GRIDENKO HIS MEN WI EVERYTHING CAN TO PRO YOU.
RIG COLO
AND WHAT OF YOU, CAPTAIN?
I'M GOING TO FIND VOLKOV AND GIVE HIM WHAT HE WANTS--
ME.
HE'S CALLING TO ME. AND IF I DON'T END THIS, THE WHOLE CYCLE OF MADNESS AND DEATH WILL BEGIN AGAIN.
I WOULD WISH YOU LUCK, CAPTAIN. BUT GIVEN WHAT HAPPENED TO EVERYONE WHO EVER TRIED TO FACE VOLKOV...
I WILL SIMPLY SAY GOODBYE.
JUST BUY DOCTOR FOX AS MUCH TIME AS YOU CAN. AND IF YOU'RE SO INCLINED...
PRAY.

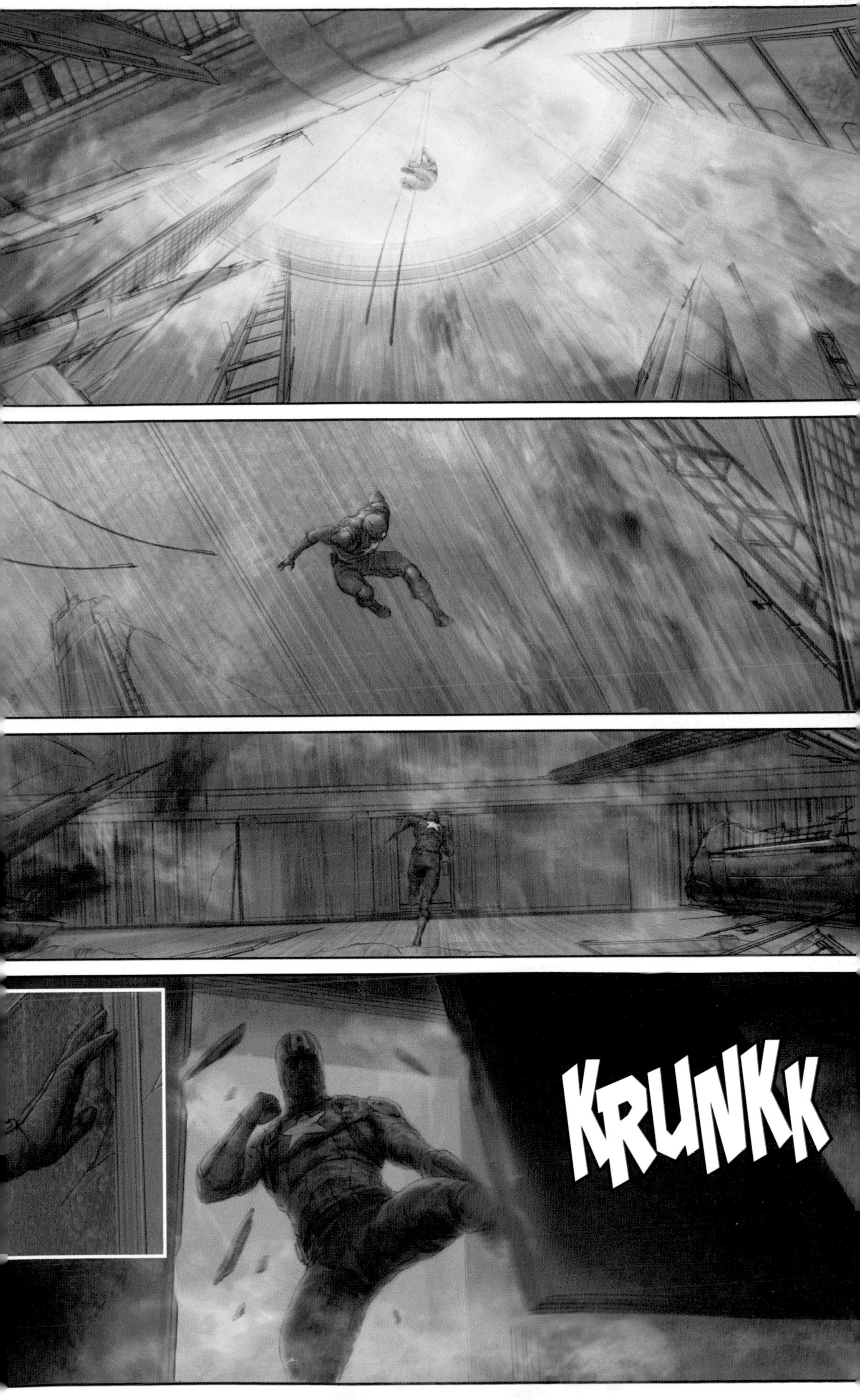
KRUNKK

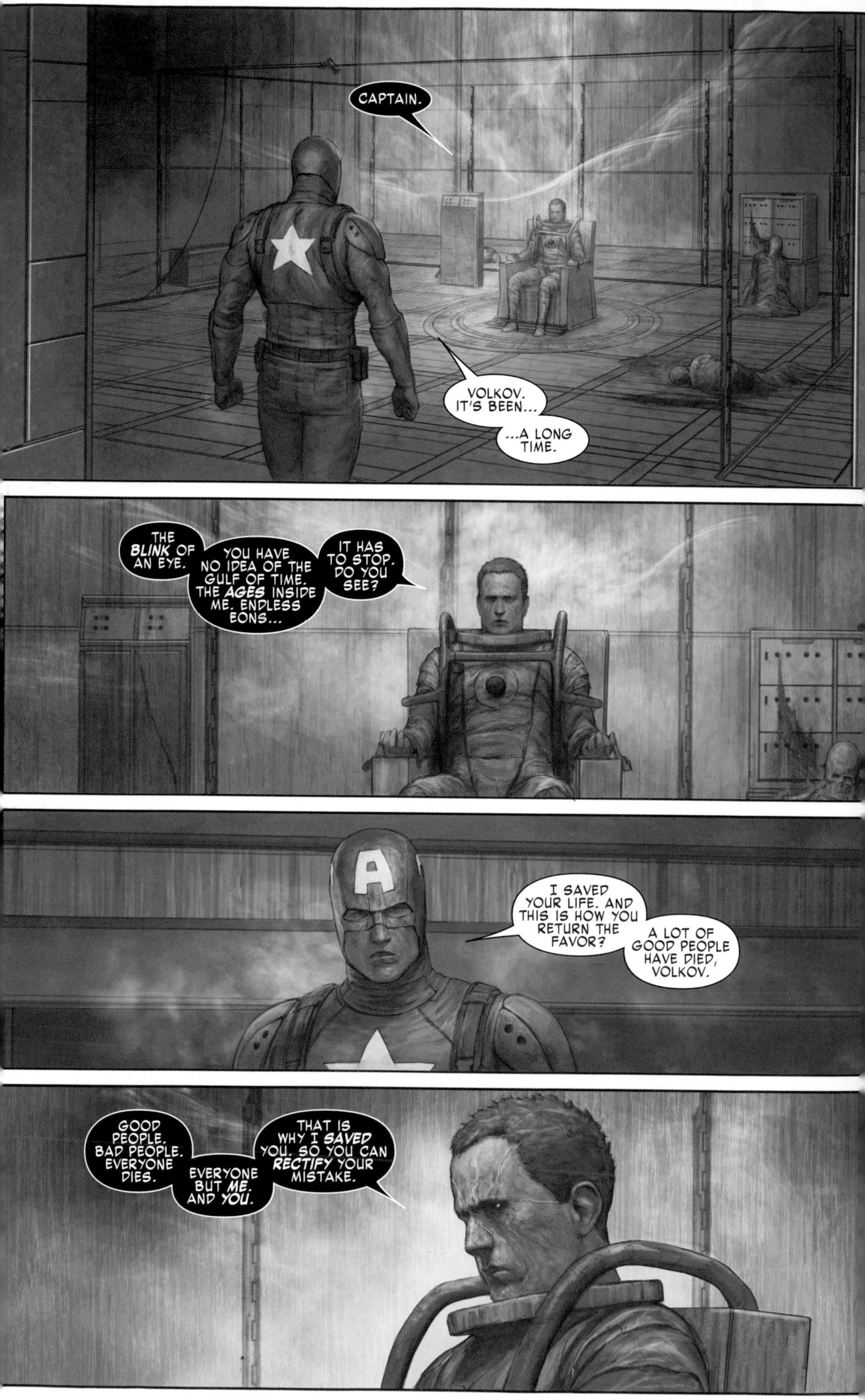
CAPTAIN.
VOLKOV. IT'S BEEN...
...A LONG TIME.
THE BLINK OF AN EYE.
YOU HAVE NO IDEA OF THE GULF OF TIME. THE AGES INSIDE ME. ENDLESS EONS...
IT HAS TO STOP. DO YOU SEE?
I SAVED YOUR LIFE. AND THIS IS HOW YOU RETURN THE FAVOR?
A LOT OF GOOD PEOPLE HAVE DIED, VOLKOV.
GOOD PEOPLE. BAD PEOPLE. EVERYONE DIES.
EVERYONE BUT ME. AND YOU.
THAT IS WHY I SAVED YOU. SO YOU CAN RECTIFY YOUR MISTAKE.

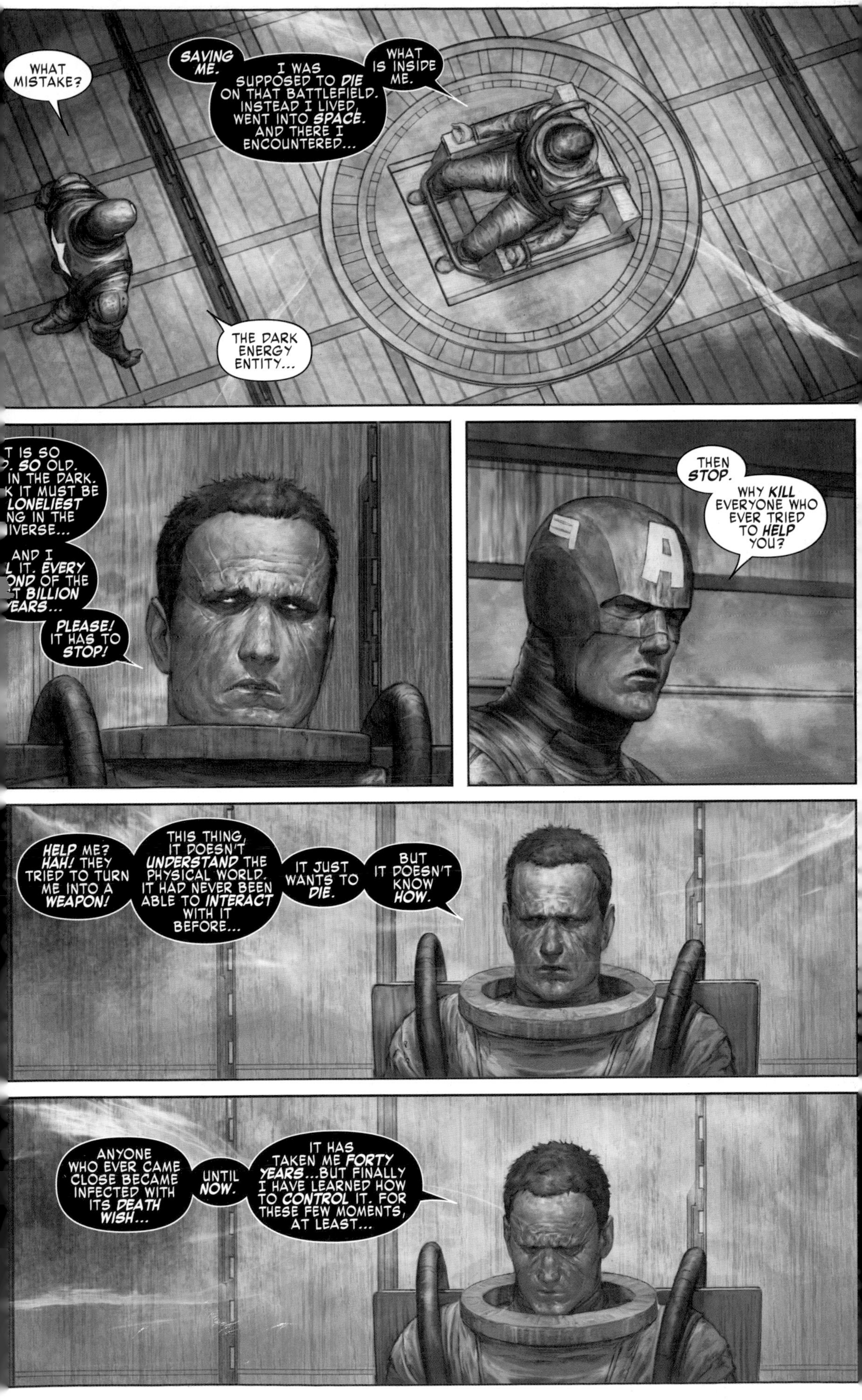
WHAT MISTAKE?
SAVING ME.
I WAS SUPPOSED TO DIE ON THAT BATTLEFIELD. INSTEAD I LIVED, WENT INTO SPACE. AND THERE I ENCOUNTERED...
WHAT IS INSIDE ME.
THE DARK ENERGY ENTITY...
T IS SO . SO OLD. IN THE DARK. K IT MUST BE LONELIEST NG IN THE IVERSE...
AND I L IT. EVERY OND OF THE T BILLION YEARS...
PLEASE! IT HAS TO STOP!
THEN STOP.
WHY KILL EVERYONE WHO EVER TRIED TO HELP YOU?
HELP ME? HAH! THEY TRIED TO TURN ME INTO A WEAPON!
THIS THING, IT DOESN'T UNDERSTAND THE PHYSICAL WORLD. IT HAD NEVER BEEN ABLE TO INTERACT WITH IT BEFORE...
IT JUST WANTS TO DIE.
BUT IT DOESN'T KNOW HOW.
ANYONE WHO EVER CAME CLOSE BECAME INFECTED WITH ITS DEATH WISH...
UNTIL NOW.
IT HAS TAKEN ME FORTY YEARS...BUT FINALLY I HAVE LEARNED HOW TO CONTROL IT. FOR THESE FEW MOMENTS, AT LEAST...

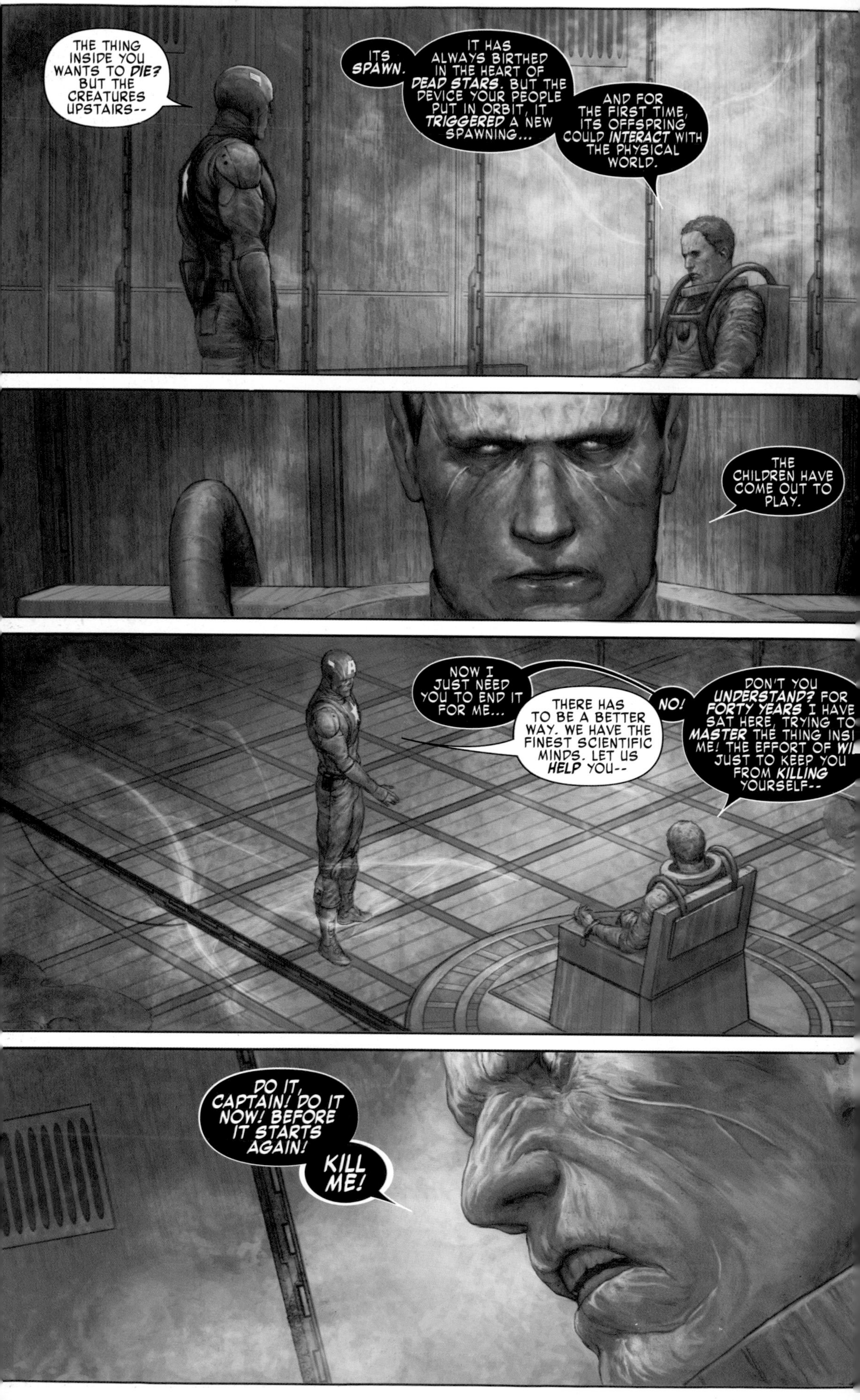
THE THING INSIDE YOU WANTS TO *DIE?* BUT THE CREATURES UPSTAIRS--
ITS *SPAWN.*
IT HAS ALWAYS BIRTHED IN THE HEART OF *DEAD STARS.* BUT THE DEVICE YOUR PEOPLE PUT IN ORBIT, IT *TRIGGERED* A NEW SPAWNING...
AND FOR THE FIRST TIME, ITS OFFSPRING COULD *INTERACT* WITH THE PHYSICAL WORLD.
THE CHILDREN HAVE COME OUT TO PLAY.
NOW I JUST NEED YOU TO END IT FOR ME...
THERE HAS TO BE A BETTER WAY. WE HAVE THE FINEST SCIENTIFIC MINDS. LET US *HELP* YOU--
NO!
DON'T YOU *UNDERSTAND?* FOR *FORTY YEARS* I HAVE SAT HERE, TRYING TO *MASTER* THE THING INSI ME! THE EFFORT OF *WI* JUST TO KEEP YOU FROM *KILLING* YOURSELF--
DO IT, CAPTAIN! DO IT NOW! BEFORE IT STARTS AGAIN!
KILL ME!

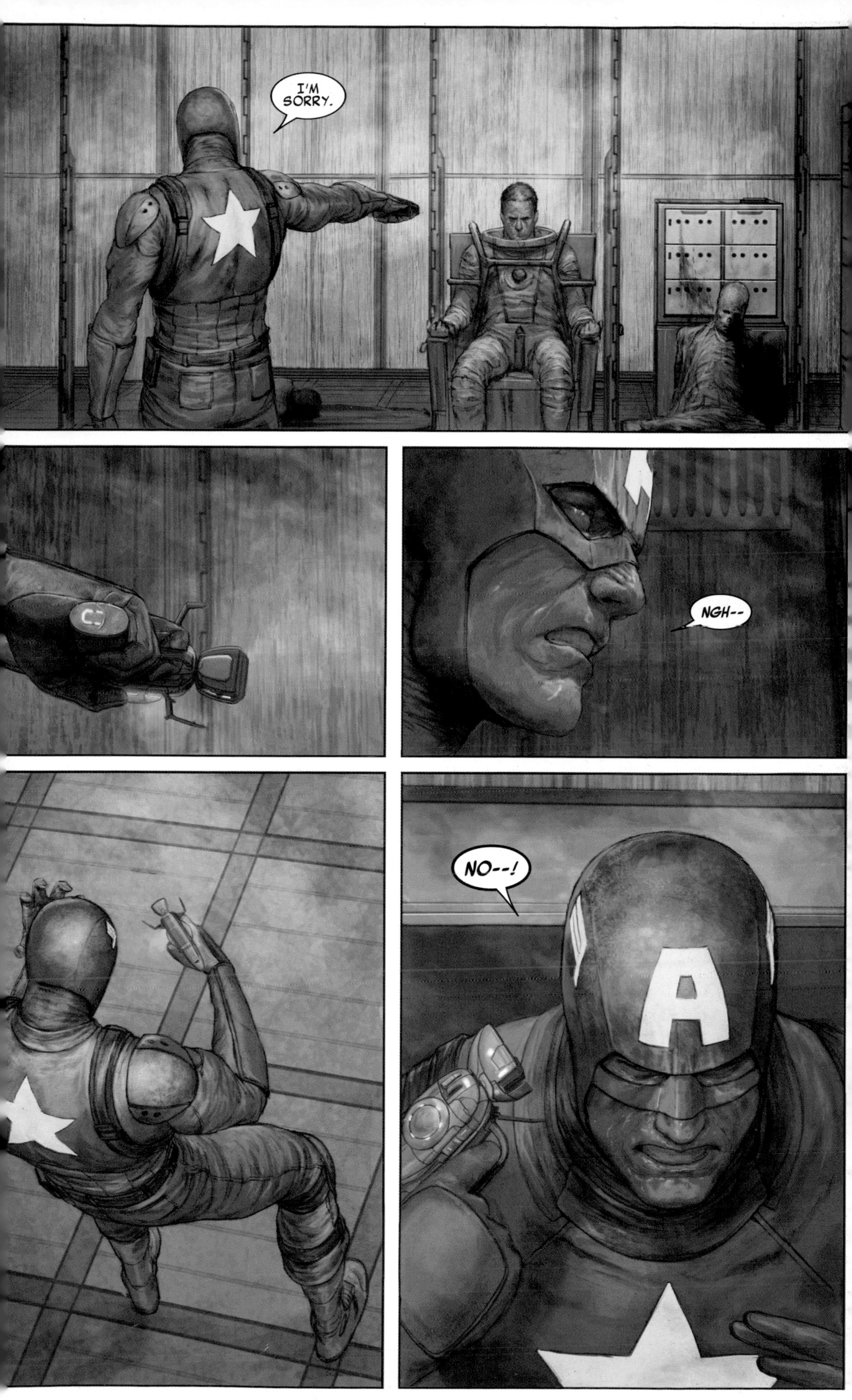
I'M SORRY.
NGH--
NO--!

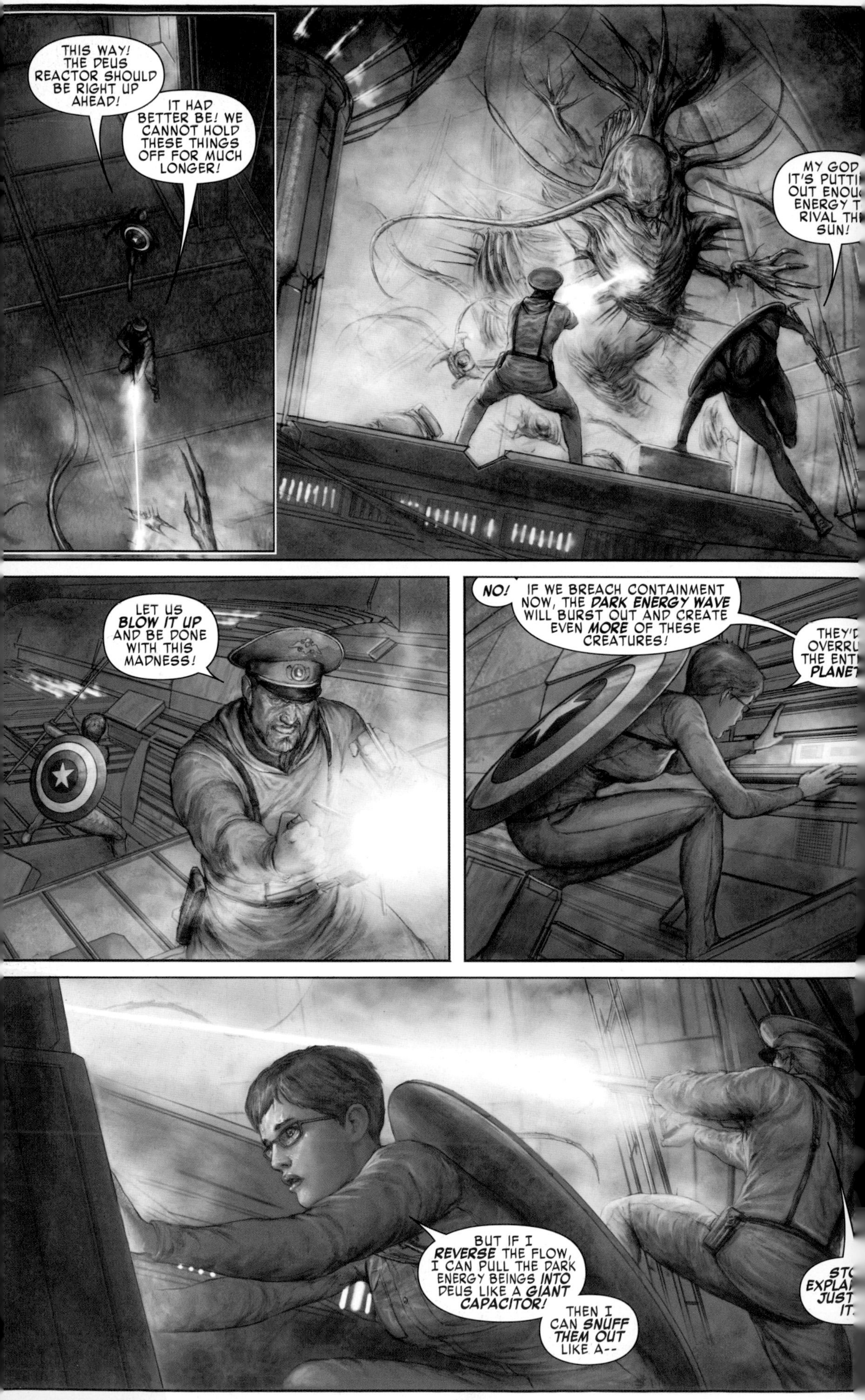
THIS WAY! THE DEUS REACTOR SHOULD BE RIGHT UP AHEAD!
IT HAD BETTER BE! WE CANNOT HOLD THESE THINGS OFF FOR MUCH LONGER!
MY GOD IT'S PUTTI OUT ENOU ENERGY T RIVAL TH SUN!
LET US BLOW IT UP AND BE DONE WITH THIS MADNESS!
NO!
IF WE BREACH CONTAINMENT NOW, THE DARK ENERGY WAVE WILL BURST OUT AND CREATE EVEN MORE OF THESE CREATURES!
THEY'D OVERRU THE ENT PLANET
BUT IF I REVERSE THE FLOW, I CAN PULL THE DARK ENERGY BEINGS INTO DEUS LIKE A GIANT CAPACITOR!
THEN I CAN SNUFF THEM OUT LIKE A--
STO EXPLAI JUST IT.

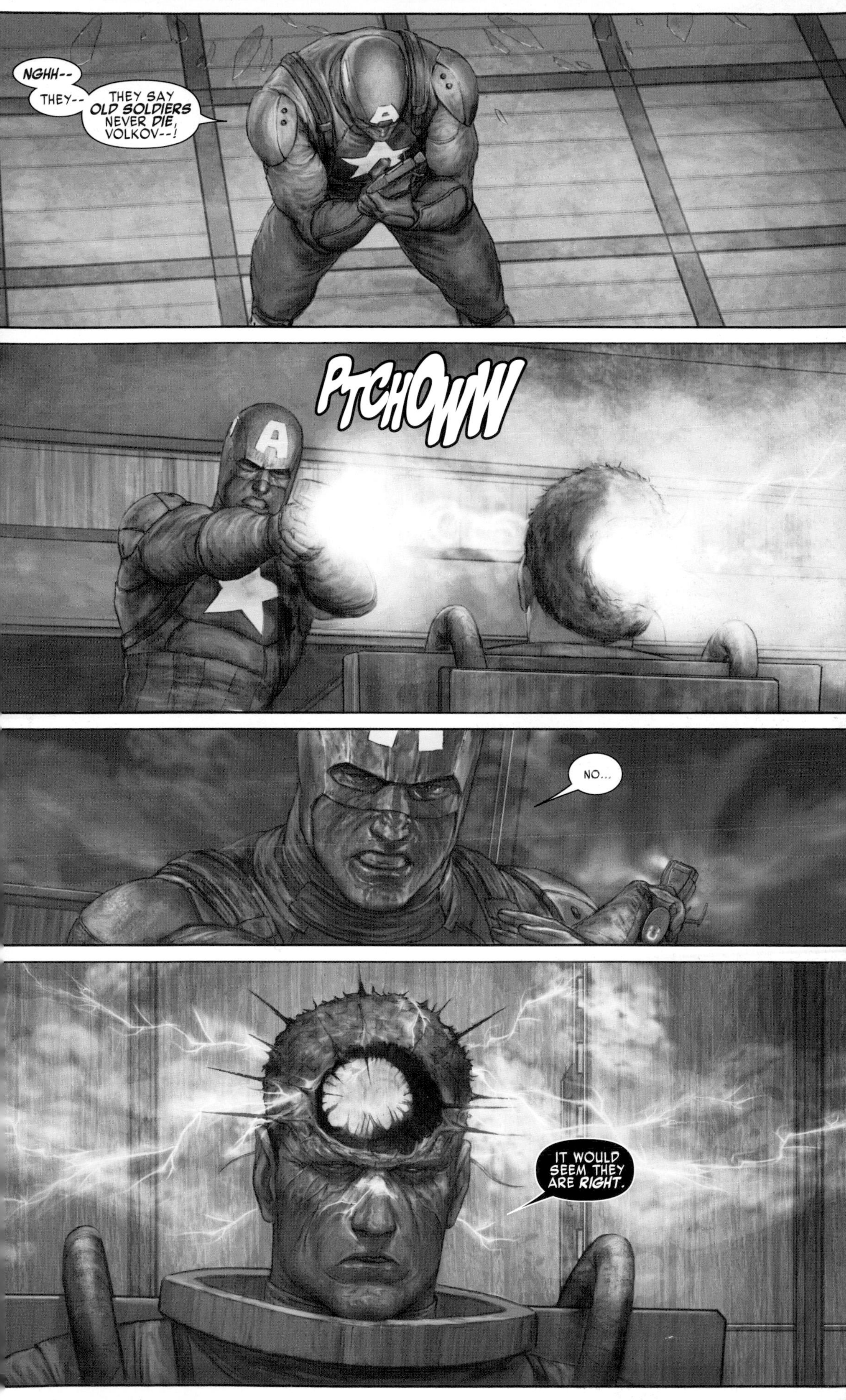
NGHH--
THEY--
THEY SAY OLD SOLDIERS NEVER DIE, VOLKOV--!
PTCHOWW
NO...
IT WOULD SEEM THEY ARE RIGHT.

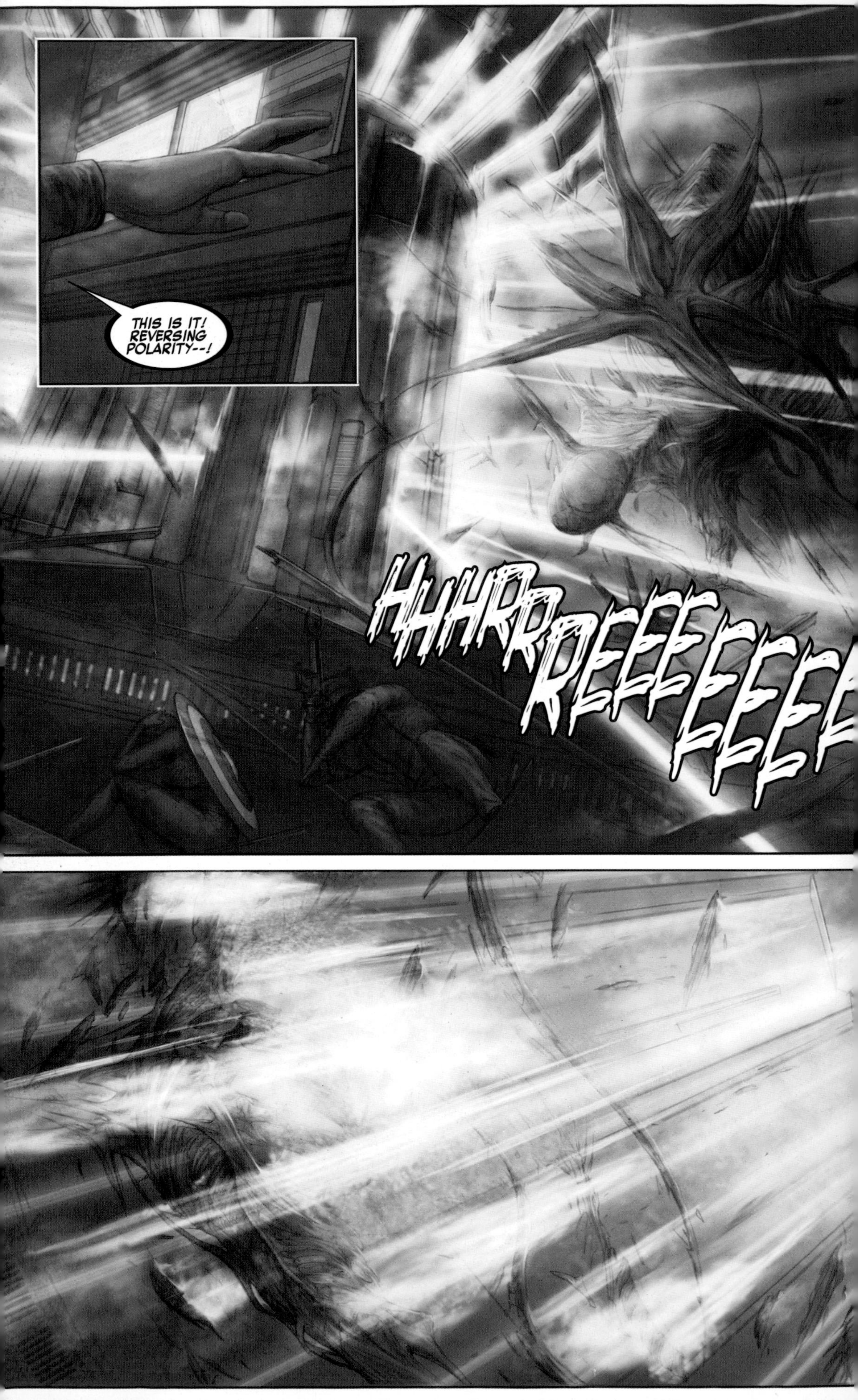
THIS IS IT! REVERSING POLARITY--!
HHHRRRREEEEEEEEE

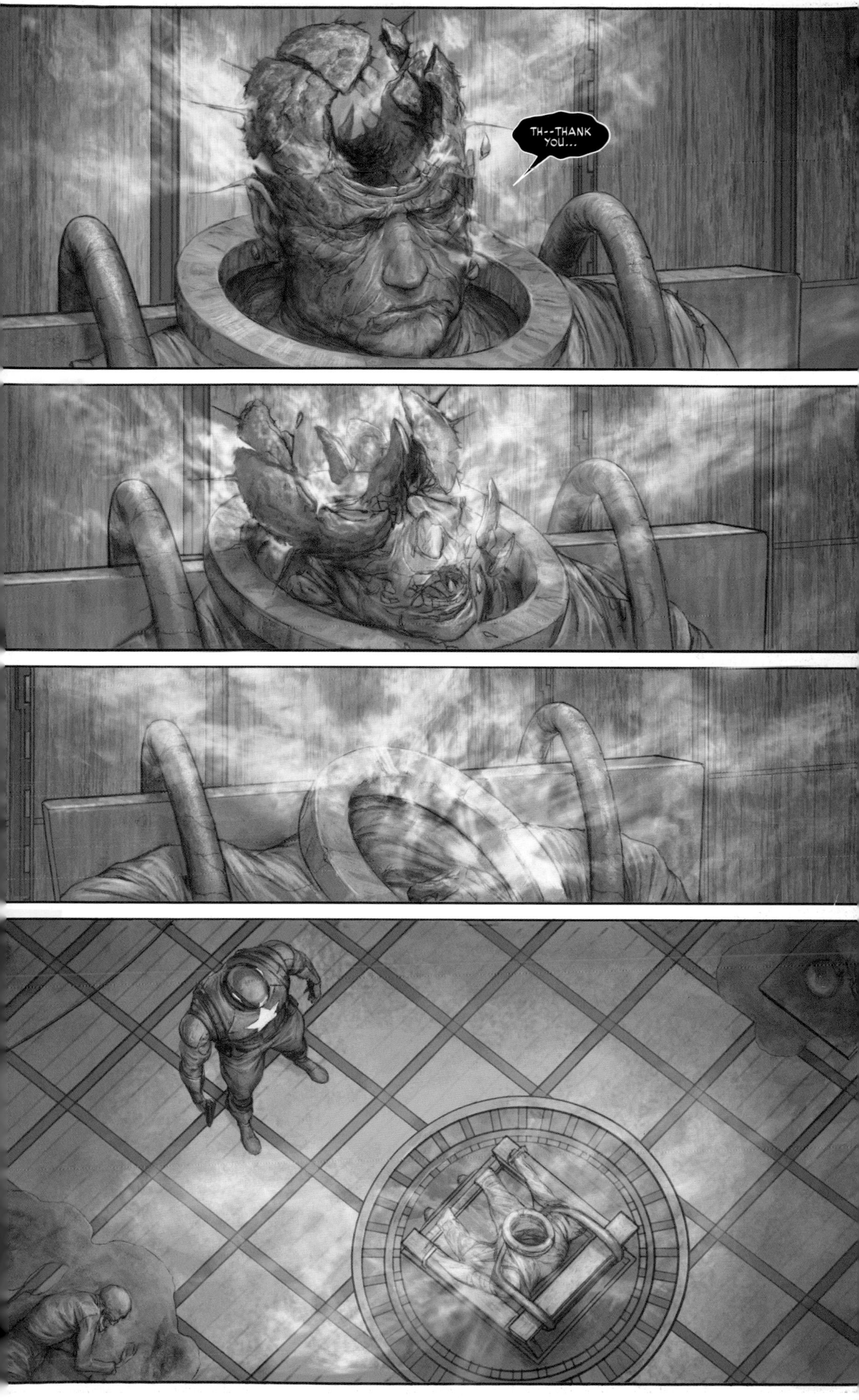
TH--THANK YOU...

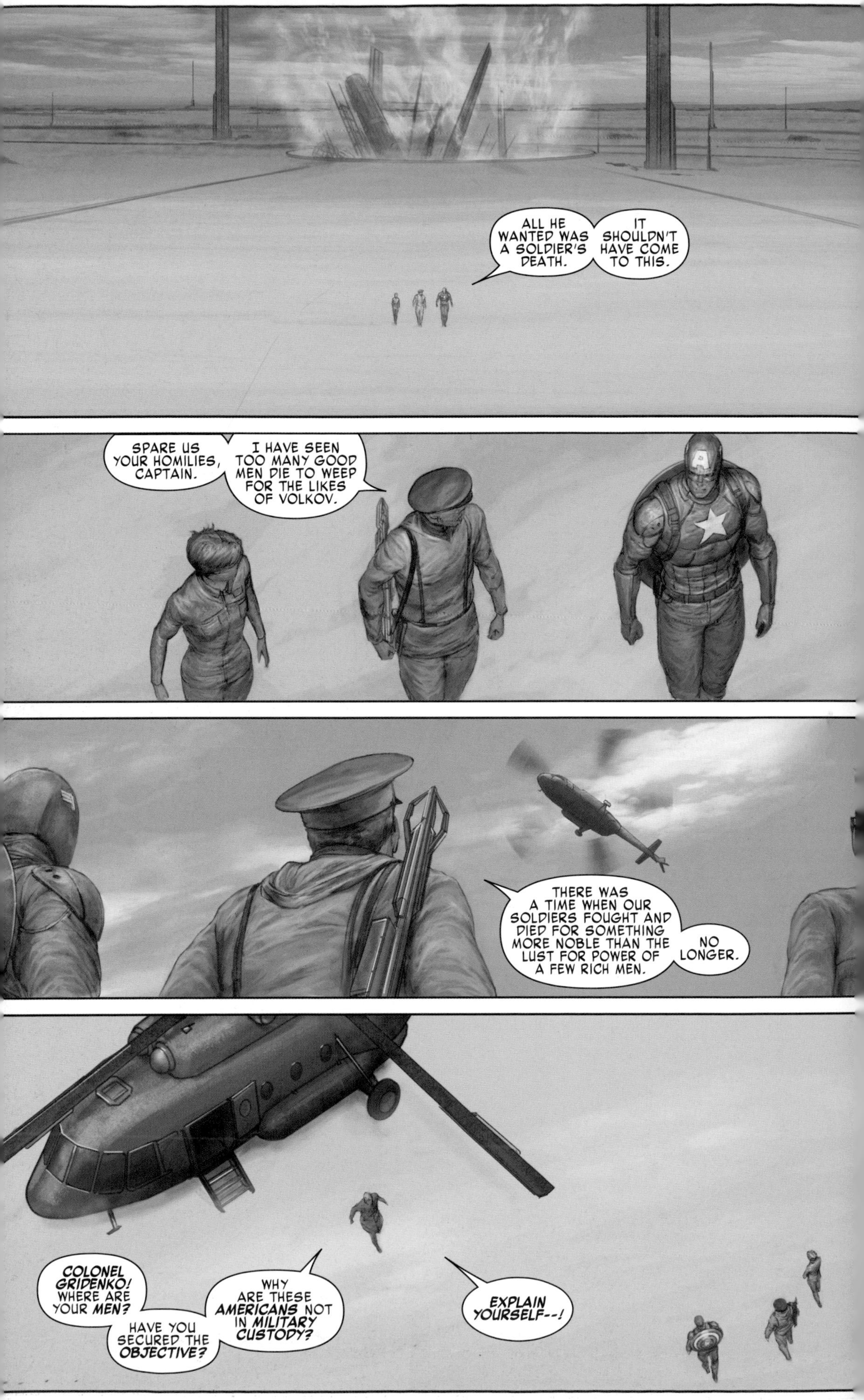
ALL HE WANTED WAS A SOLDIER'S DEATH.
IT SHOULDN'T HAVE COME TO THIS.
SPARE US YOUR HOMILIES, CAPTAIN.
I HAVE SEEN TOO MANY GOOD MEN DIE TO WEEP FOR THE LIKES OF VOLKOV.
THERE WAS A TIME WHEN OUR SOLDIERS FOUGHT AND DIED FOR SOMETHING MORE NOBLE THAN THE LUST FOR POWER OF A FEW RICH MEN.
NO LONGER.
COLONEL GRIDENKO! WHERE ARE YOUR MEN?
HAVE YOU SECURED THE OBJECTIVE?
WHY ARE THESE AMERICANS NOT IN MILITARY CUSTODY?
EXPLAIN YOURSELF--!

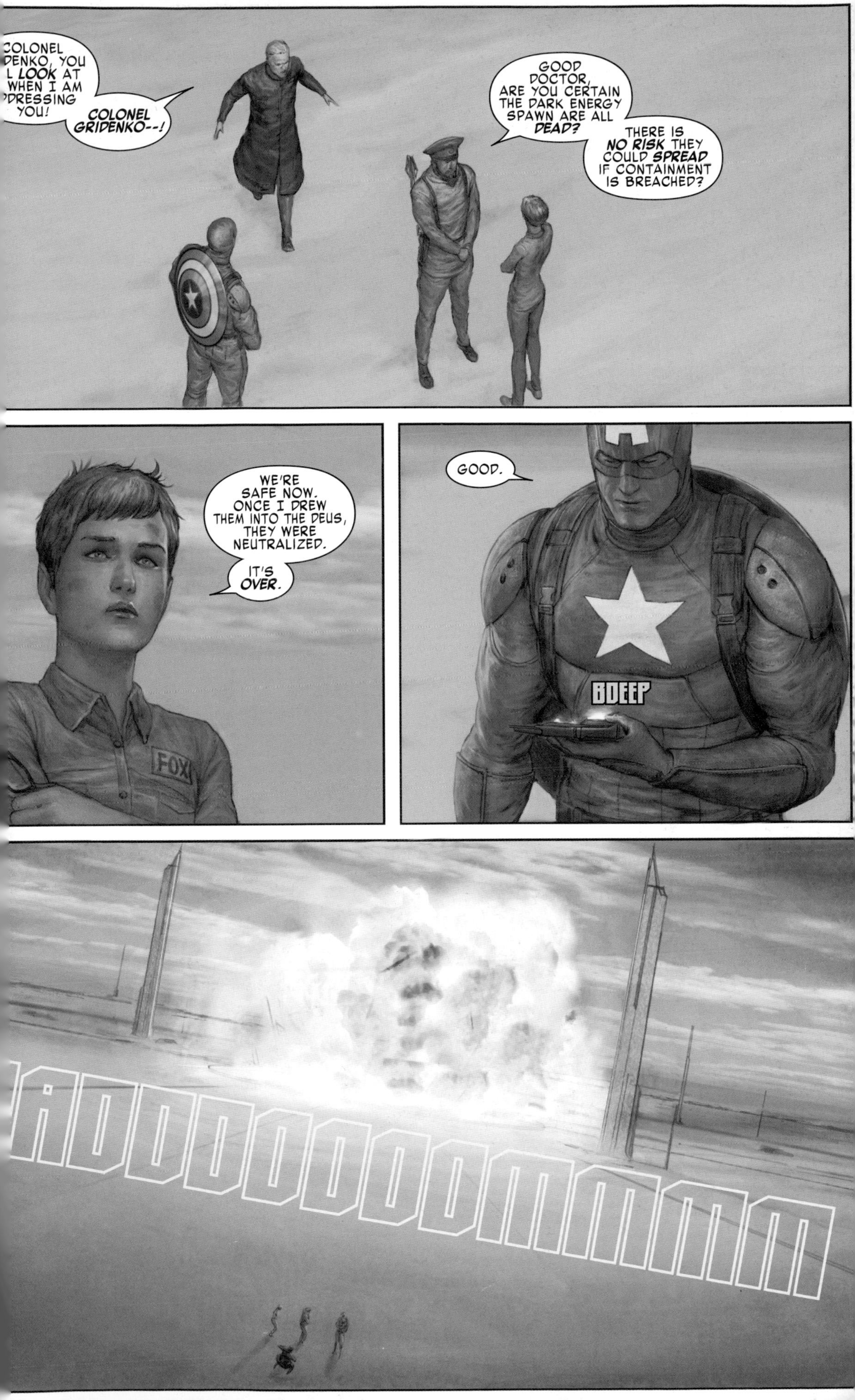
COLONEL DENKO, YOU L LOOK AT WHEN I AM DRESSING YOU!
COLONEL GRIDENKO--!
GOOD DOCTOR, ARE YOU CERTAIN THE DARK ENERGY SPAWN ARE ALL DEAD?
THERE IS NO RISK THEY COULD SPREAD IF CONTAINMENT IS BREACHED?
WE'RE SAFE NOW. ONCE I DREW THEM INTO THE DEUS, THEY WERE NEUTRALIZED.
IT'S OVER.
GOOD.
BDEEP
FOX

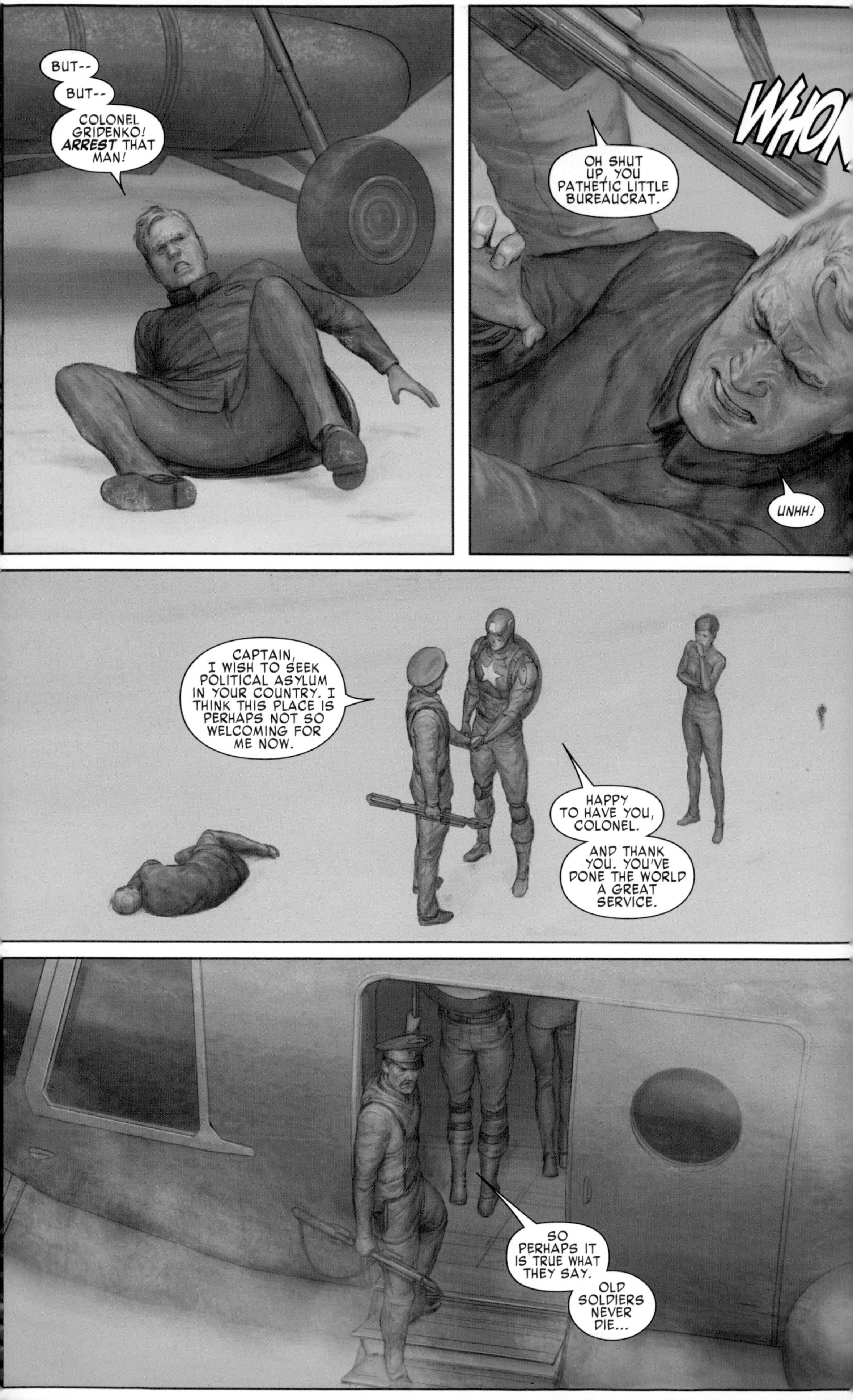
BUT--
BUT--
COLONEL GRIDENKO! ARREST THAT MAN!
WHOM
OH SHUT UP, YOU PATHETIC LITTLE BUREAUCRAT.
UNHH!
CAPTAIN, I WISH TO SEEK POLITICAL ASYLUM IN YOUR COUNTRY. I THINK THIS PLACE IS PERHAPS NOT SO WELCOMING FOR ME NOW.
HAPPY TO HAVE YOU, COLONEL.
AND THANK YOU. YOU'VE DONE THE WORLD A GREAT SERVICE.
SO PERHAPS IT IS TRUE WHAT THEY SAY.
OLD SOLDIERS NEVER DIE...

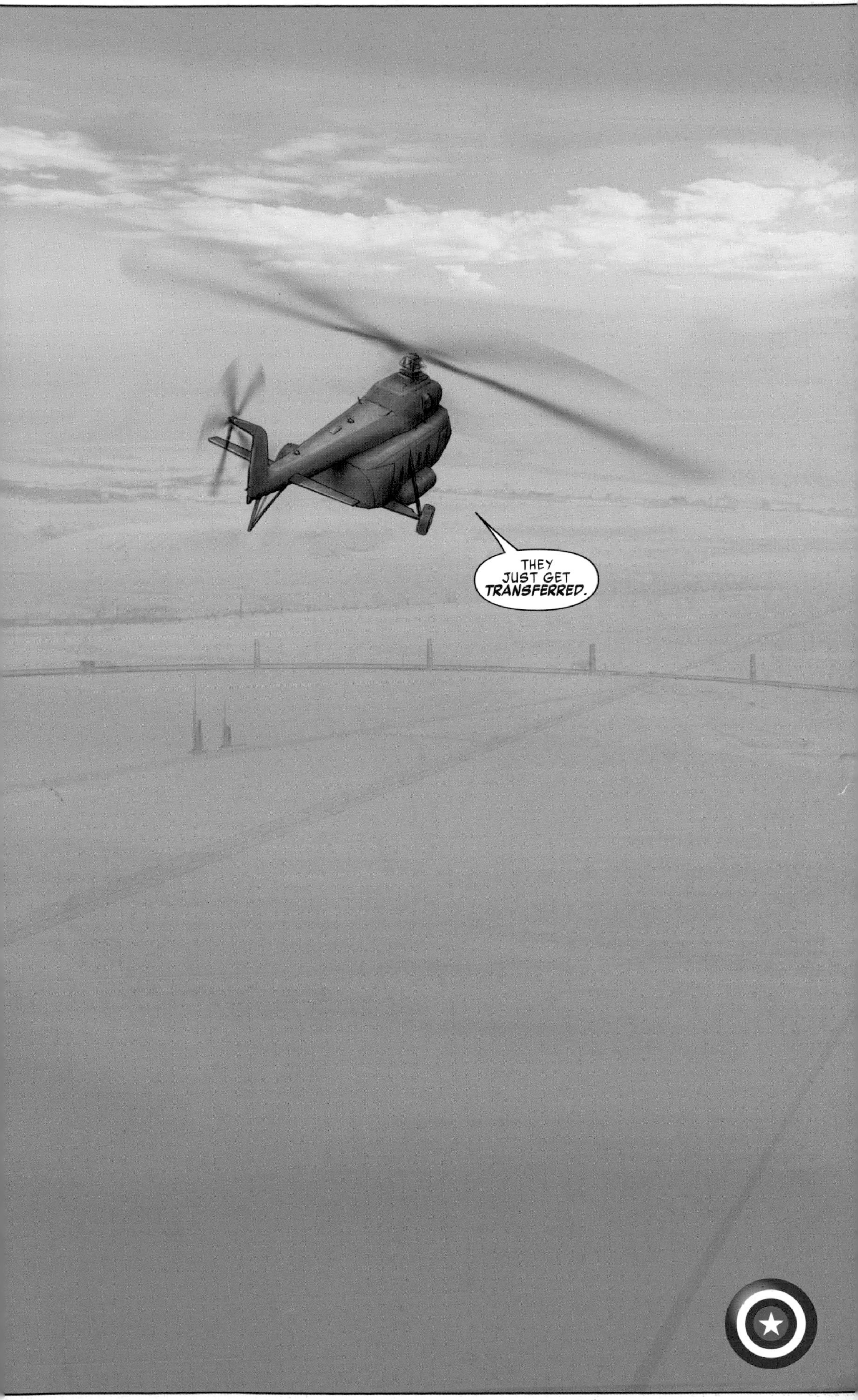
THEY JUST GET TRANSFERRED.

CAPTAIN AMERICA: LIVING LEGEND VARIANT COVER GALLERY

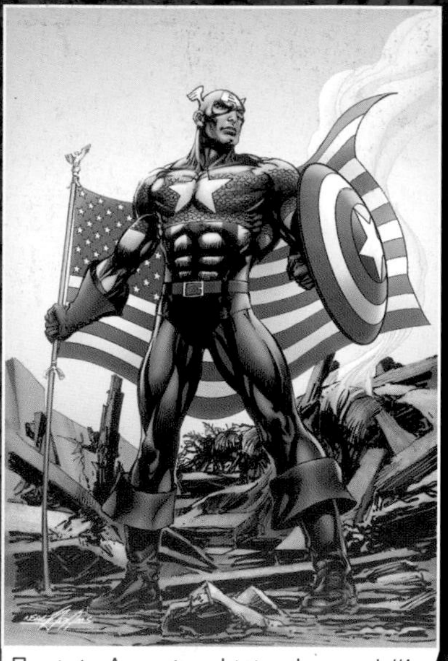

Captain America: Living Legend #1
by Neal Adams.

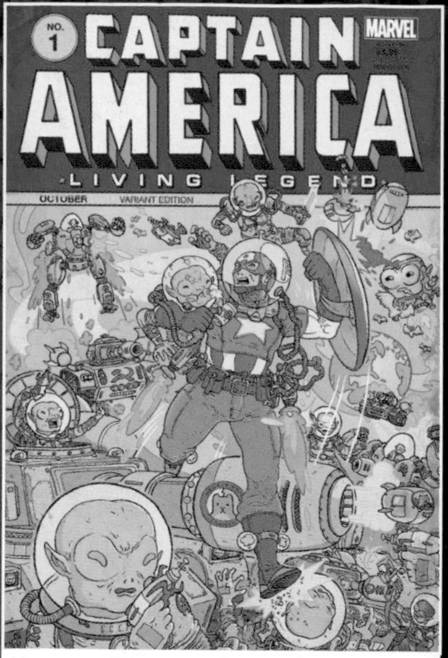

NO. 1
CAPTAIN
AMERICA
MARVEL
$3.99
·LIVING LEGEND·
OCTOBER
VARIANT EDITION

Captain America: Living Legend #1
by Ulises Farinas.

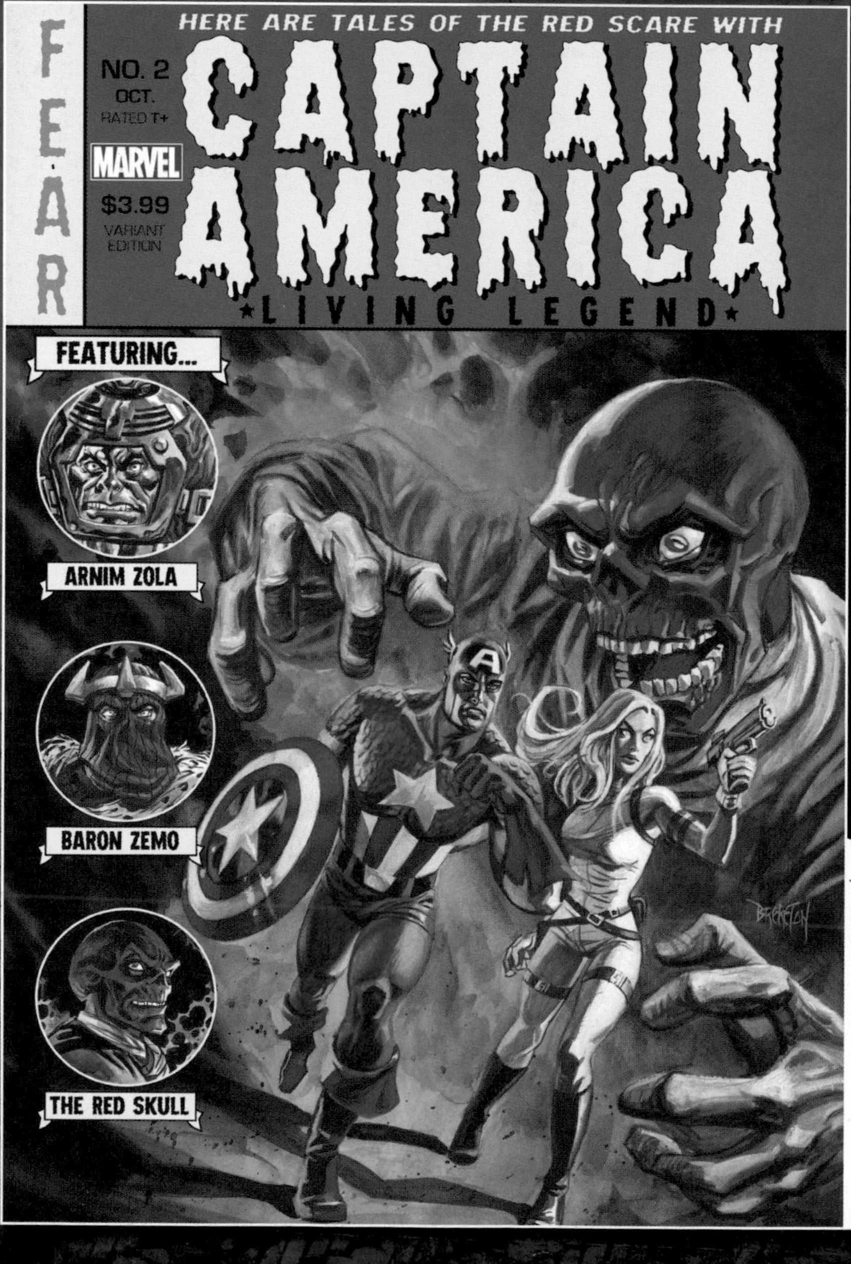

FEAR
HERE ARE TALES OF THE RED SCARE WITH
NO. 2
OCT.
RATED T+
MARVEL
$3.99
VARIANT EDITION
CAPTAIN
AMERICA
★LIVING LEGEND★
FEATURING...
ARNIM ZOLA
BARON ZEMO
THE RED SKULL
BRERETON

Captain America: Living Legend #2
by Daniel Brereton.

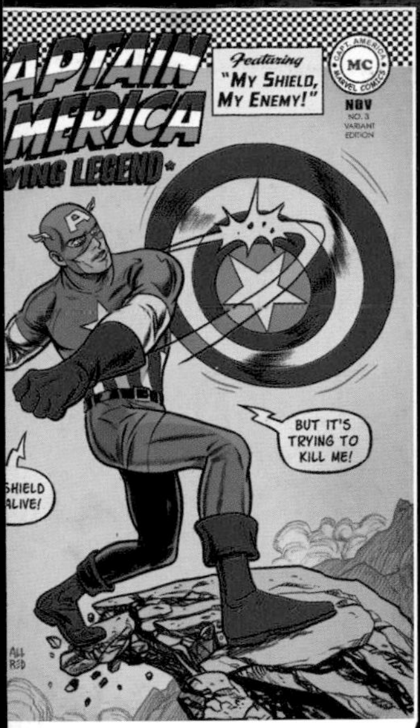
APTAIN
MERICA
VING LEGEND
Featuring "My Shield, My Enemy!"
MC
NOV
NO. 3
VARIANT EDITION
BUT IT'S TRYING TO KILL ME!
SHIELD
ALIVE!

ain America: Living Legend #3
chael D. Allred.

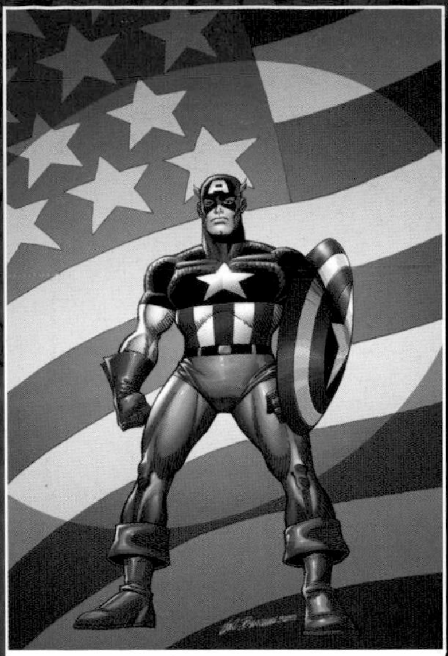

Captain America: Living Legend #3
by Sal Buscema.

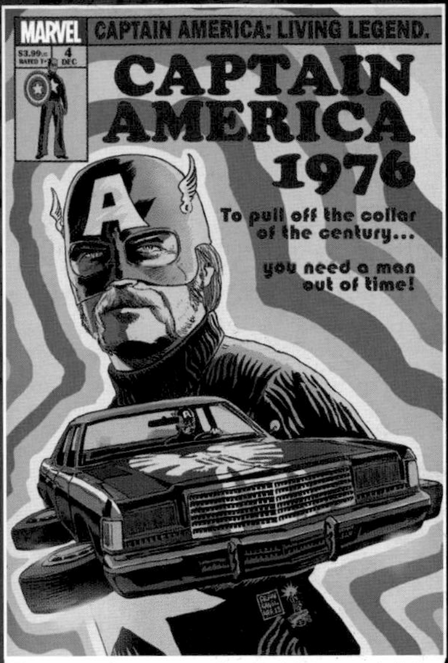
MARVEL
CAPTAIN AMERICA: LIVING LEGEND.
CAPTAIN AMERICA
1976
To pull off the collar of the century...
you need a man out of time!

Captain America: Living Legend #4
by Francesco Francavilla.

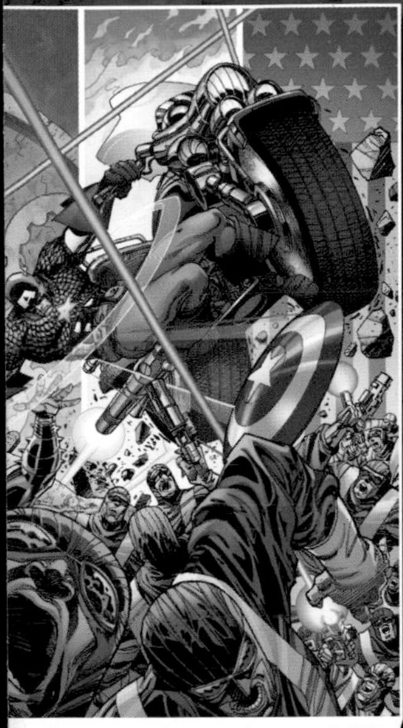

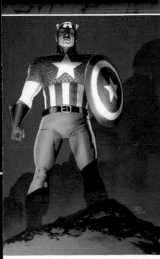

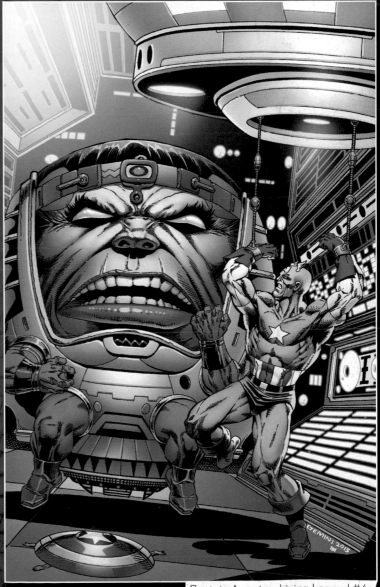

ain America: Living Legend #2
alt Simonson.

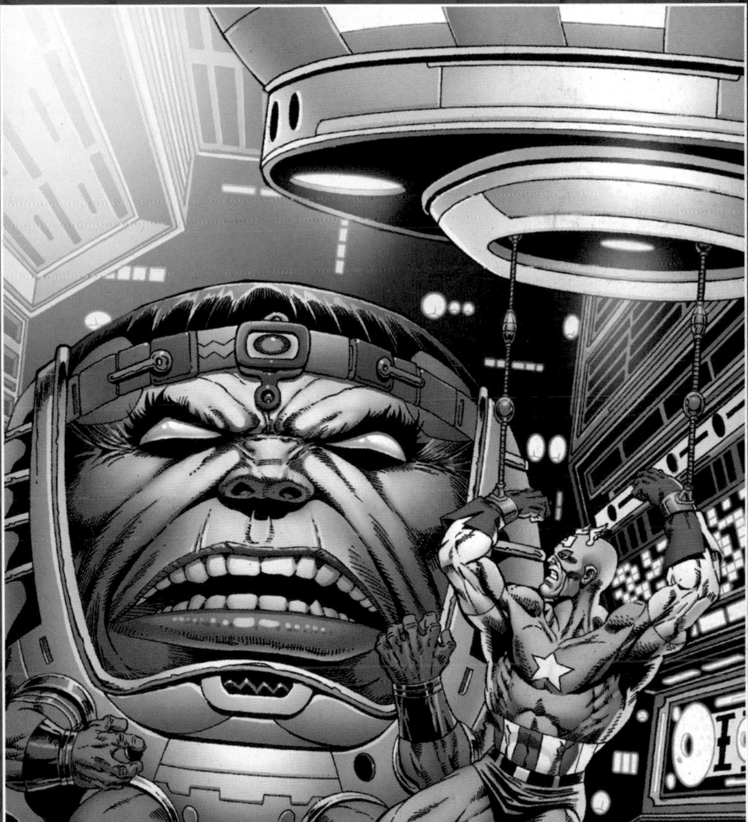
GEMINI 2013

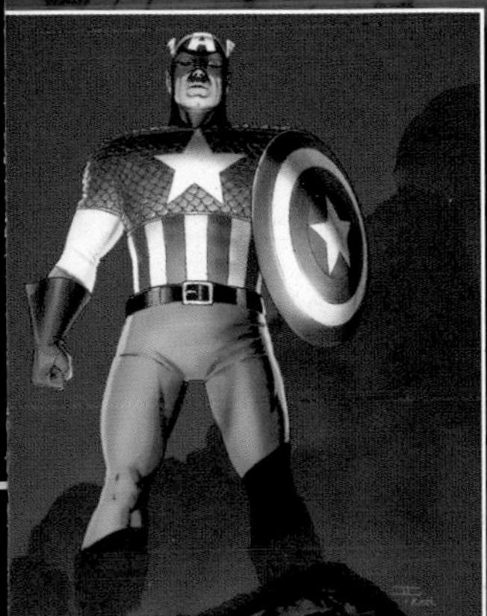

ain America: Living Legend #1
hn Cassaday.

Captain America: Living Legend #4
by Jim Starlin.

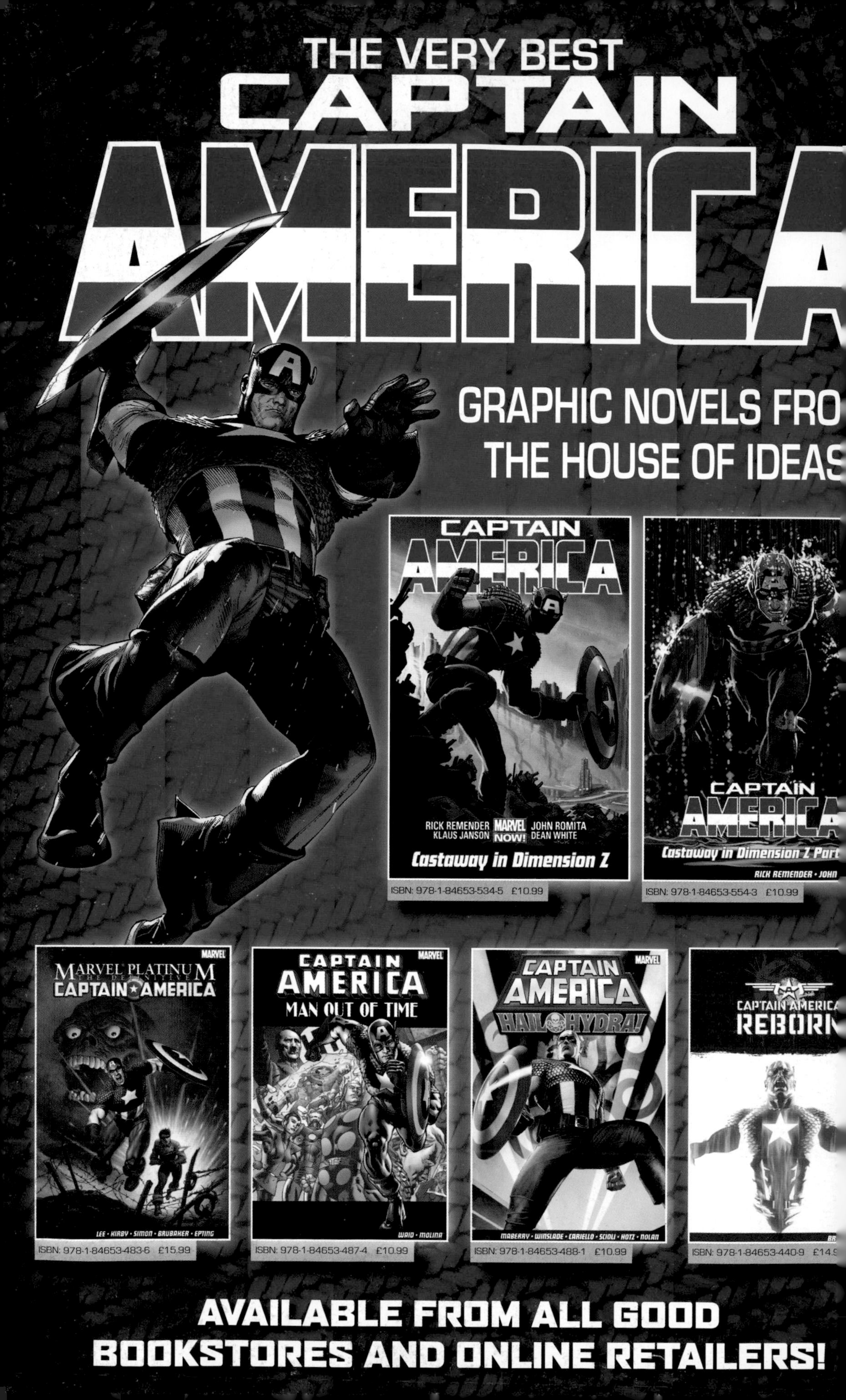
THE VERY BEST
CAPTAIN
AMERICA
GRAPHIC NOVELS FRO
THE HOUSE OF IDEAS
CAPTAIN
AMERICA
RICK REMENDER
KLAUS JANSON
MARVEL NOW!
JOHN ROMITA
DEAN WHITE
Castaway in Dimension Z
ISBN: 978-1-84653-534-5 £10.99
CAPTAIN
AMERICA
Castaway in Dimension Z Part
RICK REMENDER • JOHN
ISBN: 978-1-84653-554-3 £10.99
MARVEL
MARVEL PLATINUM
THE DEFINITIVE
CAPTAIN AMERICA
LEE • KIRBY • SIMON • BRUBAKER • EPTING
ISBN: 978-1-84653-483-6 £15.99
MARVEL
CAPTAIN
AMERICA
MAN OUT OF TIME
WAID • MOLINA
ISBN: 978-1-84653-487-4 £10.99
MARVEL
CAPTAIN
AMERICA
HAIL HYDRA!
MABERRY • WINSLADE • CARIELLO • SCIOLI • HOTZ • NOLAN
ISBN: 978-1-84653-488-1 £10.99
CAPTAIN AMERICA
REBORN
ISBN: 978-1-84653-440-9
AVAILABLE FROM ALL GOOD
BOOKSTORES AND ONLINE RETAILERS!